Thomas Cromwell

Thomas Cromwell

Servant to Henry VIII

DAVID LOADES

AMBERLEY

First published in 2013

Amberley Publishing
The Hill, Stroud
Gloucestershire, GL5 4EP

www.amberley-books.com

Copyright © David Loades, 2013

The right of David Loades to be identified as
the Author of this work has been asserted in
accordance with the Copyrights, Designs and
Patents Act 1988.

ISBN 978 1 4456 1538 7 (hardback)
ISBN 978 1 4456 1561 5 (ebook)

British Library Cataloguing in Publication Data.
A catalogue record for this book is available
from the British Library.

Typesetting and Origination by Amberley Publishing
Printed in the UK.

CONTENTS

ACKNOWLEDGEMENTS

My first and greatest debt of gratitude is due to the late Professor Sir Geoffrey Elton who supervised my PhD research at the University of Cambridge from 1958 to 1961 and who was a friend until his death in 1994. Geoffrey taught me most of what I know about Thomas Cromwell and brought Henry VIII's 'man of business' to the forefront of Tudor politics in his book *The Tudor Revolution in Government*. My second major debt is to the History Faculty of the University of Oxford, which has welcomed me as an honorary member and provided an academic home for the last sixteen years. During that period I have been fortunate to attend the Graduate Seminars in Early Modern British History at Merton College and History and Theology Seminars at Corpus Christi College and learned much from the senior and postgraduate members. It was at Merton that I met Dr Paul Cavill, then a postgraduate and now Fellow of Pembroke College, Cambridge. He has read the entire work and given me the benefit of his time and expertise. Incorporating his suggestions has saved me from a number of errors. In more recent years I have enjoyed email contact with double Booker Prize winner Hilary Mantel, and on one occasion shared a platform with her when we discussed approaches to and the value of historical fiction and academic history. Her books *Wolf Hall* and *Bring up the Bodies* deserve all the success they have achieved. Despite the unsurprising demands on her time, especially with the stage production of her work, Hilary has read my entire work and provided me with remarkable insights and detail. I am immensely grateful to her. I must also thank Jonathan Reeve of Amberley Publishing for suggesting that I tackle a book on Cromwell and Nicola Gale for seeing my work through publication. My wife, Judith, has acted as project manager and – as always – given her help, support and, in her own inimitable way, never failed to tell me what I have done wrong and how I could improve the text.

David Loades
Burford
University of Oxford
October 2013

PROLOGUE

On 4 October 1529 Thomas Wolsey, Lord Chancellor and Cardinal Archbishop of York, fell from power, leaving those in his service in limbo. One such was Thomas Cromwell, who is alleged to have lamented,

> I am likely to lose all that I have laboured for all the days of my life...

However, he was made of sterner stuff than these words would imply. Cromwell was a survivor, and, more to the point, he knew that his future must lie in the royal service. Henry VIII would have known him slightly, through his good service to the fallen minister, but Cromwell was not important enough to approach the king directly, and there was no need for him to do so. His best route lay through the good offices of the Duke of Norfolk, the king's chief councillor after Wolsey's fall. Cromwell asked for a burgess place in the forthcoming parliament, and was sufficiently encouraged by the response to begin a search. This proved far from easy, but with two days to go, and thanks to the good offices of his friend William Paulet, he was chosen to represent Taunton, a borough of the see of Winchester, and thus took his seat in what is known to us as the Reformation Parliament. He knew that this parliament was called to deal primarily with issues such as probate and mortuary fees, and so well did he employ his legal expertise in these matters that within a couple of years he had been appointed to the king's council as a legal adviser. He was also good company, and a man who could get things done. Henry liked good company, and was in need of a competent 'ways and means' man. Consequently he was able to show the king how to end his existing marriage to Catherine of Aragon, and to achieve the desired union with Anne Boleyn. This he did by using the legislative power of Parliament to break with the papacy, and set up the Royal Supremacy. Thereafter for several years, as Secretary and Lord Privy Seal, he was supreme in the king's counsels, running the administration and advising on foreign policy. In 1540 he was created Earl of Essex and Lord Great Chamberlain; but in that same year he overreached himself in his support for the reformers. He had once said that his religion was whatever pleased the king, but on this occasion he went too far, and forfeited Henry's confidence. Like Wolsey before him he fell from power, but, unlike the cardinal, the Earl of Essex was indicted for high treason, and executed in July 1540.

So who was Thomas Cromwell?

I

THE MAKING OF A MAN,
c. 1485–1522

Thomas Cromwell was born in Putney or thereabouts, being a
smith's son whose mother was married afterwards to a shearman...

John Foxe

Thomas Cromwell's origins are wreathed in obscurity. Much of what we know about his upbringing is derived from casual remarks dropped much later in his life, when he was already a man of substance. Apparently he came of a reasonably prosperous Nottinghamshire family and his grandfather, John, moved south from Norwell to Putney in around 1460 in order to take possession of a cloth fulling mill leased to him by the Archbishop of Canterbury.[1] This suggests that John was probably a younger son, but that cannot be proved. In Putney he moved into the wool processing business, married and settled down. His second son, Walter, was Thomas's father. Walter appears to have been an enterprising fellow, and something of a rogue. He features in the records as 'Cromwell, alias Smyth', a name which appears to have been derived from one of his numerous occupations, or possibly from his mother's maiden name.[2] He owned or leased land in the Wimbledon area, on which he ran sheep, and seems to have continued in the wool processing business, perhaps based on his father's fulling mill. He is described as 'shearman' in some of the records referring to him. He also ran at least one alehouse, because he was constantly in trouble for ignoring the regulations appertaining to the sale of beer, and suffered numerous small fines. He was also fined a number of times for running his sheep on Putney Common, where he had no right to be, not being a commoner. His name appears more than ninety times on the Court Rolls of the manor of Wimbledon, mostly for such infringements, although he also features in the more respectable guise of juryman and even constable.[3] This is an indication, presumably, that substance was more important than character in securing such positions, because Walter was also in trouble on occasions for drunkenness and brawling – not at all consistent with the office of constable! His elder brother, John, seems to have moved to Lambeth, perhaps to dissociate himself from all this bother. There he became a brewer, and later entered the household of the Archbishop of Canterbury, who was also lord of the manor. Meanwhile, Walter continued to hold two pieces of land in Putney parish, and two more were added by grant of Archbishop Morton in 1500. In 1495 he was constable of Putney parish, but in 1514 he blotted his copybook irredeemably by 'falsely and fraudulently' erasing evidence from the Court Roll, to which he had somehow secured access. This was the last straw as far as the steward was concerned, and he was ordered to forfeit all his copyholds in the manor. This was his last appearance on the Court Roll, and he seems to have died soon after.[4] He left no will, and what his son may have inherited from him remains a mystery. By then it did not matter very much anyway.

Walter's wife appears to have been the daughter of a Derbyshire yeoman named Glossop, although that may refer to his place of origin. She was living in Putney at the home of one John Welbeck, although whether he was her first husband is not clear. She was considerably older than Walter, and the attraction may well have been Welbeck's money, because he was an attorney by profession. They married in about 1474, and she bore him a daughter who was named Catherine in 1477. A second daughter, Elizabeth, was born around 1480, and their son Thomas around 1485. These birthdates are all somewhat hypothetical, and Thomas's later story that his mother was fifty-two when she bore him must be treated with scepticism.[5] Conception at such an age was virtually impossible. What he presumably meant was that she was past the normal age of childbearing; it is not to be supposed that he was claiming miraculous birth! The 'mother' who was living in his household in the later 1520s was his mother-in-law, not this lady, who would by his calculation have been over 100 years old by that time. Catherine later married a successful lawyer and accountant named Morgan Williams, who had come to Putney from Llanishen in Glamorgan. Morgan's brother, John, was steward to John, Lord Scales of Nayland, and an important man in Putney. Catherine's son, Richard, subsequently entered the service of his uncle Thomas, and changed his name to Cromwell. He founded the Huntingdonshire Cromwells, and was the ancestor of Oliver.[6] Elizabeth married a sheep farmer named Wellyfed, and their son, Christopher, was subsequently at school with his cousin Gregory, Thomas's son, and enters the story at a later date.

Nothing is known for certain about Thomas's childhood, although it is reasonable to suppose that he was put to school, his father being well able to afford the fees and his later intellectual interests pointing to a sound early education. Walter, however, was not an easy man to live with. He may even have had his son imprisoned for some unrecorded misdemeanour, and his wife, who might have mediated, was probably dead by then. At any rate, at the age of about fifteen or sixteen, Thomas ran away, probably stowing away on a ship bound for the Low Countries.[7] How he occupied himself and what he used for money are both unknown, but according to one later story he enlisted in the French army, or in another version was engaged as a servant to a soldier, 'carrying his pike'. In this guise he made his way into southern Italy, and was present at the Battle of Garigliano, which was fought on 28 and 29 December 1503. Garigliano was a defeat for the French, but Thomas escaped successfully from the field, and next appears as a penniless fugitive in Florence, where he was picked up in the street by Francesco Frescobaldi, a member of the prominent Florentine banking family, to whom he appealed for alms. Francesco was attracted by the young man's demeanour, and by his English nationality, that being a country of which he had fond memories, and took him into his service.[8] How long he remained in Florence is not known, nor exactly what his service in the Frescobaldi household involved. However he was an intelligent youth, and it is reasonable to suppose that he took the opportunity to educate himself in the essentials of business, and in the Italian language, both skills for which he was later to show a marked aptitude. Florence was at that time a republic, and Niccolò Machiavelli was active in its service, but it would be stretching credulity too far to claim that they met, and in any case he would have been far too distinguished to discuss his ideas with a mere English servant. In so far as those ideas may have influenced the mature Cromwell, that influence came much later in his career.[9] Frescobaldi seems to have taken Thomas with him when he travelled on business within Italy, and on one such trip left him behind as factor to a Venetian merchant. The parting seems to have been completely amicable, and how long Cromwell remained in his new employment is similarly unknown. It was probably in Venetian service that he travelled north to Antwerp, the connections between the two cities being close at that time, but once there he again abandoned his master, and took service instead with some of the merchants of the English House. Somehow he succeeded in establishing himself as a trader in his own right, dealing in English cloth and undertaking some legal work on behalf of the Merchant Adventurers, although how he could have acquired any legal knowledge so early in his career is again a mystery, unless it had been part of his experience in the house of Frescobaldi.[10]

By this time he was in his very early twenties, and had already acquired the experience of a much older man, being skilled in several languages and in merchandising. He spoke French and Spanish as well as Italian, and had a good working knowledge of Latin, which he appears to have developed by memorising large chunks of the Erasmian version of the New Testament, a benefit which was to remain with him over the years.[11] It was during his stay in Antwerp that Cromwell undertook the first of his two missions to Rome, when he was persuaded to accompany Geoffrey Chambers, who had been sent by the Guild of Our Lady in St Botolph's church at Boston in Lincolnshire to the Pope to secure an indulgence for the guild. As far as we know he had no previous connection with Boston, unless it was through a trade link with Antwerp, but Chambers clearly identified him as a useful colleague for a mission of this kind, because of his skill in languages, which he himself lacked. He picked up Cromwell on his way through Antwerp, and he soon proved to be invaluable. Chambers himself had no idea how to approach the pontiff, and would have awaited his convenience alongside the innumerable other suitors who thronged the papal audience chamber. Cromwell, however, had other ideas, and having acquired some choice sweetmeats, lay in wait for Julius when he returned from a hunting trip. How he had learned of the Pope's weakness for such delicacies we do not know, but the trick worked to perfection, and Julius granted the desired indulgence on the spot.[12] It appears that the highly developed opportunism that became so manifest later in life had put in an early appearance. According to Foxe, from whom this story is derived, this episode took place in 1510, when Thomas would have been about twenty-five. At some point between 1512 and 1514, Cromwell returned to England, and added a legal practice to his established trade in cloth, although his existing commercial ties continued to take him back to the Netherlands from time to time. More than twenty years later a merchant named George Elyot reminded him of an encounter which they had had at the Syngsson Mart in Middleburgh in 1512, and although Elyot's memory was not necessarily perfect, it does indicate that Thomas was present at the market in that year.[13] However in November 1512 a legal instrument, endorsed in a hand that closely resembles that of Cromwell, records a title to the manor of Whityngham, which seems to suggest that he was practising as a lawyer in London by that date. Some such date for his return is also indicated by the fact that by 1514 he had married. His wife, whom Chapuys referred to many years later as the daughter of a shearman, was

Elizabeth Wykys, who in fact came of an ancient gentry family, and was the niece of one who had been a gentleman usher to Henry VII. She was therefore his superior in status and probably in wealth.[14] Cromwell appears to have entered into a business partnership with his father-in-law, and was marketing his produce as late as 1524, which might seem a strange occupation for a man who was by then primarily an attorney, but is a good example of his versatility, which enabled him to pursue several occupations simultaneously. This noticeably increased both his wealth and his standing. By 1522 he was being referred to as a gentleman, and had moved into the substantial house at Austin Friars in London that he was to occupy for many years.[15] Elizabeth presented him with three children, Gregory, Anne and Grace, the first of whom must have been born not later than 1515. Gregory was later something of a disappointment to his father, and Anne and Grace both died during the plague outbreak of 1529. It seems likely from the will that Thomas drew up in that year that their mother died at the same time, but Cromwell's private life remains very much in the shadows. It is possible that Elizabeth had been married before, and the fact that Mercy Prior is recorded in his will as his mother-in-law indicates that she too had married a second time. She was resident in his house at the time that his will was drawn up, which suggests that her second husband was also dead by then. Elizabeth's father had clearly died at some point after 1524, but all these dates, except that of the will, are somewhat speculative.[16]

Meanwhile Cromwell appears to have undertaken a second trip to Rome on behalf of the Boston guild. This took place in 1517 or 1518, and was again in the company of Geoffrey Chambers, with whom by this time he could claim a good acquaintance. The story of what happened has become confused with the events of seven or eight years previously, but there is no reason to doubt that he made a second trip, or that he stayed in the English Hospice and took the opportunity to do a little sightseeing. Interestingly enough, the effect of this experience seems to have been much the same as that of a similar trip by Martin Luther a few years before. It alienated him from the whole apparatus of the Roman bureaucracy, and indirectly from the ritualism of the Roman Church. Nevertheless the mission was successful, and the Boston guild obtained its indulgences as before. At about this time also, Cromwell caught the eye of the powerful Thomas Wolsey, Archbishop of York from 1514, Cardinal and Lord Chancellor in 1515.[17] It is possible that he was introduced by his cousin Robert Cromwell (John's son), who was vicar of Battersea at this time and had business dealings with the archbishop, or perhaps the introduction was affected by Lord Henry Percy, who is alleged to have borrowed money from Cromwell and to have been impressed by his creditor's attitude. We do not know the exact date or the circumstances of their connection. It may have come at any time between 1514 and 1519, and probably arose as a result of Wolsey's decision to use Cromwell's legal expertise as a client of his business. There are no records of his being paid a regular retainer for his services, nor do we know exactly what being 'in Wolsey's service' would have meant in terms of commitment, or of his other business.[18] It is perhaps safest to assume that the archbishop began to use him on an occasional basis in about 1516, and that mutual satisfaction caused the connection to develop. According to one version he became a member of Wolsey's council in 1519, but it is not certain exactly what that would indicate, and he continued his private practice throughout the 1520s. He does, however, appear to have given up his wool business by about 1524, perhaps on the death of his father-in-law. It is not until 1520 that the records preserve the first undoubted sign of his activity on the cardinal's behalf, when he was called upon to prepare an appeal to the papal Curia against a decision of the Prerogative Court of Canterbury involving Nicholas Cowper, the vicar, and the Prioress of Cheshunt, Margaret Chawry. The prioress wrote sending 'information by the letters of Thomas Cromwell from which your Lordship will understand the merits of the case'. Cromwell apparently prepared the resulting brief, but the outcome is not known.[19] The case does, however, indicate that he was thought to be well seen in the canon law as well as the common law, and familiar with the proceedings of the Curia. Wolsey had by this time been the king's leading man of affairs for some six years, and it is entirely likely that Henry was aware of his use of Thomas Cromwell, but whether he employed him in any service involving contact with the court is not known. In August 1522 he was granted power of attorney in a suit involving two merchants of the Hanse, and in that, which describes him as 'of London, gentleman', it is clearly indicated that he was considered to be a member of Wolsey's household, although most of the records which survive from this period could equally well have been generated by his private business.[20]

In January 1522 a certain William Popely wrote to him in terms which suggest familiar acquaintance, asking him to act as attorney in a suit which he had before the king's council. The letter was written from Bristol, and indicates that Cromwell was using his commercial contacts to build his legal business, an impression confirmed by the fact that some months later John Creke wrote to him from Bilbao in Spain in the warmest terms, asking to be commended to his wife, and addressing his letter simply to 'the worshipful Thomas Cromwell, London'.[21] Any nobleman was likely to regard a commoner with whom he had regular dealings as being in his service, and the term is very imprecise. For example Cecily, the Dowager Marchioness of Dorset, wrote somewhat peremptorily to him in August 1522, requesting him to forward a 'trussing bed' and its equipment to her son Leonard, and endorsing the letter 'to Cromwell, my son Marquis servant'. Thomas, the then marquis, had been Wolsey's pupil at Magdalen College, Oxford, in the 1490s, and that may have created a relationship which caused his mother to presume in this fashion.[22] There is no other indication that Cromwell ever considered himself to be the marquis's servant, or that the nobleman saw him in that light. It seems to have been little more than a figure of speech. His legal business was varied, and no doubt profitable. It also took him out of London from time to time. Richard Cawffer wrote to him on 15 August about a dispute between himself and Lord Mountjoy, who was acting as an executor to Henry Kebyll, 'late of London, Alderman'. The nature of the dispute is not known, but it presumably related to probate, because the failure of one of the arbitrators to turn up meant that the case stood referred to the bishop. Tunstall had ordered each party to name an 'indifferent person' to advise him, and Chawffer had chosen Cromwell. He asked the latter to let him know when he was next in London, that he might instruct him, which seems an odd request to make of one whose normal address was at the Austin Friars.[23] Perhaps he was in attendance upon the cardinal, who seems to have been at Esher at the time. Another indication of his connection with Wolsey comes over the administration of the Privy Seal loan for which he was primarily responsible in the autumn of 1522. Henry

Lacy, acting on the cardinal's behalf, sent him a draft Privy Seal with a covering letter to a Mr Ellderton, instructing him to take the mayor's advice and to 'order it as he thinks fit'. Exactly what he was supposed to do is not clear, because a draft Privy Seal would have had no legal standing; perhaps Lacy was canvassing opinion as to whom in London it would be appropriate to send such demands.[24] This would seem to be a good example of the kind of semi-official way in which Cromwell operated, because in the same letter was enclosed a draft of Sir James Turberville's account, which he was asked to put in due form, a task that would seem to be more appropriate to his private practice. Other letters of the same time give a similar impression. In 1521 he acted for Charles Knyvett, who had resigned the offices which he held under the Duke of Buckingham shortly before that nobleman was executed for high treason on 17 May. Knyvett had a powerful sense of grievance, having been forced to incur over £3,000 worth of debt on his master's behalf. This debt he now sought to annul, and to recover the receiverships which he had been compelled to resign, on the grounds that all Buckingham's property was now in the hands of the Crown. This suit might well appear a forlorn hope were it not for the fact that Knyvett had provided useful testimony against the duke at his trial, and was looking for his reward. That he chose Thomas Cromwell to represent him is indicative of the fact that the latter's favour with the cardinal was well known, and Cromwell would not have taken him on if he had not judged the chances of success to be reasonable.[25] In the event their suit failed, but this did not reflect adversely on Cromwell's reputation, as he seems to have won golden opinions for his efforts on Knyvett's behalf. Perhaps the suggestion of a trade-off was a little too obvious for the council to stomach.

William Popely was obviously satisfied with his legal advice, because he wrote again in August with an odd request from a certain 'poor man', who may well have been Popely himself. He wanted to know where one Glaskerton had been on Our Lady's Eve. The reason for this request is not explained, nor why Cromwell should have been expected to know the answer. The suggestion that he was running a private detective agency among his numerous other preoccupations is not supported by any other evidence. The letter continues with the apparently inconsequential news that Popely was to be married on 'the Sunday after St Bartholomew' (31 August), and he wanted his brother's writs sent down 'by the first'.[26] This ragbag of a letter suggests a man who is completely at ease with his solicitor, and that impression is confirmed by another letter, written on 27 September referring to a case which was obviously well known between them, asking Cromwell to ensure that 'Mr Elliot may answer by his counsel', and informing him that the ship, which was presumably to bear his letter, waited only for the wind to serve.[27] Similarly Richard Chawffer followed up his letter of August with another on 22 September, expressing complete satisfaction with the advice that Cromwell had given him in response to his earlier communication, and requesting a commission (presumably from Wolsey), in the strictest form 'according to the bill I received from you'. He wants to know what action, if any, he can take against Lord Mountjoy, or whether such a course would damage his cause. His Lordship's goods in Calais are vulnerable, or he could try a suit in Chancery.[28] It is a very routine sort of letter, and one wonders why it has survived when so much of Cromwell's correspondence from these years has obviously perished. Not every letter was from a satisfied customer, and the indications are that his legal business was taking priority, because a communication from a certain Thomas Twesell in October 1522 about the cloth business 'takes it unkindly' that he has not been sent the velvet pouch which had been requested. How long the item had been outstanding is not clear, but it appears that Cromwell was allowing his merchandising to slide rather, perhaps in anticipation of giving it up a couple of years later.[29]

In addition to running an effective legal practice, and a rather less effective clothing business, Cromwell also seems to have been a money lender. In this connection his international contacts were invaluable, because he probably borrowed the money in Antwerp at a standard rate, and then loaned it onto his clients with an enhancement. He was well known, as we have seen, in the house of Frescobaldi, where he would have learned the basics of the banking business in his youth, and was friendly with Antonio Bonvisi of Lucca, also well known in London, who included Wolsey among his clients. In his cosmopolitan experience, there were many features which point towards money lending as an attractive proposition, and his entrée to the Antwerp exchange would have given him a decisive advantage.

So what manner of man was Thomas Cromwell by 1522? His unusual youth had left its mark upon him, particularly in the skills that he had acquired. He was knowledgeable about banking, and the cloth trade, and had a most unusual command of languages. He had friends in Italy, in the Netherlands, and among the merchants strangers based in London. There is, however, no reason to suppose that he was that reviled creature, an 'Italianate Englishman', nor a disciple of Machiavelli, suppositions derived from his time in Florence.[30] Nor, in spite of Foxe, was he a closet Lutheran. His trips to Rome had alienated him from the papacy, and he appears to have become sceptical about such standard devotions as the veneration of relics. However his will of 1529 reveals him to have been a man of conventional piety at that stage of his life, and there is no reason to suppose that that had changed over the previous seven years. That he was acquisitive is a reasonable supposition, but the only hint in his correspondence that that was frowned upon comes in a letter of 1532, charging him with not having paid for certain goods of the Duke of Buckingham which he had received eleven years earlier.[31] The circumstances of this charge are unknown, and it could have been the result of mere oversight. However, it remains a mystery how and where he acquired the legal knowledge which supported his main business in the 1520s, because it was not until 1524 that he was enrolled at Gray's Inn, and by that time he was well established.[32] If he learned 'on the job' as an apprentice to an established attorney, that has escaped the record, and the only possible conclusion is that he was self-taught. Presumably he started in a small way, on the back of his merchandising, because his experience on the Continent would have taught him nothing about the English common law. Apart from membership of an Inn of Court, there was no recognised qualification for the profession, so he must have started with the occasional low-grade assignment and built up his practice by personal recommendation. There are a few suggestions in the records that this might have been so. In which case his success would have built upon itself, which is a testimony to his personality as well as to his learning ability. Apart from the fact that he was highly intelligent and adaptable in his approach, we have no evidence of that personality in these early years, but he clearly had a great capacity for friendship because he corresponded with men (and a few women) all over Europe, and they nearly all seem to have held him in warm regard. About his family life we know next to nothing. His wife and his daughters are mere names, and most of our knowledge of his son Gregory comes from later years. However the fact that he gave a home to his widowed mother-in-law suggests a congenial nature, which is reflected also in his letters. That he was a hard man of business may be deduced from his growing prosperity, but of the ruthless ideologist of later legend there is not a trace.

2

THE CARDINAL'S SERVANT, 1523–1530

*The Cardinal of York, seeing Cromwell's vigilance and diligence,
his ability and promptitude, both in evil and in good, took him into
his service, and employed him principally in demolishing five or six
good monasteries...*

Eustace Chapuys

Thomas Cromwell sat in the parliament of 1523, but we do not know his constituency, or the circumstances of his election.[1] Because he was in the cardinal's service by this time, and was known to be so, it is likely that the Archbishop of York placed him in one of the boroughs whose patronage he controlled, but which one is unclear. It is, however, inconceivable that one who was fairly close to Wolsey should have entered Parliament without at least his knowledge and consent. This raises an interesting question about what double game the cardinal may have been playing, because we have the text of a speech, allegedly delivered by Cromwell in one or other of the sessions, which runs directly counter to the cardinal's declared purpose.[2] Ostensibly, Wolsey was arguing for an invasion of France, in accordance with the Anglo-Imperial treaty of the previous year, and a subsidy of 4s in the pound to support it. Cromwell's speech, however, is opposed to all such schemes. It starts with judicious flattery of the king's intentions.

> To recover again by the sword the realm of France, belonging to our most redoubted Sovereign by good and just title, and to change the sums of money which we have in sundry years received from thence into the whole and just revenues that might there from year to year be levied, if we did peaceably enjoy the same, who is here present that would not gladly dispend his goods but also his life ... to help to obtain unto our most benign sovereign his most noble succession...[3]

However, he then goes on, in equally dulcet tones, to argue against the king taking the field in person, suggesting that it would be a disaster to the kingdom if he should miscarry, bearing in mind his 'forward courage'. He would leave a daughter as his heir, and she but a child. Without suggesting the difficulties of a female succession, he points out that Mary's well-being demands her father's safety, not the kind of risks which he would be taking on campaign. If the king's warlike energy demands action, let him attack the Scots, who are a perpetual threat to his northern borders, 'for though it is a common saying that in Scotland is nought to win but strokes, for that I allege another common saying, who that entendeth France to win, with Scotland let him begin'.[4]

He therefore discreetly opposes the subsidy that Wolsey had demanded, but ends on the same flattering note on which he had begun: 'I beseech God send our most dear and most redoubted sovereign prosperous succession and fortunate achieving of all this his noble enterprise.' This speech has been rightly described as a masterpiece of eloquence and discretion, full of mature wisdom and sharp insights. If it was ever delivered, no doubt it helped to persuade the Commons to reject the grant asked for, and to replace it with a much smaller tax. Instead of £800,000, Wolsey would have to be content with £152,000, spread over three years.[5]

The cardinal was apparently deeply chagrined at this rebuff, but one wonders whether his disappointment was as great as he wished to make it appear. He had been very active in the promotion of peace between England and France since at least 1514, and the great Treaty of London of 1518 had been largely his handiwork. Since then he had been exercised to restrain his master's martial ardour. He was, however, the king's servant, and bound to follow Henry's policies when these were clearly articulated. Consequently he had negotiated the treaty of 1522 with the Emperor, which had committed England to war against France, and set out to raise the necessary money by way of forced loans. By this means he raised over £350,000, but this, as he knew well, was nowhere near enough to cover the cost of the Army Royal which Henry proposed to lead. In fact it was £40,000 short of what was actually spent on the Duke of Suffolk's raid in the autumn of 1523, and on the activities of the Earl of Surrey on the Scottish borders, which fell well short of open warfare.[6] Hence his reluctant consent to meet Parliament in April 1523, with the object of raising the enormous sum of almost £1 million. This was based on accurate estimates of what would be required, and was by no means exaggerated. The convocations, which met at the same time as Parliament, made the unprecedented grant of 10 per cent of all clerical incomes, but that was spread over five years, whereas Wolsey's need was for cash in hand. However, the House of Commons proved to be difficult, with or without Cromwell's help, and in spite of the cardinal's state visit, clearly designed to intimidate, would grant only the smaller sum. That was accomplished with much bitching and grinding, and the first instalment of the new tax was not to be paid until the spring of 1524.[7] However, in spite of Wolsey's vigorously expressed disappointment, in fact the rebuff suited his purposes very well. Another forced loan in the autumn of 1523 failed even partly to close the financial gap, and the Army Royal was never launched. In spite of the king's obvious frustration, with which Wolsey was quick to sympathise, nothing could be done in 1524 or 1525, and the cardinal's peace policy eventually prevailed at the Treaty of the More in August of the latter year.[8] Although he could not admit it for obvious reasons, the House of Commons' refusal of his subsidy request in April 1523 was not quite the setback that it appeared to be. This raises the intriguing possibility that Thomas Cromwell was acting as Wolsey's agent in his well-known speech, and the reason why a complete text survives in the handwriting of one of Cromwell's scribes is because it was carefully crafted in advance with the cardinal's consent and approval. No one commented upon this at the time because the two were ostensibly so much at odds, and if anyone observed the oddity of one of Wolsey's servants contradicting his master, their comments have not survived. The speech as recorded was cleverly designed to avoid giving offence to the king, and seems to have impressed with its force and subtlety, because when Cromwell next sought a place in Parliament in 1529, Henry was 'well contented' that he should be a burgess, provided that he obeyed the king's orders, which suggests that his value as an orator was well appreciated.[9]

It may therefore have been with a wry sense of satisfaction that Cromwell wrote to his friend John Creke, who was in Bilbao at the time, on 17 August 1523, that he

> ... with others have endured a parliament which continued by the space of seventeen whole weeks, where we communed of war, peace, strife, contention, debate, murmur, grudge, riches, poverty, perjury, truth, falsehood, justice, equity, deceit, oppression, magnanimity, activity, force, attemperance, treason, murder, felony, conciliation, and also how a commonwealth might be edified and also continued within our realm. Howbeit in conclusion we have done as our predecessors have been wont to do, that is to say as well as we might, and left where we began.[10]

The session had not been a rich one in legislative terms, and no doubt Wolsey would have written similarly if he had been so inclined, but it would be wrong to read into this humorous letter any deep disillusionment with Parliament as an institution. Rather it expresses a measure of frustration with this particular session, which the cardinal, who was also Lord Chancellor, had managed with such apparent incompetence. That may, however, have been planned by Wolsey, who had no opinion of parliaments, and avoided them whenever possible. By demonstrating the futility of such meetings, which became mere talking shops that did nothing to alleviate the king's poverty, he was no doubt hoping to convince the king that further sessions would be a waste of time, and indeed as long as his influence prevailed Parliament was not called again.[11] Cromwell, however, learned much about its potential power in his weeks as a burgess. It had the ability to frustrate or implement the king's policies, and it discussed every subject under the sun. Although it had a defined professional competence, the constraints upon it were self-imposed and the result of tradition rather than law. With proper management those limitations could be transcended. It only needed a minister with the right skills and the king's backing to turn Parliament into an effective instrument of the royal will, and that he was to remember in due course.

Meanwhile, he turned back to his legal practice, and to his regular activities on Wolsey's behalf. It is often difficult to determine which was which. In January 1523 he had been given authority, with others, to call in the cardinal's debts, a position of household responsibility, whereas in May he was asked by John Robinson of Boston to get Robert Pynson to print a large number of letters and briefs 'for which he will send', which seems to have nothing to do with Wolsey or his service.[12] At the same time his admission to Gray's Inn must have owed something to his position with the cardinal, and may have been the result of prompting by his employer, because he entered as a qualified lawyer, which he surely was not unless his years of experience were taken in lieu. It is difficult to be sure. In December 1523 he was making presentments before the alderman of Breadstreet ward in the City of London concerning nuisances about St Mildred's church, and in November he was appealed to by Henry Wykys, his brother-in-law, for assistance in selling a house in Chertsy. In November also he was in correspondence with Sir Peter Vavasour concerning the cheating ways of one Wim Bank, who was withholding his rents in the Low Countries. Vavasour was promising to come to London to consult him.[13] All this would seem to belong to his private business, but the Bill which he drafted on behalf of John Palsgrave, one of Wolsey's clerks, for a Chancery suit in which Palsgrave was suing the executors of one Henry Wilcocks for the moiety of a benefice in Leicestershire, or the licence to a Hanseatic merchant to pass into France in pursuit of Hanseatic goods seized there, must be activities undertaken on the cardinal's behalf. The latter was an extraordinary concession in view of the state of war between the countries at the time.[14] Also as a result of his service to Wolsey he was instructed to set up an investigation into a dispute within the family of the Earl of Oxford concerning inheritance; and he received a petition addressed to him as 'councillor to the Lord Legate' from Edward Smything requesting the recovery of some cloths painted by Smything which had been, he alleged, wrongfully detained. In December 1524 he dealt with a case of breach of covenant in Yorkshire, and in May 1525 drafted a lease of some church lands in York, while in June he received a letter from one Cowper requesting his aid in providing a relative to a benefice.[15] These are just a few examples of what was obviously an intensely busy life, but one which enabled Cromwell to prosper. In July 1526 George Monoux, an alderman of London, promised him 20 marks (£13 6s 8d) for the successful outcome of a suit which he had in hand, and in June 1527 a detailed inventory of Cromwell's house shows him to have been well set up with the goods of this world.[16]

The evidence for his use of this prosperity is conflicting. One Lawrence Giles wrote to him in fulsome terms, professing his inability ever to repay his generosity and observing that God helps those who help the poor, but his correspondence with John Checkyng, his son's tutor in Cambridge, is more equivocal. Checkyng, who was a Fellow and Tutor at Pembroke Hall, took on his son Gregory, then aged about twelve, and Gregory's cousin Christopher Wellyfed, at some time in 1527. Christopher was obviously a bright boy, and Checkyng's reports on him were favourable from the start. Gregory, however, was a different matter, being slow and somewhat obstinate. His tutor tried at first to blame the poor teaching he had hitherto received from John Palsgrave, and made the best of his progress thereafter, bearing in mind that his own reputation as a tutor was at stake.[17] However it did not really work, and the best that could be said for Gregory was that he was diligent, which meant that relations with his father became increasingly strained. Checkyng was obviously providing board and lodging for the boys as well as teaching, and found it very difficult to persuade Cromwell to pay the bills. In June 1528 he acknowledged receipt of £6 13s 4d, but it was not enough to cover his expenses. He was, he professed, in debt and did not know which way to turn for cash. It particularly riled him that Wolsey's prosperous servant was not even willing to pay for the bedding which Christopher had accidentally destroyed by setting fire to it when dozing over a lit candle.[18] Eventually, in July 1529, Cromwell threatened to take the boys away, whether, as he alleged, because he was disappointed with their progress, or possibly because he had become wearied by Checkyng's constant calls for money. The tutor said that he would be relieved by this development, 'because they had been no profit to him', but hastened to deny responsibility for their lack of progress. Gregory, although not bright, was well seen in the classical authors, and Christopher had done excellently. He had been, he added, responsible for the education of six scholars who had subsequently become Fellows of Colleges, so there was nothing wrong with his track record.[19] Altogether the experience was an unfortunate one, which does not reflect much credit on either party. We do not know whether Checkyng's constant requests for money were justified or not, but Cromwell was clearly much less than generous in his treatment of the tutor. Nor did he make any gift to Pembroke Hall, which would have been expected of a wealthy man in the circumstances. Gregory's letters to his father confirm Checkyng's diagnosis. They show a rather stupid lad, anxious to make a good impression by appearing hard-working but only really enthused by the day's hunting, to which they had been treated by a local landowner and of which he reported that they saw 'such game and pleasure as I never saw in my life'.[20] Such an experience was clearly worth many hours of Cicero or Tacitus, and his tutor's frustration is understandable. Cromwell got the message, unpalatable though it must have been, and did not join his son with him in reversion in any of the innumerable offices which he subsequently held. Since such an arrangement was common, almost customary, he cannot have had any illusions about his son's capacity for business, although he did make a courtier of him subsequently, so he was not completely stupid.

As far as we can tell, and in spite of his gift for languages, Wolsey did not use Cromwell in any of his complex foreign negotiations, and with one possible exception he did not travel abroad in his master's service.[21] However, the interpretation of this is more likely to have been positive than negative; the cardinal wanted to keep him close at hand because his legal and administrative skills were in such constant demand. Nor did he use him much in his political manoeuvrings at the court, or take any trouble to introduce him to that environment. Instead he delegated much of the routine work of providing for his educational foundations at Oxford and Ipswich to the man who can probably be described most accurately as a secretary. This led to an immense amount of work, because it involved the dissolution of nearly thirty small religious houses, the disposal of their property, the renegotiation of their leases and other land arrangements, the transfer of their properties to the new foundations and the establishment of those colleges.[22] There was, or was intended to be, no religious significance attached to those houses selected for closure. Each was dissolved on the grounds of its lack of viability, either in numbers or resources. Because Wolsey was the Cardinal Legate, he had the authority to do this, and to redistribute the lands of the houses so dissolved. There was no question of the secularisation of such property, because the colleges were ecclesiastical foundations, and those monks and nuns who wished to remain in their habits were transferred to other foundations. Nor was there any suggestion of Lutheran sympathies on Wolsey's part, because he maintained his campaign against heresy, burning Lutheran books and interrogating those suspected of such views.[23] Nevertheless the complaints against his actions were numerous and vociferous, coming both from the gentry and the commons. Travellers had been provided with free hospitality at such monasteries, and they were notoriously lax landlords, which meant that many of the protests came from those who found themselves having to renegotiate their leases with the much tougher Thomas Cromwell, which usually meant enhanced rents, and the more rigorous exaction of other dues. Such objections were even transmitted to the court by aristocratic enemies of Wolsey and in 1527 the cardinal was warned that 'the king and noblemen speak things incredible of the acts of Mr Alyn and Mr Cromwell'; although if this was intended to damage either the legate or his agents, it appears to have failed at this juncture.[24]

Cromwell was also accused of taking bribes in his capacity as land agent, and this seems to have been justified up to a point, because he certainly accepted payments from some heads of houses, either to secure generous pensions for themselves or to fix leases of former abbey properties for their friends or kindred. A few houses were inspected but allowed to stand, and the suspicion is that financial inducements were offered in such cases. All this is difficult to prove because the line between a legitimate fee and a bribe was (and is) hard to define, and Cromwell undoubtedly took payments for the work which he undertook, sometimes from his clients – or victims – as well as from his employer. Such payments look suspicious, but it is by no means certain that they were improper at the time, and the accusations of bribery rest largely on the hostile testimony of Reginald Pole. Pole undoubtedly knew Cromwell and his work at first hand, but he wrote his account some years later, when Thomas had done far more to earn his animosity.[25]

On 5 January 1525 Thomas Cromwell and John Smyth were appointed attorneys for the new foundation of Cardinal College in Oxford, documents were drawn up in anticipation of its establishment, and in February a list was compiled of the twenty-one religious houses that either had been or were about to be dissolved to provide the funding.[26] At the same time Sir William Gascoigne, William Burbank and Thomas Cromwell were commissioned to survey the lands and possessions of half a dozen of them, including Medmenham and Wallingford, and Cromwell and Smyth were given the additional responsibility of acting as attorneys for four others which had obviously been dissolved already. It was not until 13 July that Wolsey was licensed to establish his new foundation 'on the site of dissolved priory of St Frideswide', and he made his foundation grant of property a week later, on 21 July.[27] At some time between then and 10 February 1526 John Higden was appointed dean of the new college, because on that day Cromwell and Smyth were also named as attorneys for an additional grant made by Wolsey to Higden in that capacity. The chronology of the dissolutions that made these grants possible is not very clear, but most of them seem to have taken place in 1525 and 1526 and Cromwell was present at the majority of them, representing the Lord Legate, who was otherwise engaged. It is perhaps not surprising that the odium attached to these moves should have stuck to him rather than to his master. He was described at one point as the 'most hated man in England', and his friend Stephen Vaughn expressed concern for his personal safety. Indeed there seems to have been an obscure plot aimed at his life in 1527, but the details are vague and there is no suggestion that such threats put him off in any way at all.[28] He seems rather to have relished the work, which involved surveying and estimating the value of the property of the dissolved houses, making careful inventories, and disposing of their moveable goods, which consisted mostly of altar furnishings, bells and household implements. The latter were sold and a careful record kept of the moneys accruing, while lands were for the most part leased out for enhanced rents, over which Cromwell proved himself to be a tough negotiator. All this work required a detailed knowledge of the law, particularly as it related to real estate, and this he possessed in full measure. The indications are that this work was far more arduous than Wolsey, with his rather grand view of the situation, ever realised, but his agent was supremely diligent and effective. It is perhaps not surprising that in April 1527 Henry Lacy should write to Cromwell congratulating him on his promotion through the cardinal's favour, and addressing him as a member of Wolsey's council.[29] Lacy was well informed about such matters, so it is likely that this elevation in status had occurred recently.

Cromwell's involvement with Cardinal College did not, however, end once the grants of property had been made, because he appears to have been both Receiver General and site manager for the new foundation. The first *valor* of the lands of Cardinal College was drawn up by him on 30 September 1526, at the beginning of the accounting period which was to run from Michaelmas to Michaelmas, and showed a yearly revenue of £2,051 9s 4d. However, the building work at the college had hardly commenced at that time, and on 31 December Cromwell reported that the money so far dispensed on that work came to £4,684 17s 7d, so he was obviously being allocated funds from elsewhere in Wolsey's enormous resources.[30] Just what was counted as the income of the foundation is not entirely clear from the surviving documents, because at Michaelmas 1527 Cromwell accounted for a gross income of £4,096 1s 5d, which had apparently accrued over the previous year, and this does not match either of the accounts previously submitted. To make the confusion worse, on 19 December 1527 the Receiver General returned another set of 'the expenses of Cardinal College', covering the period since 16 January 1525, and showing income of £9,828 11s 4d, and expenditure of £8,882 3s 4d. Whether this covers ordinary as well as extraordinary income is not clear, but it does appear that Wolsey's brainchild was costing him about £4,000 a year, of which half was covered by the landed endowment which had been transferred from the dissolved monasteries.[31] By this time, however, the college was up and running because on 31 October 1527 Cromwell submitted a claim for his expenses, which included the cost of bringing a number of scholars from Cambridge, whence they had been tempted by generous offers, as well as for time spent on Wolsey's other foundation at Ipswich, and a trip to York.[32] In April 1528 the cardinal was apparently considering adding to the endowment of his Oxford foundation, for in a report on the 2nd of that month, in addition to praising the work being done on the college and the excellence of its chapel establishment, Cromwell said that he had been to Wallingford in Oxfordshire 'about the dissolution of that house', and had sent the evidences to John Higden, the dean of the college. Rather belatedly, on 12 June 1528, Pope Clement VII issued a Bull in confirmation of the new foundation. Apart from tidying up the legal side in Chancery, the work of foundation was then complete, and although building work was still proceeding,[33] Cromwell was able to turn his attention to other aspects of the cardinal's service. A final *valor* of the college lands, taken on 29 September 1528, showed an income of £2,263 15s 1d for the previous year, so Wolsey had added rather more than £200 to the endowment of 1526, although whether that came from Wallingford is not known.

Cromwell's involvement with the cardinal's other foundation at Ipswich appears to have been less formal, and more in the way of general oversight. In September 1528 William Capon, the dean of the college, wrote to Wolsey with a general progress report, and noted that Mr Cromwell had been there for several days. He was not altogether happy with the building work, and suspected that the masons were not being paid enough to guarantee their diligence, but there is no suggestion that this was Cromwell's fault. On 20 December he wrote again, with a more positive report of progress of the building, and the news that, in spite of being incomplete, the college was up and running.[34] This had no doubt been helped by the transfer to the college of the lands of St Peter's manor in Ipswich, which had happened in that same month. No accounts survive for the work on the Ipswich college, but Cromwell did report to Gardiner in January 1529 that there had been a flood in the nearby marshes, and that he had been exceptionally busy with the legal aspects of the foundation, which indicates the nature of his oversight.[35] William Capon wrote to him in April 1529 that the Bishop of Norwich was being difficult over the dissolution of Broomshill and Rowburgh, minor houses over which he claimed jurisdiction, and whose resources had also been allocated to the college. This perhaps suggests the nature of the legal difficulties with which Cromwell was wrestling. He was also responsible for the flood defence works, and later claimed the credit for paying the workmen enough to ensure that they stuck to their job, and thus prevented a much worse disaster than that which had actually occurred. By far the larger part of Cromwell's correspondence during the years 1525–29 relates either to the dissolution of the religious houses or to the foundations for which their resources were destined. However, his more general business was not neglected. He was written to on a number of occasions by his friends in Boston, usually asking for favours but in suitably amicable terms.[36] His accounts also show that he was continuing to lend money, and in February 1529 he noted that £2,116 3s 2d had been due to him over the ten years previous, of which £542 os 1od was owed on obligations 'whereof the date has expired'. Interestingly only £170 of this large sum had been entered into on the cardinal's behalf, and these were mostly very small sums, where Cromwell had obviously paid bills as they arose.[37] He also received petitions from clergy in search of benefices, from noble patrons (including one from Anne Boleyn in favour of a servant of hers), and news from his friends in the Netherlands and in Spain. The latter were now usually addressed to him as 'Councillor to my Lord's Grace', and it is clear that by 1528 at the latest he was very close to Wolsey, which was to be a circumstance of great importance in the crisis which was now looming. Among those drafting documents on his behalf, running errands and generally acting as his agents occur the names of Thomas Wriothesley, William Brabazon and Ralph Sadler, who were clearly his most trusted servants, and whose fortunes were tied to his in the great move which was impending by the summer of 1529.

Then in July 1529 he wrote his will, or rather he completed a will upon which he had been working for some months.[38] Why he should have done this when he was forty-four years old and apparently in the best of health is something of a mystery, but it was probably connected with the death of his wife, Elizabeth, which seems to have occurred towards the end of 1528. His young daughters Anne and Grace also died while the will was in preparation, and these domestic tragedies may well have turned his thoughts towards his own mortality. It is an interesting document in many ways, starting as it does with the bequest of his soul to 'the great God of heaven, my maker and redeemer', and with a petition to the Virgin Mary and the whole company of heaven to be intercessors for him.[39] Nothing could have been more correct and orthodox, because such a formula betrays no hint of the Lutheran sympathies of which he was subsequently accused. Later on in the substance of his will he continues, 'Item I will that mine executors shall conduct and hire a priest being an honest person of continent and good living to sing for my soul by the space of seven years next after my death, and to give him for the same forty six pounds thirteen shillings and four pence, that is to say vi li xiiis iiiid yearly for his stipend.' Such a provision would have been unthinkable had he been the crypto-Protestant he is sometimes represented as being.[40] The piety of this will is strictly conventional, and, although consistent with the biblical humanism which we know from other sources that he professed, could not cause offence even to the most conservative of minds. Stephen Vaughn and Ralph Sadler, his servants, and John Williamson, his brother-in-law, are named as executors, but it is just possible that he intended it to be seen by Wolsey. That might account for its rather self-conscious orthodoxy, but there is no tangible reason to suppose that he was thinking along these lines. The substance of his bequests are the setting up of a use for his son Gregory, until he shall come to the age of twenty-two whereby the revenues of his lands will be secured, and the distribution of his moveable property among his kindred and servants. Typical of these provisions is that for his niece Alice Wellyfed, who is left 'to her marriage xx li. And if it happen her to die before marriage, then I will the said xx li shall remain to her brother Christopher', and for his mother-in-law Mercy Prior, who is left some silver plate and the exhortation to his executors 'to be good unto her during her life'.[41] It is altogether a generous document, making several bequests to the poor and to the marriage of poor maidens, and it enables us to get closer to the human side of Cromwell than any number of business letters. Unfortunately we do not know how the death of his wife affected him. Between 1520 and 1528 numerous friends asked to be commended to her, and the fifteen years or so that they spent together appear to have been happy, but we can form no impression of her as a person. After

1525 Thomas spent much time travelling, but her letters to him (if she wrote any) do not survive. There is a single reference to her in his will as 'my late wife' and his request that 'poor indigent folk' should pray for all Christian souls does not include any specific reference to her. But then neither does it include any reference to his daughters Anne and Grace, to whom we know he was close. In spite of this last will and testimony, Cromwell's nearest and dearest remain shadowy background figures, belonging to that private life about which he was so reticent.

By 1529 Wolsey had been the king's right-hand man for rather more than fifteen years. They had had their ups and downs, but his influence still remained unsurpassed. In 1525 the cardinal had taken the blame for the failure of the Amicable Grant, which he was bound to do, although the fault had been mainly Henry's. This had temporarily weakened the king's trust in his minister's judgement, because Henry was genuinely unable to see the truth of the matter, and confidence had not been restored until the end of the year.[42] Then in 1527 Henry had been less than frank about his feelings for Anne Boleyn, and, having confessed his doubts about the viability of his marriage, had allowed Wolsey to undertake a diplomatic mission to France for the purpose of finding him another bride. In fact, unbeknown to the cardinal, he had already proposed to Anne, and been accepted, so the mission was a wild goose chase, and offered evidence of a lack of trust between them. Wolsey was chagrined by this, as well he might have been, but more to the point identified Mistress Boleyn as a potential rival for the king's ear, and this had placed him in a considerable dilemma.[43] If he should do his duty, and promote the annulment of the king's marriage in Rome, he would create a formidable power at court and run the risk of losing his unique relationship with Henry. If, on the other hand, he should fail in Rome, not only would he risk Anne's wrath and indignation, but he would inevitably forfeit Henry's favour completely. The Boleyns realised this and, as Anne's influence over the king became greater, regarded the cardinal with steadily increasing suspicion.[44] They read the situation correctly, but for the time being held their fire as he appeared to be the only man capable of resolving the king's problem. He had, after all, a foot in both camps, and consistently overemphasised his influence in the Curia. Then in 1528 he appeared to have succeeded, and Anne became positively polite to him, exchanging gifts in friendly fashion. He had extracted a commission from Clement to enable the king's 'Great Matter' to be heard in England before himself and Lorenzo Campeggio, the Cardinal Protector of England. What he did not know was that Campeggio was under orders to delay proceedings as far as possible, and in no way to find in the King of England's favour.[45] So the Legatine Court which assembled in May 1529 was a sham, and Wolsey was the dupe. At the end of July Campeggio adjourned the court on the pretext of keeping the Roman terms, without reaching any decision, and the fraudulent nature of the proceedings became clear. The king's fury knew no bounds, and Anne was equally enraged. This gave the cardinal's many enemies at court their opportunity, and a series of articles was drawn up against him. Henry, however, bided his time. He may have realised the truth about Campeggio's mission, but the Roman cardinal was beyond his reach, and was allowed to depart in peace, leaving him free to deal with Wolsey in his own way. It was obvious by the middle of August that the latter had lost his master's favour, but it was not clear how far the king's indignation would go, or what the consequences would be.[46] The tension was racked up further by the fact that Henry accorded a private audience to him at the beginning of October, and it began to be speculated that he would survive the crisis. However, on 4 October he was charged with offences under the statute of praemunire, and on the 18th deprived of the Great Seal. As a prince of the Church he could of course have defied the king, although not over the chancellorship, which was in Henry's gift, but he chose not to do so. Instead he pleaded guilty to the absurd charge of praemunire, and all his properties and promotions were declared forfeit.[47] His servants, including Thomas Cromwell, were left in limbo, because without resources he could not pay them or reward them in any way, and Cromwell ran the risk of being exposed to the popular fury over his role in the monastic dissolutions.

It is against this background that Cavendish's famous story of his encounter with Thomas must be set. Cavendish was Wolsey's gentleman usher, and was writing many years after the event, but his account nevertheless has a ring of truth about it.

> It chanced me upon All Hallows day (1 November) to come into the Great Chamber at Esher in the morning to give mine attendance, where I found Mr Cromwell leaning in the great window with a primer in his hand, saying Our Lady Matins, which had been since a strange sight in him.[48]

Obviously in spite of his will he had no great reputation for piety in Wolsey's household. On this occasion, however,

> he prayed no more earnestly than he distilled tears as fast from his eyes. Whom I saluted and bade good morrow; and with that I perceived his moist cheeks, the which he wiped with his napkin. To

whom I said, 'Why Mr. Cromwell, what means this dole? Is my lord in any danger that ye do lament for him, or is it for any other loss that ye have sustained by misfortune?'

Given the circumstances of early November this might seem a disingenuous question, but Thomas apparently answered, 'Nay, it is for my unhappy adventure. For I am like to lose all that I have laboured for all the days of my life, for doing of my master true and diligent service.'

Cavendish apparently sought to reassure him that he had done nothing without his lord's commandment, and nothing of which he had any need to be ashamed:

'Well, well,' quoth he, 'I cannot tell; but this I see before mine eyes, that everything is as it is taken; and this I know well that I am disdained withal for my master's sake, and yet I am sure that there is no cause why they should do so. An evil name once gotten will not lightly be put away.'[49]

His mood of despair did not last, however, because even before his conversation with Cavendish had come to an end, he had formed a remedial plan of action. He would take the bull by the horns and ride to the court, where he would 'make or mar, or ever I come again', perhaps hoping that he had attracted sufficient good opinions for his loyal service to overcome the collapse of the cardinal's fortunes. As we shall see, his hopes were justified, but not without further effort on his part. That same afternoon, having assisted in paying off Wolsey's menial servants, a process in which he persuaded his master's chaplains (whose benefices were unaffected by Wolsey's disgrace) to help, he sought permission and rode to London.⁵⁰ There he picked up a plan which he had already formulated, because a letter from his servant Ralph Sadler, dated that same day, makes it clear that he had earlier sent Sadler to speak to John Gage, the vice-chamberlain of the household, about the possibility of securing a place in the parliament which had been called on 9 August. This was now urgent, as the assembly was due to meet on 4 November, but Sadler had not been idle:

> I spake with Mr Gage and according to your commandment moved him to speak to unto my Lord of Norfolk for the burgess room of the parliament on your behalf. And he accordingly so did without delay like a faithful friend. Whereupon my said Lord of Norfolk answered the said Gage that he had spoken with the king his highness and that his highness was very well contented that you should be a burgess...⁵¹

provided that he ordered himself in accordance with such instructions as Norfolk should give him from the king. These conversations must have taken at least a few days, and Cromwell's gloom on 1 November may have been occasioned by the fact that he had not at that time received Sadler's encouraging letter, and his urgent ride to the court that same afternoon may well have been prompted by the need to know what progress his quest had made. It was one thing, however, to secure the king's approval and another to find a seat, because Henry did not offer any help in that connection. It is natural to assume that Norfolk, who controlled several boroughs, was the relevant patron, but this appears not to have been the case. Having approached his friend Sir Thomas Rush unsuccessfully to secure a nomination for Orford in Suffolk, he then asked Sir William Paulet, who had been Wolsey's steward in the diocese of Winchester, to get him selected for one of the Winchester boroughs.[52] This worked, and in the nick of time, on 3 November, he was named as one of the burgesses for Taunton. We do not know who was displaced to achieve this, but on 4 November Cromwell was able to take his seat in the House of Commons, and the first step in his escape strategy had been taken.

How he used his opportunity is a matter of some controversy, because helping his employer and helping himself were not clearly distinguishable. He appears to have persuaded the cardinal to grant annuities to certain key members of the court, and took the credit for these gifts himself, which would not have been hard to do. Residing at Esher, and out of touch with affairs, Wolsey was wholly dependant upon Cromwell for his hopes of redemption. In December, for instance, he wrote to him asking him to find some way to assuage the displeasure of Lady Anne: 'All possible means must be used for attaining her favour ... I commit me to your wise handling.'[53] The following month Anne sent a token to the disgraced minister, so it does not appear that Cromwell's efforts were altogether in vain. The unknown factor in this equation is of course the king's own attitude. He seems to have allowed the cardinal's enemies to promote a Bill of attainder against him early in the session, and then permitted Cromwell with a 'wise and pithy' speech to talk it out. He had evidently decided that Wolsey's submission was sufficient, and by the new year he had pardoned his praemunire and reinstated him at York.[54] For both these developments his good servant took a share of the credit, and justly so because he never seems to have relaxed his efforts on the cardinal's behalf, but it was the king who was responsible, and it is not surprising that rumours of his reinstatement should have been rife by January 1530. His redemption, however, only went so far; neither St Albans Abbey nor the palace of Richmond were recovered, and Wolsey's treasured creations at Oxford and Ipswich remained forfeit. On 22 November William Capon wrote to Cromwell from Ipswich to say that the king's commissioners had been to the college and removed various items, but that he had not relinquished his title to them, and asked for instructions as to how to proceed.[55] We do not know what answer he received, but the handover of both colleges seems to have been completed by February 1530, when John Williamson sent Cromwell copies of the surveys which had been made. He, more than anyone else, would be able to judge their accuracy. Meanwhile Wolsey continued to be almost pathetically dependent on his servant, addressing him as 'my only comfort and my only help ... mine own good Thomas and my only refuge and aid'.[56] Whether Cromwell was deserving of this trust is another matter, but on the whole the evidence is positive. He did his best for Wolsey's treasured colleges, and may have been responsible for Henry's decision to continue the foundation in Oxford as his own, a move which seems to have been made by the end of December. In 1546 the King's College became Christ Church. Whether he deserves any of the credit for the king's decision to allow the Archbishop of York to proceed to his diocese (which he had never visited) at the beginning of April is uncertain, but Sir John Gage did choose him to write to with a warning not to allow the cardinal to make a grand procession of his journey to the North, because the king would hold him answerable for any unnecessary display.[57]

Meanwhile Wolsey's health was giving cause for concern. On 19 January de Augustino, his physician, wrote to Cromwell urgently requesting that Dr Butts, who served the king in the same capacity, should be sent down to Esher and should bring some electuaries with him. What was wrong with him we do not know, but the crisis seems to have passed because he was soon writing to Cromwell again in the same pleading tone as before. He will do nothing without his advice, and begs him to come down to Esher. How often Cromwell made that trip is not clear, but it was not often enough to satisfy Wolsey. On 6 February he was disappointed not to have seen him the previous night, and on 10 March he was expecting a visit in the morning.[58] Obviously they had much to discuss, not least the diocese of Winchester from which Wolsey was soliciting a pension. It may have been the result of his poor health, but the cardinal's letters during the spring of 1530 became increasingly querulous. Perhaps he suspected his servant of playing a double game, and not without justice because Cromwell was naturally seeking to turn his constant presence in the court to his own advantage. As early as 3 February 1530 Stephen Vaughn wrote from Antwerp to congratulate him on his success; 'you now sail in a safe haven,' he declared, obviously in response to news of the king's favour, and on 13 April Cromwell carried out a profitable exchange of lands with the king. This cost him £500 as he had little land to offer, but was well worthwhile, because in addition to the profits of the lands secured, such an exchange was a sure token of the royal grace.[59] Interestingly enough, a subsidy assessment of Wolsey's household made in January 1530 includes both John and Robert Cromwell, who were presumably kinsmen, but makes no mention of Thomas.[60] This may have been for the simple reason that he was no longer resident, but it may also represent another step in his gradual detachment from the cardinal. If that was the case, neither of them was admitting it; William, Lord Sandys, wrote to Cromwell on 17 June about the keepership of the manor of Farnham on the assumption that he spoke for Wolsey, who was still the bishop there in spite of his forfeitures, and at the end of the same month Cromwell wrote to the cardinal what can only be described as a friendly letter about diverse pieces of business which they had in hand. On 30 July Wolsey wrote to him again, expressing appreciation for all the pains that he had taken. Whatever was left of his estate he owed to Cromwell's efforts, for which he would requite him when he was able. However he also complains of his renewed illness, and how he cannot sleep for weeping, which makes the reader suspect that he was already in the grip of that ailment which was to carry him off in November.[61] On 18 August it was noted that Mr Cromwell had such opportunities of access to the king that it was to be hoped that he would remember Wolsey in his misfortune, and a few days later Thomas replied to his letter of the 30th, discussing various bits of business and ending, 'I am, and during my life shall be, with your Grace in heart, spirit, prayer and service, to the uttermost of my power.'[62] There is no reason to suppose that he was being dishonest, but his access to the king had opened opportunities which he could not afford to ignore, and he was briefly in the position of the man who serves two masters. Either Wolsey would be restored to grace or he would be forced to cut his ties with him, no matter what professions he might make.

If Cromwell was being less than straight with the cardinal, Wolsey was also not being entirely frank with his servant. We do not know what they discussed at Esher before his departure for the North, but there is no mention in the surviving correspondence of the latter's attempts to collect Continental support for his reinstatement, let alone of his surreptitious efforts to open negotiations with the papacy.[63] Cromwell was his agent for domestic affairs, and broad though his remit was, it did not include this sort of business. There is no trace in Cromwell's papers of the near fiasco over the Treaty of Cambrai in 1529, which played a large part in the original withdrawal of the king's confidence, nor of his interest in the papal election of 1523, and there is no mention of these later negotiations either. Wolsey's agent in these transactions was his Italian physician Augustine Augustino, who proved less than trustworthy when he was arrested at the beginning of November 1530, although whether he was responsible for the original incriminating leak is not clear. Wolsey was arrested on the same day, but whereas Augustino was whisked straight off to the Tower for interrogation, the cardinal was allowed to make his own way south under escort, while the case against him was assembled. Although he had been planning a grand enthronement ceremony in York, in fact he never made it further north than Southwell, being arrested at Cawood on 4 November.[64] On his way to London his various ailments, and the general misery of his circumstances, caught up with him and he died (not without a suspicion of self-harm) at Leicester Abbey on 29 November. Just as he had been no party to the negotiations which brought about Wolsey's final downfall, so Thomas Cromwell was not affected by his passing. He had done his duty as long as it was relevant, but by December 1530 an altogether more appealing prospect was opening up before him.

While all this was going on he continued his private legal practice, taking full advantage of his position at court and in the cardinal's confidence. On 4 June 1527, for example, Sir John Vere wrote an appreciative letter to Cromwell, saying that 'your sending to Edward Hardy made him more pliant than either I or Sir Giles

Capell could achieve' with the result that the dispute between Hardy and one Kneewill was settled.[65] We do not know the nature of Cromwell's intervention, or what the dispute was about, but this tribute indicates that he earned his fee. Francis Lovell was involved in a matrimonial tangle in March 1528, and sought his guidance as to how to proceed, and in December of the same year he arbitrated a dispute between Ralph Dodman, alderman of London, and John Creke over certain bonds which had been delivered in Bilbao. His position with the cardinal meant that clergy frequently appealed to him to sort out problems relating to their benefices, and cases could be cited from both Bangor and Norwich, which usually involved the payment of fees.[66] His remit was wide, and in December 1529 he arbitrated another dispute, this time jointly with Nicholas Lambert, alderman of London, in a domestic row between two London grocers, and took bonds from them to abide by their decision. Some of his commissions seem to have come from the king, although it would be wrong to suppose that he was actually in the royal service at this time. For example Sir John Russell wrote to him on 1 June 1530, when Wolsey was already in the North, instructing him on Henry's behalf to make out a patent for a particular office, which was clearly in the cardinal's gift as archbishop, and may have been the treasurership which had been discussed earlier. He was also to draft a letter for Wolsey's consent, and to drop a hint that the king had not forgotten his former minister. The archbishop held the seal for this appointment, so his consent was essential, although in view of what was to happen five months later, the hint may have been less than reassuring. Russell also went on to say that Henry was speaking well of Cromwell, which may be taken as an indication that he would be prepared to take him into service when the circumstances permitted.[67] However, in spite of the temptation, there is no evidence to suggest that, unlike Stephen Gardiner, he rushed to abandon the fallen chancellor. As long as Wolsey was alive, and irrespective of misunderstandings between them, he continued to regard himself as the cardinal's man, and Henry seems to have understood this position and accepted it. Once Wolsey was dead, however, the rules of engagement changed. His last service to his former master came at the end of November 1530, when he arranged his obsequies and settled his debts as far as he was able. A list of the cardinal's personal effects was also drawn up, although in the absence of a will it is difficult to know what happened to them.[68] It is reasonable to suppose that once his accounts were settled what was left would have been divided among his remaining servants, and that Cromwell took the lion's share.

3

THE KING'S SERVANT, 1533–1536

What if [Henry] *should shortly after change his mind, and exercise in deed the Supremacy over the church of the realm ... or what if the Crown of this realm should in time fall to an infant or a woman. What shall we then do? Whom shall we sue unto? Or where shall we have remedy?*

Bishop John Fisher

So when did Cromwell enter the king's service? There are indications that he may have been involved in drafting the anticlerical legislation in the autumn of 1529, but the evidence is inconclusive and he may have been functioning simply as a member of a House of Commons committee.[1] The best guess is probably January 1530, but at that stage he would have been a comparatively humble member of the administrative staff, and evidently did not consider that to be incompatible with his relationship to Wolsey. Some such step would explain Stephen Vaughn's remark about his sailing 'in a safe haven'. The story told much later of a dramatic interview with the king, during which he presented Henry with a blueprint for ending his matrimonial troubles and promised to make him 'the richest prince in Christendom', is almost certainly a fabrication.[2] Neither Cavendish nor Hall, who were contemporary observers, mention any such event, and indeed Cavendish speaks explicitly of his growing gradually in favour during the year 1530. What does seem to have been the case, however, is that after about a year, Cromwell had become a member of the king's council. In 1531 this was not the honour which it would have been ten years later, when the formation of the Privy Council had consolidated that inner ring, to which he certainly did not belong. Cromwell was what would have been known at the time as a Councillor at Large, who would be summoned only when his particular expertise was required. That expertise was in the law, and he was what would have been known a few years earlier as a 'Councillor Learned'.[3]

As such, he may well have been called upon to give an opinion on the king's marriage, because during 1530 Henry was groping his way towards a new policy. Having run up against a stone wall of papal and Imperial obstruction, he was looking for a way to declare his independence and circumvent them both by getting a verdict declared within England. Such an idea was not altogether new. As long before as 1515 he had spoken of having no superior on earth, in connection with the Standish affair, but that had not been followed up or particularly noted outside England. More importantly, and much more recently, his specially established 'think tank' on the situation had come up with a more considered judgement to the same effect.[4] This group, which consisted of Nicholas de Burgo, Edward Foxe and Thomas Cranmer, had been set up in 1529 on the urging of Anne Boleyn to find a solution to the problem. Henry must have been kept in touch with their workings because before its report was produced, in the summer of 1530, Henry was instructing his agents in Rome to urge the *privilegium regni*, which claims that, by the ancient privileges of his kingdom, no King of England could be cited to appear outside of his realm, and that any issues of ecclesiastical jurisdiction had to be settled domestically. Decisions of the early councils were invoked in support of this, but unsurprisingly his agents could find no reference to it in the Vatican Archives.[5] Nor did those scouring the libraries of Europe for evidence to support his case find anything relevant, even when they were allowed to look. The search at home proved to be more fruitful, and it must have been some word of that which the king was using in his urgent quest. His researchers turned up a letter in the so-called *Leges Edwardi Confessoris*, which purported to have been written by the second-century Pope Eleutherius to King Lucius of Britain, declaring that all jurisdiction belonged to him as a Christian king, including that over the Church. That King Lucius was a myth and the letter a forgery was not appreciated by anyone at the time. More substantially, according to Aelred, King Edgar had reproved the morals of the clergy, and claimed that such a judgement belonged to him as king.[6] According to Ralph de Diceto, because of the scandal of the rivalry of two Popes, Urban and Clement, England had refused obedience to any Pope after the death of Gregory VII in 1085, but that was manifestly untrue, and altogether the list of authorities was not impressive. Equally questionable was the quotation from Bracton, saying that the king was *vicarius dei*, and his rule the rule of God, because he had no superior. Bracton was no canonist, and his statement in any case is not clear. The Old Testament was also appealed to, the reforms of Jehosophat being particularly relevant. Jehosophat had established spiritual judges in all the cities of Israel, and appointed priests and others to hear appeals at Jerusalem, which seemed to Henry to constitute a biblical precedent for what he wanted to do.[7] While the king had God-ordained sovereignty, he might from time to time delegate a part of that authority to the priesthood, which kings of England had manifestly done for centuries, without forfeiting his rights in that respect. Such powers may never be alienated finally from the king's divinely granted prerogative. Consequently Henry was speaking of himself as Emperor and Pope in his own realm as early as September 1530. These ideas were familiar in English jurisprudence, so it is not surprising to find the Duke of Norfolk airing them to Chapuys before the end of 1530.[8] However, when the king canvassed them in a specially convened meeting of lawyers and divines in October 1530, and asked whether Parliament had the right to enact that the king's cause be heard by the Archbishop of Canterbury, notwithstanding the Pope's prohibition, he was met with a flat negative.[9] It is not known whether Cromwell was one of the lawyers consulted, but if so then the verdict was a defeat for him as well, because although he was not a member of the king's 'think tank', it is fairly clear that he was exploring the same ground. He may well have been one of the lawyers whom the king was consulting in a general sense. Henry was angry at the rebuff, and postponed the next session of Parliament until January 1531 because there seemed to be little point in convening it if it was unable to help him in his dilemma. Instead he took the dramatic step of indicting the whole clerical estate of praemunire on the grounds that the exercise of ecclesiastical jurisdiction itself constituted a breach of the statute, which was, in a sense, an extension of the indictment to which Wolsey had pleaded guilty the previous year.[10]

When the convocations met in January 1531, the clergy soon found themselves bargaining with the king over the terms of a settlement. This was undoubtedly Henry's intention, because to have pressed ahead with the indictment would have created enormous problems, not least how to fund a church whose entire property had been declared forfeit. They eventually settled for fines, or grants as they were called, of £118,000; £100,000 for Canterbury and £18,000 for York. Before this could be accepted, however, there was an exchange of articles with the king, whereby the clergy requested five years to pay, and Henry demanded that convocation recognise his ecclesiastical jurisdiction. After considerable debate, and further exchanges with the Council, in early February an agreement was reached, whereby the king accepted the delayed payment, and the clergy accepted the king's supremacy over the Church. This last clause proved to be particularly contentious, and was agreed to only with the saving clause 'in so far as the law of Christ allows'. This form of words, which could mean everything or nothing according to how they were interpreted, was apparently suggested by Cromwell, who, with Thomas Audley, sat in on the convocation debate on the king's behalf.[11] It was not mentioned, except by implication, when Parliament confirmed the royal pardon later in the same session. It was stated instead that the exercising of spiritual jurisdiction

> shall be by authority of this present pardon, acquitted, pardoned, released and discharged against His Highness, his heirs, successors and executors, and every of them, of all manner offences, contempts and trespasses committed or done against all and singular statute and statutes of provisors, provisions or praemunire and every of them.[12]

Henry was at pains to reassure the clergy that he did not mean by this any extension of the powers which he already exercised under the statutes, and that, although he saw himself as 'Supreme Head and Protector' of the Church, he did not intend to exercise spiritual functions in his own person. Bishop Fisher was not reassured. In continuing to object to the agreement now reached, he asked the pertinent question,

> What if he should shortly after change his mind, and exercise in deed the supremacy over the church of this realm. Or what if he should die and his successor challenge the continuance of the same? Or what if the crown of this realm should in time fall to an infant or a woman that shall still continue and take the same upon them? What shall we then do? Whom shall we sue unto? Or where shall we have remedy?[13]

All contingencies which were to arise in due course. However, for the time being Henry took his money and professed himself satisfied. This may partly have been because he was finding his relations with the papacy increasingly difficult, and partly because at about the same time he received a courteous letter from the newly formed Schmalkaldic League. This explained and justified the stand that the Lutheran princes had taken at the Diet of Augsburg in the previous year, in terms which might have been designed to appeal to Henry, emphasising as it did the jurisdictional dispute with the papacy, and playing down the doctrinal aspects. This letter was probably the work of Philip Melanchthon, who was at the same time working on his *Apology of the Augsburg Confession*, which was an irenic response to the Catholic Confutation which had appeared towards the end of

1530.[14] For whatever reason, the king was markedly less hostile to the Lutherans in 1531 than he was either before or after, and in May he responded to the League's letter in non-committal but positive terms.

This attitude may also have been conditioned by the fact that he was pursuing Tyndale with offers of reconciliation. William Tyndale had fled to the Continent in 1525, having failed in his bid to persuade Cuthbert Tunstall, the Bishop of London, to support his plans for a translation of the Bible into English. Since then he had produced an English version of the New Testament, which various agents had smuggled into England. This had provoked savage proclamations in March 1529 and June 1530 against erroneous books, which had named Tyndale, along with Simon Fish and John Frith, as one of those whose works were contrary to the Catholic faith.[15] By the end of 1530 this campaign was being orchestrated by Sir Thomas More, and although Henry did not dissent from it, there are signs that his own position had shifted slightly. Tyndale had also written *The Obedience of a Christian Man*, certain aspects of which appealed to the king, and this had suggested the possibility of recruiting him to the propaganda campaign in favour of the annulment of Henry's first marriage, which was then beginning to gather momentum.[16] It is also possible that he was listening to the advice of Thomas Cromwell, whose Christian Humanism was beginning to edge in an unorthodox direction at the same time. Although certainly not a Lutheran at this (or any other) stage, he was very much the king's man on his marriage issue, and as such would have suggested the recruitment of Tyndale as a supporter. This would be made more likely if he knew of Henry's reaction to the *Obedience*, which he almost certainly did because he was in alliance with Anne Boleyn at this time. It was therefore Stephen Vaughn, Cromwell's friend and servant, who was chosen to go across to Antwerp to sound him out.[17] The choice of Vaughn for this mission is made more significant by the fact that, on a previous visit to Brabant, questions had been raised about his orthodoxy, and More had an unfriendly eye upon him. He wrote to Tyndale as soon as he arrived, which was probably before Christmas 1530, and reported to the king on 26 January. In spite of having some difficulty in locating the reformer, he had eventually got a letter through, offering him a safe conduct for his return. It is not clear whether the condition of defending the king's position was made at this time or not, and Vaughn described his instructions as contradictory, but Tyndale's response was in any case a polite refusal. He feared a trap, and although he did not say so, clearly did not trust the king's word.[18] In view of the fierceness of the dispute with Thomas More in which he was engaged, this was a sensible decision, and bearing in mind that he could not in conscience have promoted Henry's matrimonial cause, the only rational thing to have done. Vaughn, however, also reported to Cromwell at the same time, and said things which he would not have ventured to say to the king. He doubted very much whether Tyndale would ever return to England while More was in office, and, having answered More's attack on him, would write no further polemic, but would concentrate rather on his translation of the Old Testament. Tyndale was a wiser man than Henry took him for, and he wished to God that he was back in England.[19] Obviously he considered it to be safer to commend Tyndale to Cromwell than to the king. This is confirmed by a subsequent letter, written by Vaughn on 25 March, with which he enclosed a copy of Tyndale's latest answer to More, and an anxious enquiry as to whether it would be safe to let the king see it. His concern was justified because, in the spring of 1531, convocation was still pursuing known evangelicals, including Edward Crome and Hugh Latimer, with charges of heresy, and it was only a rapid climbdown by the latter which protected them from prosecution.[20] Cromwell may well have recommended submission, because he was beginning to emerge as a discreet patron of evangelical causes, and was a party to a suit which Richard Tracy and his father's executors brought against the chancellor of Worcester diocese. William Tracy had left a will in which he had expressed a belief in justification by faith alone, which was classic Lutheran doctrine, and which the Archbishop of Canterbury pronounced heretical. The chancellor had then caused his body to be exhumed and burnt. His executors, with Cromwell's support, successfully sued the chancellor for exceeding his powers and won damages of £300.[21] The money, however, was unimportant by comparison with the principle involved, whereby the ecclesiastical jurisdiction was curtailed. Henry could hardly object to such a decision, which was very much in accordance with the views expressed in his pardon of the clergy, and if Cromwell was testing the waters of Henry's acquiescence, then he had done so successfully.

They were treading a tightrope, because when Vaughn ventured to send a copy of a part of Tyndale's *Answer to More* to the king on 18 April, with a commendation of the author as a loyal subject, he provoked what must have been a completely unexpected rebuke from Cromwell. It seems that the latter was instructed by Henry to reply on his behalf, and the surviving draft of the letter bears much evidence of revision. It is an inconsistent document including many harsh words against Tyndale, but ending with a postscript in which Cromwell urges his agent to carry on as before![22] It is perhaps not unreasonable to suppose that the postscript was added after Henry had vetted the main letter. Anyway there was no royal rebuke for Cromwell, and no recall for Stephen Vaughn. On 20 May the latter, quite unabashed, was telling the king that Tyndale earnestly wanted a reconciliation, and was longing for the day when Henry would authorise an English translation of the Scriptures.[23] Either he had missed the point of the letter he had earlier received, or Henry had changed his mind about the validity of his mission. That this may have been the case is indicated by Vaughn's next letter to Cromwell, dated 19 June, with which he enclosed an unnamed book of Luther's, which would have been a rash thing to have done had not some word of the king's shift of position reached him. However he hesitated to send a copy of Melanchthon's treatise on the Augsburg Confession to Henry, in case it should fall into unfriendly hands, and in that he was undoubtedly wise. Tyndale, Vaughn went on to explain, had now completed his translation of Jonah, and encouraged George Joye, another evangelical exile, to translate the prophecies of Isaiah. Both these works had been printed in Antwerp, and would appear in England in due course. He sent this letter in two copies,[24] presumably fearing interception, and that was a wise precaution, because Henry's attitude appears to have been completely schizophrenic. On the one hand he was allowing John Stokesley, the Bishop of London, and Sir Thomas More to wage a fierce war on heretics, and on the other encouraging Vaughn and Cromwell in their dealings with Continental Lutherans and their fellow travellers. Thomas Bilney went to the stake in August 1531, and Richard Bayfield in November, which could not have happened without the king's permission. On 3 December another proclamation denounced

Tyndale as a spreader of seditious heresy, and at the same time More was trying to extract from George Constantine relevant details of his dealings with Vaughn, who was understandably apprehensive.[25] Nevertheless on 14 November he wrote again (in two copies) to Cromwell, enclosing a copy of Robert Barnes's *Supplication unto King Henry VIII*, and urging that he present it to the king and commend its author. Since Barnes had fled from England two years earlier, and made his way to Wittenburg, where he became a pupil of Luther, this might seem an exceptionally rash course to have advocated, and we do not know whether Cromwell followed up his suggestion.[26] Probably not in view of the fate of Richard Bayfield at about that time. In a letter dated 6 December he urged Vaughn to be extra careful and watchful, in order not to give More any pretext to move against him; Vaughn replied a few days later, declaring that he was neither a Lutheran nor a 'Tyndalian'. This profession may have been honest in terms of his doctrinal allegiance, but scarcely explained his dealings with the reformers, and may well have been inserted for the benefit of the king, to whom it was clearly intended to be shown.[27] Henry may even have been convinced, because Vaughn was able to continue his search for Lutheran books on Cromwell's behalf, and the latter was able early in 1532 to secure a safe conduct for Barnes to come to England. Unlike Tyndale, Barnes was willing to take that risk, and even had a private audience with the king. Although his supplication was offensive to the monarch in the sense that it advocated justification by faith alone, it also explained a number of Lutheran tenets in terms which were acceptable to Henry, and contained a fulsome declaration of loyalty to his sovereign.[28] The king would have been looking for some endorsement of his position on his marriage, and over that it is likely that Barnes was non-committal, because rather to everyone's surprise, Luther himself had emerged as a strong supporter of Catherine, brushing aside Henry's Levitical arguments as irrelevant. He recognised the king's need for a male heir, and advocated bigamy as a solution to the problem. Henry was unimpressed, but he did not abandon his cautious interest in the Lutheran alliance, nor take any action against Barnes, Vaughn or Cromwell.

It is possible that this mild response was due to the latter's increasing influence in the king's counsels, because there is some evidence to suggest that Henry was beginning to perceive his dispute with the Pope as a jurisdictional issue only, which did not impinge upon the Catholicity of his faith.[29] This was Cromwell's view throughout, and his interest in Lutheran works was focused mainly on the German's quarrel with the Church as an institution, rather than on debates about justification or the Eucharist. In his daily dealings with the king, he would have been very careful to stress this distinction, which increased the former's confidence in him at no cost to his own conscience. It is not, therefore, particularly surprising that an attack should have been launched in Parliament against the clergy, while the fires of Smithfield were still consuming heretics. This took the form of the Supplication against the Ordinaries, which was introduced into the Commons towards the end of February 1532.[30] This may have been designed to take the place of whatever the Duke of Norfolk had been hoping to produce from a meeting held on 14 February. At that meeting he had urged that matrimonial jurisdiction belonged to the king 'who is emperor in his kingdom', and not to the Pope. However the House was clearly not yet ready for so radical a notion, and nothing resulted. Instead the Commons turned back to what they understood and appreciated better – bashing the churchmen. The first draft of this document was produced in house, and it is not known by whom, but its consistency with what was shortly to become government policy make it likely that the councillors in the Commons played a leading part.[31] The supplication was redrafted several times, and the penultimate version is in the hand of Sir Thomas Audley, which makes it clear that by then it had become an official measure. As such, it was part of a two-pronged attack upon the Church, the other prong being the threat to papal revenues which eventually emerged as the Act in Conditional Restraint of Annates. The draft of this Bill is partly in Thomas Cromwell's hand, and that points to the strategist who was behind these congruent measures. It is indeed possible that the first draft of the supplication dates from the session of 1529, when such matters were very much in the minds of members. It was not introduced in that session, but an awareness of its existence might well have prompted Cromwell or Audley to seize on it as being relevant to the business of 1532, and might also account for the fact that it was rewritten. Cromwell revised the first part of the document completely, removing a reference to the role of the bishops in Parliament, so that it became a direct attack upon the legislative functions of convocation, where laws were made 'without your royal assent or knowledge, or the assent or consent of any of your lay subjects'.[32] The revised supplication went on to complain about the 'light and frivolous' causes for which laymen were summoned before the spiritual courts, and particularly of the *ex officio* procedure and the use of false witnesses. The complaints went on to cover the use of excommunication for 'small and light' causes, the excessive fees charged by the spiritual courts, and nepotism and simony in the conferring of benefices.[33] The evidence suggests that this supplication was deliberately revived in 1532 as a part of a strategy of applying pressure to the English Church to make it more willing to do the king's bidding over his marriage. It did not become an Act, but was nevertheless submitted to Henry, who passed it to convocation for their comments. The result was a resounding defence of clerical privileges, penned by Stephen Gardiner, the newly appointed Bishop of Winchester, and the king was not pleased, passing it back to the House of Commons with the message that it would 'smally content' them. This proved to be an understatement. The Parliament pressed its attack through a statute providing for the diversion of annates from the Pope to the Crown, and made it clear that Henry had accepted their supplication, and would act upon it. Gardiner, who was the king's secretary, and who had misjudged the situation completely, hastily penned a treatise on *True Obedience* in order to redeem his career, and the convocation surrendered their legislative independence to the king.[34] This last was what mattered, and, on receiving the news, Sir Thomas More resigned as Lord Chancellor, recognising the defeat of his own campaign, which had been waged in alliance with the Church. By astute parliamentary management, Cromwell had won the first round in his battle for the king's mind. Henry had battered the clergy into submission, and it now remained to see what use he would make of his victory.

On 16 May 1532 the Submission of the Clergy, which embodied complete surrender on the question of jurisdictional independence, was offered to the king at Westminster. An interesting group of councillors was present on that occasion: George, Lord Abergavenny; John, Lord Hussey; John, Lord Mordaunt; Sir William Fitzwilliam; and Thomas Cromwell. None of these was a senior councillor, and Cromwell's closeness to the king can be deduced rather than proved. He had only just become an office holder, having been appointed Master of the King's Jewels on 14 April, but the others were all household officers, and with the exception of Hussey were to be associated with Cromwell over the next few years.[35] Archbishop Warham had been opposed to the surrender, but had lacked the resolution to withstand it. He was a long-standing royal servant and had no wish to be seen as resisting the king's wishes on so important a matter. What he might have done about implementing the new powers which he had been given by implication we do not know, because he died on 22 August, and that left the way open for Henry to proceed to the next stage of his plan. Cromwell could not have anticipated Warham's death, but it came very opportunely for the campaign which he had been discreetly waging for the last two years, to persuade the king to act unilaterally.[36] The Church as an institution would no longer oppose him, and now he had the opportunity to appoint a compliant archbishop. At the same time, and with the same ultimate objective in view, Henry pursued his plan for a face-to-face meeting with Francis I. Whatever course of action he followed in order to rid himself of Catherine, it was bound to be opposed by the Emperor, and Francis, who was constantly at odds with Charles, even when not actually at war with him, was naturally looked on as an ally. The King of France appreciated this point perfectly, and wished to take advantage of it to seal his friendship with Henry, whose position athwart the Emperor's lines of communication between Spain and the Low Countries was potentially of great value to him. After considerable negotiation a meeting was therefore arranged to take place at Calais in October 1532.[37] Anne Boleyn was to accompany her lover, and in order to give her a suitable dignity for the occasion, he created her Marquis of Pembroke on 1 September. Whether he had any other plans for her at this stage is not clear. There was speculation that they might marry in Calais, and they may in fact have done so, but if so, then it was kept very secret.[38] Francis proved affable, but his queen refused to receive her on the grounds of her ambiguous status, which suggests that even the most private of assurances that she was actually married to Henry was not forthcoming. Nevertheless the king seems to have convinced her, and himself, that a way out of his matrimonial difficulties had now been found. Thomas Cromwell, who was by this time a member of the inner ring of the council, accompanied him to Calais and persuaded him to proceed from words to actions. At some point in late November or early December the couple slept together for the first time. Their decision to do so was no doubt aided by the fact that they were weatherbound in Calais, but it still represented a decisive change in their relationship, thanks to the opportune death of Warham, and Cromwell (if he knew about it) was no doubt suitably gratified.[39]

It had taken time to induce Henry to move from the brave words of 1530 to the resolute action of November 1532, and this change has been attributed to the influence of Thomas Cromwell. It was probably at the end of 1531 that Cromwell had advanced from being a Councillor at Large to membership of the inner ring, and the Supplication against the Ordinaries was his first major service to the Crown. There is no doubt that he was responsible for converting the Commons draft of 1529 into the supplication as that was presented to the king, or that it was a cautious but deliberate step on the road that he had mapped out. How completely Henry understood this at that time we do not know, but it is never safe to underestimate the king's intelligence, and it is quite possible that he had grasped the fact that he was heading for a breach with the papacy. His mindset, however, was entirely traditional, and his arguments with the Curia had so far been conducted in terms of precedent and history, so it is likely to have been no easy task to persuade him to so radical a course.[40] Anne had been urging unilateral action since at least 1529, so that when the king eventually came round to the same point of view, her consent was natural. Should she become pregnant, Henry would now have no option but to marry her and declare (by whatever means) his existing union to be null and void. In view of Clement's attitude, a formal breach with Rome would then become inevitable. In late January or early February her condition was established, and the fuse which led to the Act in Restraint of Appeals was lit. An unreliable tradition maintains that they were married on 25 January, but that may well have been the date upon which her pregnancy was discovered.[41] Meanwhile it was essential that the jurisdictional structure necessary for such a sequence of events should be completed by the appointment of an acquiescent archbishop. Henry had already renounced any claim to exercise spiritual jurisdiction in his own person, so the settlement of his marriage would be a matter for the archbishop's court, and he had to be sure that the archbishop would be willing to do his bidding. His choice fell on Thomas Cranmer, the Archdeacon of Taunton; not the most obvious choice, but one who had the essential qualification. Cranmer was wholeheartedly and honestly the king's man over his 'divorce' issue. He had been a member of that group which had produced the *Collectanea satis copiosa* in 1530, and the idea of consulting the European universities had been his.[42] He had also written a tract, now lost, on the divorce issue, and had lodged with the Earl of Wiltshire (Anne Boleyn's father) while he wrote it. In the autumn of 1532 he had been sent off on a diplomatic mission to the Emperor, to whom he was introduced as the king's 'new theologian', and it was during that mission that he was recalled to be the next archbishop. Cranmer was appalled by the summons. Not only did he have no episcopal experience, but he had recently married, his bride being the niece of the Lutheran divine Andreas Osiander. Marriage was forbidden to priests, let alone to an archbishop, and the appointment would mean at least many years of secrecy.[43] It is to be hoped that he consulted Margaret, because the sacrifice would be mainly hers, but there could really be no hope of avoiding it and remaining the king's good subject. So in mid-January he returned to take up the unwelcome office, and Henry applied to Rome for his pallium. In spite of his marriage, he was not a Lutheran, and his doctrinal and ecclesiastical positions were very close to those of the king. In short he was an ideal man for the job, and returned to a situation in which his first task would be to declare the king's marriage to Catherine to be null and void, and to confirm the nuptial which had already taken place between Henry and Anne. In spite of being aware of Cranmer's antecedents, Clement made no difficulties about granting the pallium, and he was consecrated on 30 March 1533.[44] It was therefore as a papally confirmed archbishop that he prepared to ignore the Pope's prohibition and to pronounce on Henry's first marriage. We do not know what Cromwell's reaction to this appointment may have been, but he certainly knew Cranmer and knew the way that he was thinking. It is just possible that he may have suggested him to the king, because he understood the importance of the office, and indeed had set up the task which Cranmer inherited. It is hard to believe that he was not delighted.

While Thomas Cranmer awaited his consecration, Parliament had taken the essential step to make his decision final in English law; it enacted the Restraint of Appeals. This measure, which was introduced into the Commons on 14 March, was based upon the position already conceded that the king was the fountainhead of all jurisdiction, spiritual as well as temporal. However it went further and prohibited all appeals to the papacy, on the ground that the English Church was sufficient to fulfil the offices of the spirituality 'without the intermeddling of any exterior person or persons'. Spiritual jurisdiction descended from the king or from his Imperial crown, God having given to him authority to render justice in all manner of causes arising within the realm.[45] The king was no 'exterior person' as far as the Church of England was concerned; he was its Supreme Head, the implication being that all Christian princes should exercise similar control. The draft of this Act was amended a number of times, both by Cromwell and the king, with the intention of making it as little contentious as possible, because the government really needed a swift and sure resolution of the king's matrimonial problems. Apart from the thumping theoretical assertion in the preamble about the realm of England being an empire, Cromwell made sure that the Act was strictly practical, concentrating on the costs and delays of the present system. The complaints in the Act are strictly confined to the political interference of Rome within the realm, and the remedies proposed are similarly political.[46] The implication is that this new law is only an extension and revision of the statutes already in place, and that an Act of Parliament could modify the canon law and provide protection against spiritual censures. The Act develops the Royal Supremacy, and places the king at the head of the spiritual jurisdiction. It also, however, indicates that the law necessary to make that jurisdiction effective is a matter for Parliament, which is thus built into the Supremacy in a most fundamental way. All use of the papal authority becomes a usurpation, and the habits of many generations are thus dismissed as fraudulent. On account, however, of the way in which these measures were wrapped up in talk of precedent and 'ancient chronicles', the Bill appeared less revolutionary than it really was, and it rapidly passed both houses, receiving the royal assent on 7 April.[47] Thanks to Cromwell's skilful manipulation of the text, Henry now had his law in place, and in the following month Cranmer's court at Dunstable pronounced his marriage to Catherine null and void, and his marriage to Anne good, in open defiance of the papal prohibition, which was now irrelevant.

By this time there is no doubt, not only that Cromwell was a senior councillor and a member of the inner ring, but that it was he who was guiding Henry's most sensitive policies. His fingerprints are all over the Annates Act, and the plans for Anne Boleyn's coronation, which took place on 1 June. The ceremonial was not his responsibility, but he did succeed in persuading most of the senior nobility to attend a function which they regarded with distaste. The Duke of Suffolk, for example, functioned as High Constable for the day, in spite of being well known for his opposition to the marriage.[48] His duchess, Mary, the king's sister, did not attend, but she was laying sick at Bradgate and died shortly after. Even Cromwell, however, could not conjure a display of enthusiasm out of the citizens of London, and in spite of Anne's studied affability, caps remained on heads and few voices cried out 'God save her'. The king pretended not to notice, but the message would not have been lost on Cromwell, who knew that it would fall to him to implement what was clearly an unpopular policy. The next stage of this was to persuade Catherine to accept her demotion to Princess Dowager of Wales, which the logic of her divorce required. A few days later she was visited at Ampthill by a delegation of councillors, armed with cogent arguments. Cromwell was not among them, but he had drawn up the articles, and it was to him that the browbeaten delegation reported on their return. He cannot have expected any other outcome, and is alleged to have commented wryly that God had done her a disservice in not making her a man, because her courage surpassed that of all the heroes of history and legend.[49] Henry, however, was neither impressed nor amused. He had Catherine moved to Buckden in Cambridgeshire, and reduced her household as a penalty for her intransigence. Shortly after, on 11 July, Pope Clement finally got around to condemning Henry for his abandonment of Catherine and his relationship with Anne, giving him until September to return to his lawful wife.[50] The king, however, had burned his boats, and treated the papal sentence with contempt, no doubt to Cromwell's huge relief because this demonstrated, even more than his marriage had done, Henry's commitment to the policy which they had thrashed out between them. There could now be no turning back, and the future rested on the child which Anne was carrying. However on 7 September she was delivered of a daughter and there was no option but to try again. In spite of respectful congratulations, Cromwell must have cursed his luck, because it would now be at least another year before dynastic security, which had been his objective from the beginning, could be assured.

Meanwhile, he was not spending the whole of his energies on the high politics of the realm. His surviving correspondence shows him to have been active in a multitude of ways. In October 1531 for example he drafted a number of letters concerning various aspects of the king's business, and in 1532, when Gardiner, the king's secretary, was absent on a diplomatic mission to France, Cromwell seems to have stood in as assistant secretary.[51] In January he wrote to the Bishop of Winchester, saying that the king was missing him, and was so pestered with business that he did not know which way to turn. This letter was presumably intended to reassure Gardiner, whose absence from the court was causing him anxieties, and may indicate that Cromwell had been responsible for suggesting him for this mission, since both his going and his coming home were at Henry's discretion.[52] Cromwell also seems to have acquired a reputation as a general 'Mr Fixit' about the court. In January 1531 a priest wrote to him, asking for his help over a matter of debt – 'except only for the help of your mastership, I am utterly undone' – and in February one Reginald Lytylpace wrote from Norwich, 'I hear that you are in the king's service, and in high favour', which suggests that the said Reginald was a little behind the times. In April Henry Darrell solicited his 'continued favour' to his son (who had a place at court with the clerk controller), John Gostwyck (who was not without other contacts at court) besought him to continue his good work in 'the Welsh matter', and the Corporation of Salisbury asked for a commission of Gaol Delivery.[53] Even the nobility expressed their gratitude to this upstart politician. In July 1531 the Earl of Huntingdon solicited his favour for a servant of his, expressing appreciation for past kindnesses, and in August the Earl of Northumberland thanked him for manifold favours in the process of soliciting his intervention with the king to redress a legal decision which had gone against him.[54] We do not know the outcome of either of these letters, but probably their lordships were satisfied with the service that they received.

Parliament was due to reassemble on 15 January 1532, and the management of the session was clearly in Cromwell's hands. On 31 December Sir Thomas Denys sent him a Bill to be signed by the king, and begged to be excused attendance on the grounds of a sore leg which prevented him from riding. At about the same time John, Lord Audley, also asked to be excused, and referred his proxy to the king. In the course of so doing he expressed his gratitude to Cromwell for the handling of his debts, and professed himself entirely dependent upon the king's graciousness.[55] Cromwell sat in the Commons and was the brains behind the Annates Act, so these requests suggest that he was responsible for the whole business of the session, and although only the king could grant a right of absence, the petitioners obviously knew who to apply to. Parliament was not, of course, his only concern. He was also considering the state of Ireland, where William Skeffington was acting as deputy for the absent Duke of Richmond. On 2 January 1532 Piers, Earl of Ossory, wrote to him, outlining a situation of which he thought that the king should be aware, and warning him against the pretensions of the Earl of Kildare. Since, however, the feud between the Butlers, of whom Piers was the head, and the FitzGeralds, led by Kildare, was notorious on both sides of the Irish Sea, it is unlikely that Cromwell paid much heed to the warning, because Gerald, the 9th Earl of Kildare, was appointed deputy on 5 July following, an appointment which the council soon had cause to regret.[56] Sometimes it is hard to know whether Cromwell's surviving letters relate to his official position as councillor or to the private legal practice which he carried on at least until the end of 1532. In March, for instance, his old friend John Creke wrote to him asking for a loan of £10 until Michaelmas; and in April the Marchioness of Dorset asked for his help in respect of two benefices in Essex over which she claimed patronage, but which were also claimed by the Bishop of London, which sounds like a plea for legal assistance.[57] He also seems to have acted as a financial agent, perhaps in consequence of his moneylending activities. In May 1532 he received an acquittance for £533 6s 8d paid into the king's coffers, of which £333 6s 8d was in part payment of £2,000 owed to the king by Sir Thomas Seymour, the Mayor of the Staple at Westminster, from which it seems that Cromwell had assumed responsibility for these payments. In June he received a letter from Sir Richard Tempest, reminding him to obtain for his son-in-law Thomas Waterton 'long days of payment to the merchant for the Lordship of Burne', which sounds like another financial wangle.[58] Sometimes there is no doubt that it is his status as a councillor which is being appealed to, as when Augustine Augustino wrote from abroad with news of the Emperor or the Turk, or Lord Edmund Howard (Catherine's father) appealed to his 'faithful friendship' to promote a suit to the king. Howard was, as he put it, 'highly kinned' – he was brother to the Duke of Norfolk – but he could not trust his brother to promote his cause with the effectiveness of his faithful friend.[59] This probably says more about Cromwell's perceived relationship with the king than about his actual relationship with Edmund Howard!

During 1532 and 1533 he acquired a number of minor but lucrative offices. In January 1532 he was appointed Receiver General of all the lands allocated to the king's new college in Oxford. This was in effect a continuation of the office which he had held from Wolsey, but it was a new appointment, and probably a recognition of the part which he had played in transferring those revenues when Wolsey's foundation was taken over. On 14 April he was named to the somewhat more prestigious office of Keeper of the King's Jewels in succession to Robert Amadas, who had just died. This was hardly a 'cabinet ranking' post, but it did involve quite a lot of confidential business, and regular access to the monarch, which Cromwell enjoyed anyway. For the first year he shared this position with Sir John Williams, but did most of the work himself, as his general position dictated.[60] In July 1532 he was also appointed Master of the King's Wards, and this was also a very useful promotion, carrying with it a great deal of royal patronage. Placing the king's wards was highly responsible work, and given the competition which existed for wardships also carried with it substantial fees and even larger bribes. Cromwell did not deserve his subsequent reputation for rapacity, but there is little doubt that he absorbed significant financial inducements from hopeful applicants, because the right to control a ward's estates was a highly profitable business. Unlike the 'tegs' and ambling nags which were the small change of inducement, these sums do not feature in his correspondence, which is hardly surprising.[61] They would have been smuggled through the official accounts of his office. It may have been news of his appointment to this position which caused him to be described by one correspondent as 'Receiver General of Attainted lands', an office which is not otherwise known to have existed, and for which no evidence survives of Cromwell in possession. In April 1533 he was named as Chancellor of the Exchequer, which was not then the prestigious position which it subsequently became, but was rather an administrative post of the second rank. What it did give him was an office within the financial establishment, and an opportunity to familiarise himself with its procedures, which was useful in terms of the governmental strategy which was then developing.[62] On 8 August 1533 Cromwell became Recorder of Bristol, a position which he would have exercised by deputy, but which provides additional evidence of his desire to keep in touch with the mercantile elite outside London; and on 12 September he became Steward of Westminster Abbey. In view of the subsequent fate of the abbey this has a slightly sinister look about it, but was almost certainly offered by the abbey as a means of having a friend in high places, which was already thought of as desirable given the pressure which the Church was under. All these posts were accepted by Cromwell, and the chances are that he solicited them, at least the ones in the gift of the Crown. By late 1533 he did not hold any major office, either in the administration or the court, but was admirably positioned to assess the needs and assets of government. Whether Henry recognised what he was about is another matter, because the king did not have that kind of imagination, but he did appreciate his skill in handling Parliament, and that was what mattered for the time being. During the summer of 1533 Henry was absorbed by his new wife, Queen Anne, and her forthcoming confinement. Secure, as he thought, in the friendship of France, neither papal nor the Imperial threats impinged upon him.

Meanwhile what of Cromwell's own surviving child, his son Gregory? He seems to have remained at Pembroke Hall, although no longer under the tutelage of John Checkyng. On 31 July 1531 a certain John Hunt reported that he was in good health and diligent in his studies, and in October Gregory wrote twice to his father; the first time to confirm Hunt's tidings, and to say that the same applied to his cousin Wellyfed, and the second to ask for his father's blessing. This slightly odd request suggests that all was not well in relations between the two at that point, and that perhaps Thomas was inclined to blame his son for his lack of academic progress.[63] The fact that his first letter was sent from Tapysfield, the Earl of Oxford's seat near Castle Hedingham in Essex, and thanks the earl for his 'good cheer', may provide sufficient explanation. How long Gregory stayed in Cambridge, and whether he stayed at Pembroke Hall is not altogether clear. On 30 June 1532 one Henry Lokwood wrote to Cromwell from Christ's College, thanking him for his favours bestowed on the college, and sending commendations to his 'loving pupil' Gregory.[64] Gregory in any case did not spend all his time in Cambridge, and seems not to have returned to Austin Friars during the vacations. In January 1531 he and his minder, one Nicholas Saddler, were staying with Margaret Vernon, the Prioress of St Helen's, who dutifully reported to Cromwell that both were in good health and that Saddler was of 'very good condition'. Mr Copland, she reported, gives them a Latin lesson every morning, and Nicholas made sure that Gregory benefited fully from it. 'Your son,' she concluded hopefully, 'is a very good scholar.'[65] Where Margaret Vernon and her establishment fit into the story of Gregory's education is not very clear, or whether Nicholas Saddler's attendance was John Hunt's idea or Thomas Cromwell's. He was presumably paid, but unlike John Checkyng, did not have to sue for his payments. By 1532 Gregory was between sixteen and nineteen years old, and his formal training would have been coming to an end in any case; he disappears from the records for the next five years, and lived all his life under the shadow of his mighty father, so it is perhaps not very surprising that the story of his life in Cambridge is somewhat shadowy and confused. In spite of some flattering reports, he was clearly not a great scholar, and what impression his time at Pembroke Hall may have left on him is not clear either. He was his only son and heir, but the impression left by the surviving evidence is that Thomas found him a disappointment, an expense and something of a nuisance.

Nevertheless by the summer of 1533, Cromwell had every reason to be pleased with life. Not only had he earned his king's gratitude by clearing a path through the legal jungle which had surrounded Henry's first marriage, he had done so in such a way as to set up a governmental strategy that, by using Parliament, would enable him to establish the Royal Supremacy in an unprecedented form.

4

THE ROYAL SUPREMACY, 1533–1536

Where by divers sundry old authentic histories and chronicles it is
manifestly declared and expressed that this realm of England is an
Empire, and so hath been accepted in the world, governed by one
supreme Head and King ... unto whom a body politic compact of
all sorts and degrees of people, divided in terms and by names of
spirituality and temporality, be bounden and owe to bear next to
God a natural and humble obedience...

Act in Restraint of Appeals

The Royal Supremacy was established in the spring of 1533, by the king's marriage to Anne Boleyn, by the verdict of Cranmer's court in its favour, and by the Act in Restraint of Appeals. There were, however, loopholes in the Act. It did not specifically cover heresy cases, for instance, and it was not clear whether it was retroactive. Catherine's supporters were therefore able to argue that the statute made no difference to her appeal, which had been launched in 1529, and she herself continued to look to Rome for a judgement in her favour.[1] Nevertheless the resort to Parliament was highly significant, because a statute was supposed to be the act of the whole realm, in which the Lords and Commons were involved alongside the king. It also carried the force of law, which a royal edict did not. Traditionally the competence of Parliament extended to ecclesiastical jurisdiction, but not to 'matters spiritual'. Thus it was able to redefine the rights of sanctuary, which impinged upon the secular jurisdiction, but not those of the doctrine of justification, which did not. The issue between 1529 and 1533 had therefore been in the nature of a boundary dispute. To what extent were the clergy of the realm the king's subjects, and to what extent the Pope's? It is not surprising that Henry decided that issue early on, but not clear what it meant in jurisdictional terms beyond the hoary matter of benefit of clergy, which Parliament had been whittling down for many years.[2] The *Collectanea satis copiosa* had been directed to the question of territoriality – whether English cases could be cited outside the realm – and argued that they could not, but did not attempt to define what constituted a spiritual cause. It had been Thomas Cromwell, armed with Marsilius of Padua's *Defensor Pacis*, who had persuaded the king that his matrimonial cause was a jurisdictional matter rather than a spiritual one, and therefore within the competence of Parliament.[3] This crucial shift came at some point in 1532, and marks the beginning of Cromwell's dominance in the king's counsels. No record tells us when this happened, and it was probably gradual rather than sudden, but it had certainly happened by November, when Henry began to use Anne as his wife, and may well have married her. By January 1533 the Bill in Restraint of Appeals was already in preparation, and Cromwell prepared the draft, because it would be his duty as the chief parliamentary manager to see it safely through. By implication, and in the light of what happened subsequently, it appears a revolutionary measure, but at the time it was quite possible to see it differently. It claimed to be re-establishing an ancient order, validated by 'sundry old authentic histories and chronicles', whereby the king had heard ecclesiastical disputes by virtue of his God-given authority as a Christian prince.[4] The claims of Rome are of human origin and are thus to be disregarded, and the Pope's sanctions ignored. This flew in the face of all tradition, but who was to say that its claims were not valid? The failure to mention heresy may well have been deliberate, because it was quite radical enough without that, but nevertheless it passed an anticlerical Parliament within a fortnight, and may well have been seen by many members as no more than an extension of the laws which had already been passed in respect of clerical fees in the session of 1529.[5]

The clergy were not happy, but the convocations had already submitted to the king over the question of their legislative powers, and were in no position to resist this new assault. A less institutional means of expressing opposition therefore seemed to be called for, and this took the form of the prophesyings of a certain Elizabeth Barton, known as 'the nun of Kent'. Elizabeth was by origin a serving maid, who had been born in about 1506. In 1525, at the age of nineteen, she was taken ill with what appear to have been epileptic fits, in the course of which she spoke in tongues, giving voice to sayings of 'wondrous holiness in rebuke of sin and vice', and strange-sounding prophecies. She thus became accepted as a charismatic mystic, and quickly acquired a popular following. This in turn attracted the attention of Dr Edward Bocking, a monk of Christchurch, Canterbury, who investigated her case and became convinced that she had experienced genuine religious ecstasy.[6] He arranged for her to be admitted into the nunnery of St Sepulchre's in Canterbury, where her special gifts would be better cared for. Under Bocking's protection, her reputation spread, and she soon began to attract the attention of the great. She had audiences with Archbishop Warham and with Bishop John Fisher, both of whom were impressed by her sanctity, and by her utterances. She also met Cardinal Wolsey in 1528, and is alleged to have predicted his downfall. Sometime in 1529 she was seen by the king, although the story that she was offered a place at court by Anne Boleyn is probably a fabrication arising out of the fact that she was seen by Gertrude, Marchioness of Exeter.[7] She was not unique. At about the same time a Holy Maid existed in Ipswich and another in Leominster. However by 1530 her prophecies were beginning to take on a political edge and Catherine of Aragon wisely refused to see her. Thomas More, who was equally unhappy with the way in which policy was developing, likewise avoided her. By 1533 her clerical minders were obviously exploiting her. She claimed that an angel had appeared to her and commanded her to tell Henry that he ought to mend his ways and 'take none of the Pope's right or patrimony from him'. He ought also to destroy all men of the new learning, a politically loaded message if ever there was one.[8] Worse was to follow. She, or her heavenly control, pronounced that if he married and took Anne to wife, the vengeance of God would light upon him and he would die a villain's death. In support of her testimony, she claimed to possess a letter written from Heaven by Mary Magdalene, 'in letters of gold', but was unable to produce it as evidence of her veracity.[9]

Such sayings were extremely dangerous, although not treasonable as the law then stood, and from the end of 1532

Cromwell was keeping a watching brief on the maid and her associates. Henry bided his time, and then with Anne safely crowned and visibly pregnant, he struck. Elizabeth Barton, Edward Bocking and several clerical members of her circle were arrested and thrown into the Tower to be interrogated by Cranmer and Cromwell. Since she belonged to Canterbury, she was under the archbishop's jurisdiction, but Cromwell seems to have undertaken the bulk of the examination. He was under no illusions about the political importance of these utterances;

> If credence should be given to every such lewd person as would affirm himself to have revelations from God, what readier way were there to subvert all commonwealths and good order in the world...[10]

His investigations quickly revealed that Elizabeth had maintained contacts with friends of the discarded Catherine, and that alone was suspicious. Through his associates in the world of London printing, he was able to seize all 700 copies of the Nuns Book before they could be distributed, and burned the lot, along with all the other writing about her that he could lay his hands on. In November 1533 there was talk of an indictment for high treason, and Fisher and More were accused of misprision for not revealing her guilt, but in the event what happened was less dramatic. On 23 November the nun and some of her associates were paraded at Paul's Cross, where they were denounced as frauds by John Salcot, the Abbot of Hyde, Winchester. She was a vain whore who had been misled by her confessor, Bocking. Salcot seems to have succeeded in whipping up the crowd to a frenzy of derision, perhaps because he insinuated sexual misdemeanours as part of the heady brew of his rhetoric.[11] This no doubt made a good show, but the substantial breakthrough was made by Cromwell in the course of relentless interrogation, when he asked her to reveal past events that she could not possibly have known about. At this she broke down and confessed that 'all that she said was feigned of her own imagining, only to satisfy the minds of those who resorted to her, and to obtain worldly praise', which prompted Cranmer to call them 'mischievous visions ... containing much sedition'.[12] This was very satisfactory, but it left unanswered the question of what was to be done with them, because it was all verbal, and not directed against the king except in a very general sense. An indictment for high treason would be thrown out by a scrupulous jury, and that would not do at all. Perhaps this was a matter for the king, and one of Cromwell's remembrances towards the end of the year reads, 'To know what the king will have done with the nun and her accomplices.' The king apparently willed an Act of Attainder, although it is difficult to imagine Henry coming up with that solution, because it has Cromwell's fingerprints all over it. The nun and five of her minders were duly accused of high treason in a Bill that was presented in the House of Lords on 21 February, although, thanks to Cromwell's manoeuvres, the Marchioness of Exeter was spared. It appears to have encountered no opposition, and received the royal assent at the end of the session, on 30 March.[13] Having been given due notice of the end, they were executed at Tyburn on 20 April. According to Burnet, Elizabeth Barton made a 'good end', in words which it is difficult to imagine her inventing for herself:

I am the cause not only of my own death, which most justly I have richly deserved, but of the deaths of all those persons who are going to suffer with me. Alas! I was poor wretch without learning, but the praise of the priests about me turned my brain...[14]

Assuming that Burnet was quoting a genuine source, Thomas Cromwell's influence is easily discernible here, because this is exactly what he would have wanted her to say. As a reward she was hanged rather than burned, which was the normal punishment for the female traitor. Her companions suffered the full penalties of high treason, being hanged, drawn and quartered. No one was left in any doubt about the fate which awaited anyone tempted to follow in her footsteps – which no one did.

John Fisher was included in the Act, but escaped with a fine of £300. This may also be ascribed to Cromwell's influence, who on 27 February, while the Bill was still in the House of Lords, had attempted to persuade the bishop to seek the king's mercy for his misprision.

If you beseech the king's grace ... to be your gracious lord and to remit unto you your negligence, oversight and offence committed against his highness ... I dare undertake that his highness shall benignly accept you into his gracious favour, all matters of displeasure past before this time forgotten and forgiven.[15]

Fisher had not yielded to this tempting offer, but the imprisonment and loss of goods to which he was in theory liable were not imposed. In effect the old man had escaped with a warning. Thomas More, whose name had also been mentioned in this connection, was not eventually included in the Bill at all, because not only had he avoided meeting the nun, he had also denounced her as a 'lewd ... and wicked woman'. He had, he admitted, originally believed her to be inspired, but had been deterred by talk of treason. It pained him, he wrote, that ever the king could have thought him guilty. Nevertheless, his exclusion from the Act was due to the friendly offices of Thomas Cromwell rather than to any generosity on Henry's part. The king was not graciously inclined to one who had embarrassed him by resigning the chancellorship in order to protect his conscience. Hostile prophecy was in the air in the latter part of 1533 and early in 1534, but the accusations often seem to have been malicious or self-interested. Ralph Wendon, for instance, a Warwickshire priest, was alleged to have spoken of a prediction that a queen should be burned at Smithfield and 'trusted that it might have been that whore and harlot Queen Anne'.[16] However, when Cromwell investigated he found plain evidence that his accuser had a grudge against Wendon, and the matter was dropped. In 1534 the parson of Chesterton in Huntingdonshire was accused by his curate of keeping a 'false and abominable' prophet, but it appeared on enquiry that the curate was after his job, and that case proceeded no further either. Even Mrs Amadas, the widow of Cromwell's predecessor at the Jewel House, was apparently declaring that the king 'was cursed with God's own mouth', and that before midsummer (1534) England would be conquered by the Scots. However, since she also accused Henry of having designs on her virtue, for which there was not a scrap of evidence, Mrs Amadas was judged to be unbalanced, and no action was taken against her.[17] What is clear from these and other similar cases is that, once a matter was brought to his attention, and appeared to be serious, Cromwell would investigate, usually by interviewing one or both of the parties involved, and that in many cases no further action was taken. Although where an accusation was substantiated, he was quite willing to let the law take its course, he was very far from running a 'reign of terror' against suspected dissidents.

One reason why he was willing to do this was that the law was substantially augmented in the course of 1534. It could be argued that the Buggery Act of 1533 was a part of this campaign, criminalising as it did any acts of homosexuality. This may well have been aimed at a celibate clergy, but equally it may have been a consequence of Henry's somewhat prurient morality. The fact that Cromwell drafted it and saw it through does not prove that he had a part in originating it, and indeed there is little other evidence of any sensitivity on his part towards this kind of activity.[18] The fierce language of the Act probably reflects one of the king's less endearing prejudices. On the other hand the work of the first session of Parliament in 1534 was clearly directed towards clarifying and establishing the Royal Supremacy, and here his guiding hand can certainly be detected. The Act for the Submission of the Clergy basically gave statutory form to the surrender of the convocations in the summer of 1532. It confirmed the incompetence of the clerical assemblies to make any new canons without the king's consent, and shifted the ultimate court of appeal in ecclesiastical causes to the king's Court of Chancery, which effectively made such appeals a part of the royal equity jurisdiction.[19] It also omitted the saving phrase 'as far as the law of Christ allows' from its description of the king's title. It thus gave the existing canon law a statutory basis, which was revived by the Act of 1559 and remained in place until the creation of new canons for the English Church in 1604. The name of the Pope was of course to be everywhere deleted. The second Act in this sequence is that restraining the payment of annates to the

Pope. This starts by reciting the statute of 1532, which the king had subsequently activated by letters patent, and then proceeds to lay down a procedure for the appointment of archbishops and bishops. Where hitherto the king had submitted a name to the Pope for confirmation, and had occasionally allowed the pontiff to provide one of his own servants to the vacancy, now a different method was decreed. The king was to suggest a name to the dean and chapter of the relevant cathedral, who were then expected to elect the nominated party. This was the so-called *congé d'elire*, or right to elect. The fact that it was a fiction was disclosed by the next paragraph, which declared that if the chapter failed to elect within a given time, the right of appointment reverted directly to the king.[20]

And furthermore be it ordained and established by the authority aforesaid that at every avoidance of any archbishopric or bishopric within this realm ... the king our sovereign lord, his heirs and successors may grant unto the prior and convent or dean and chapter of the cathedral churches or monasteries ... a licence under the great seal, as of old time hath been accustomed, to proceed to an election of archbishop or bishop of the see so being void, with a letter missive containing the name of the person they shall elect and chose ... and if they do defer or delay their election above 12 days next after such licence and letters missive to them delivered, that then for every such default, the King's highness, his heirs and successors at their liberty and pleasure shall nominate and present, by their Letters Patent under their great seal such a person to the said office and dignity so being void as they shall think able and convenient for the same...

The next statute in this sequence is that 'for the exoneration of exactions paid to the see of Rome', otherwise called the Dispensations Act, which transfers to the Crown in Parliament the right to grant all such dispensations as had hitherto been sought from Rome, and forbids the payment of any dues whatsoever to the Pope,

> provided always that this act nor any thing or things therein contained shall be hereafter interpreted or expounded that your Grace, your nobles and subjects intend by the same to decline or vary from the congregation of Christ's church in any things concerning the very articles of the Catholic faith or Christendom; or in any other things declared by Holy Scripture and the word of God necessary for your or their salvation...[21]

He was acting thus, he declared, 'to repress vice and for good conservation of this realm in peace, unity, and tranquility', not out of any desire to reform or amend the faith. So, early in his legislative campaign, he declared his quarrel to be jurisdictional, or even personal, against a particular Pope, and not implying any sympathy with the heretical ideas then current. Thomas Cromwell may well have drafted the Dispensations Act, but he knew better than to stray from the narrow path of orthodoxy which the king had laid down. When he was concentrating, Henry was very insistent upon this interpretation of his actions.[22]

In spite of the king's defensive language, these acts nevertheless transgressed the traditional boundaries between secular and spiritual law, although there is little sign that the members were aware of doing anything very new. Cromwell's careful presentation, and management of the discussion through

Humphrey Wingfield, the Speaker, carefully suppressed any talk of innovation. Not very much is known about Wingfield, who was a lawyer and a burgess for Yarmouth, but he must have been brought to the king's attention by Cromwell, part of whose business it was to know the biographies of as many members as possible.[23] The Act which most conspicuously broke new ground, however, did not involve the spiritual authorities, except by remote implication. This was the Succession Act, rendered necessary by the king's second marriage, and by the fact he had a daughter by that marriage. The succession to the crown had hitherto been deemed to be determined by the will of God, through the mysterious workings of male primogeniture, but that could hardly apply in Henry's case. In the absence of any siblings of his father, the nearest males to the throne were James V of Scotland and Henry Brandon, the sons of his sisters Margaret and Mary, both unacceptable, although for different reasons.[24] When the king's judges had been invited to decide a disputed succession in 1460, they had declared so high a mystery to be beyond their competence, and that of Parliament, but no such modesty seems to have afflicted the Lords in 1534. Without a qualm they decreed the obvious; that the succession would pass to any son born to his 'dearly and entirely beloved wife, Queen Anne' or to any subsequent wife. However in the absence of any such son, the crown was to pass to his daughter Elizabeth, the 'issue female' born to the said wife, and to the heirs of her body. In the absence of any such heirs, the next-born female should succeed, and so on.[25] This was to distinguish the Crown from any private inheritance, because there the law was that all female children should inherit equally. In other words the inheritance was to be divided, which would clearly be inappropriate to the

Crown. The purpose of the Act was stated to be the avoidance of a disputed succession, which had so afflicted the realm in the past; but also to obviate any possible claim by the Pope, who,

> contrary to the great and inviolable grants of jurisdiction given by God immediately to Emperors, Kings and Princes in succession to their heirs, hath presumed in times past to invest who it should please them to inherit in other men's kingdoms and dominions, which thing we your most humble subjects both spiritual and temporal do most abhor and detest...[26]

Mary was not mentioned, having been ruled illegitimate by the dissolution of Henry's marriage to Catherine, and nor was Henry Fitzroy, the Duke of Richmond, equally a bastard and therefore incapable of succession. This was the first time that Parliament had given 'a form of succession to the Crown', and it was accepted without demur as being the only sensible way out of what was potentially a very difficult situation, but of course it was predicated upon the acceptability of the king's second marriage, and the rejection of papal jurisdiction – neither of which had won universal acceptance.

Thomas Cromwell had devised this, as well as the other Acts of the session, and his services to the king were beyond price. Partly in recognition of this, and partly of his general usefulness, shortly after the session ended, Henry appointed him to be his principal secretary in succession to Stephen Gardiner.[27] Gardiner had disgraced himself in his master's eyes by responding ill-advisedly to the Commons' Supplication against the Ordinaries. He had subsequently redeemed that lack of judgement, in part at least, by writing a treatise on *True Obedience*, which said all the right things about the Royal Supremacy, but he never recovered the confidential relationship which he had enjoyed before the summer of 1531. As a result he had spent much of the last three years on diplomatic missions to France, where he did well enough although his efforts were not helped by a somewhat abrasive personality that he seemed to be unwilling or unable to control.[28] He may have been lucky to retain his diocese of Winchester, and was undoubtedly fortunate to hang onto the secretaryship, especially as he was not around most of the time to discharge its duties. It appears that he was able to do that because he had in effect an assistant secretary in the person of Thomas Cromwell, who was discharging most of the duties of the office well before he was appointed to it. Cromwell rapidly turned the secretaryship into the great clearing house of Tudor government, but that was on account of the personal position which he already held rather than any institutional strength in the office.[29] The king's secretary had for years been an office of personal service. He was the man who wrote the king's letters and drafted confidential memoranda, but he was not an officer of state. His position was one of potential influence because of his guaranteed access to the king, but it seems that Gardiner's predecessors had not exploited that situation, and that he himself had only done so to a limited extent, perhaps because he spent so much time away from the court. Cromwell, who was already a councillor of state with a finger in many pies, conferred a new status on the office. 'Master Secretary' was the key man in the king's administration, and across his desk passed every kind of business, important or trivial. It was he who decided whether the innumerable cases of sedition which reached him were worth pursuing or not, and to make arrangements for investigation when that was considered necessary.[30] He corresponded with foreign envoys, conducted confidential dialogues with Eustace Chapuys, and brokered innumerable patronage deals. His judgement was usually sound, and he did not underestimate Henry's intelligence or engagement with affairs. This was no easy task, because the king was erratic. Sometimes he was so absorbed by his hunting or other pastimes that he had to be pursued for days to sign important papers, but on other occasions he showed himself to be the master of the most intricate negotiations. Above all, he could never be taken for granted, not even by his wife, let alone his secretary.[31] Fortunately Cromwell, like Wolsey, had a formidable work rate and an army of reliable servants and assistants, which enabled him to keep on top of this massive pile of paper. Ralph Sadler, Richard Williams and Thomas Wriothesley are just the most obvious members of this formidable team, men who could be relied upon to serve on commissions, and who performed delicate missions on the secretary's behalf; mostly within England but overseas if necessary.[32]

The secretary also had custody of the king's personal seal, the signet. This was no longer used to authenticate his private correspondence – the royal signature or sign manual having taken over that duty – but it was still used in a great many more formal ways. For example, by custom, all grants made by the Crown were supposed to follow a bureaucratic procedure, whereby the prospective grantee put in his petition, which received the king's approval by way of his signature endorsed on the document itself. This then constituted a warrant to the signet office to make out another warrant to the Privy Seal, and that in turn authorised Chancery to issue the actual grant under the Great Seal. It then had full legal force.[33] Petitioners often tried to short-circuit this elaborate system by proceeding straight from the signed Bill to the Great Seal, a process known as the 'immediate warrant', but Cromwell discouraged this because it meant a loss of fees to the signet and Privy Seal offices. In 1536 he promoted an Act of Parliament which put the full course of the seals on a statutory basis, and secured these payments even if the clerks had been bypassed. Not surprisingly, the use of the immediate warrant declined sharply, which was no doubt part of the intention.[34] The signet was also used to activate Chancery in other ways, for instance in the authentication of original writs, which were used to start actions at the common law, and in the issuing of subpoenas. The court of Star Chamber used the Great Seal for all its work, but in other respects by the sixteenth century Chancery had lost its central place in general administrative work. This was taken over by the Privy Seal office, which collected administrative orders from all the king's officers, and distributed them to the servants, who were to carry out the actual work. Cromwell seems to have contemplated replacing it in this function with the signet, which would have been a logical step bearing in mind the way in which he was concentrating business in his own hands.[35] However, before he could carry out that reform he became Lord Privy Seal himself (1536) and his priorities changed. The Privy Seal also became the Privy Council Seal after 1540, and was used to guarantee the repayment of royal loans. Nevertheless Cromwell's practice proved stronger than his theory in this respect, and without any deliberate action on his part, the signet gradually took over from the Privy Seal in the validation of administrative orders, thus becoming the main working seal of government.[36] It was only later in the sixteenth century that it lost that function in turn to the sign manual, and retreated to its original purpose as a route to the Great Seal; by which time all the seals served primarily a formal and ceremonial purpose.

The secretary had a busy time in the next session of Parliament, which assembled on 3 November 1534. First he had the difficult job of explaining what the Royal Supremacy meant, without appearing to do anything new. So the statute was entitled 'An Act concerning the King's Highness to be Supreme Head of the Church of England, and to have authority to reform and redress all errors, heresies and abuses in the same'. Starting with the bland assumption that 'the King's Majesty justly and rightfully is and oweth to be the Supreme Head of the Church of England', it then went on to enact that he must be so taken and reputed by all his subjects, an enforcement clause that was a proper exercise of parliamentary jurisdiction.[37] However, it then went on to state that what this meant was the right to wield 'any manner spiritual authority or jurisdiction'; in other words it was to be interpreted as conferring the full *plenitudo potestatis*. It is not very clear from the wording of the statute whether this was deemed to be mere recognition of an existing situation, or the conferring of additional powers. Cromwell knew perfectly well that for the king to try heresy cases would imply a revolution in the courts, but quite possibly Henry saw it merely as an example of his God-given power, in which case the statute conferred enforcement only. That would appear to be the implication behind his decision to try John Lambert personally in 1538.[38] It is unlikely that this Act created any new qualms among those already opposed to the Supremacy, who must have anticipated its provisions, but the next Bill upon which Cromwell was engaged was altogether different. Having pleaded the Pope's financial exactions as one of the reasons for banning appeals to Rome, this Bill transferred all such payments to the king, and went on to impose a 10 per cent tax on 'all possessions of the church spiritual and temporal'. Such a tax was to be assessed and collected by commissioners appointed under the Great Seal and sent into every diocese.[39] The only concession to clerical sensibilities was that the diocesan bishop was to serve as a commissioner *ex officio*. When it became an Act, this had the effect of transforming the £4,000 or so which had been paid to the Pope into something like £40,000 paid into the royal coffers. Convocation was not asked for an opinion, and the measure attracted hardly a squeak of protest from the bishops in the Lords, who must have been expecting some such demand following the enactment of the Supremacy.[40]

Cromwell used these acts as a means of tightening his grip on the Church. It is unlikely that the king paid much attention to them because they came under the broad heading of administration rather than policy. The same was probably true also of the next Bill to engage his attention, which tackled the perennial problem of lawlessness in Wales. The difficulty here lay less in the principality, which was under effective royal control, than in the Marcher lordships, especially those still in private hands. There a mixture of Welsh and English law was used, and it was regularly complained that the former was too easy on felons, allowing composition, for example in cases of homicide.[41] The stewards and other officers of the private lordships were likewise suspected of being slack in both investigating and prosecuting serious offences, while their tenacious defence of their traditional liberties inhibited the power of the Council in the Marches to interfere. It was therefore decreed that whenever a complaint of serious lawbreaking in the Marches should be received, it should be investigated in the nearest English county, and if a true Bill was found, tried within the same jurisdiction. The justices in the same counties were empowered to award process into the Marches, which the officers there were bound to implement – a halfway step to the abolition of the franchises altogether, which occurred two years later.[42] The Council in the Marches was at the same time given enhanced powers, and the effective Rowland Lee, the Bishop of Lichfield, was appointed president. Lee was a zealous law enforcement officer and acquired something of a reputation as a hanging judge. The Treasons Bill of 1534 was an altogether different matter, and the evidence suggests that Henry was actively involved in its preparation. Treason was, after all, the crime which concerned him most intimately. The object of this Bill was to plug a perceived gap in the great Treasons Act of 1352 upon which the existing law was based. That measure had decreed that anyone 'compassing or imagining' the king's death, or that of his consort or heir, should be deemed guilty, but had not explained what 'imagining' might mean in this context.[43] It was therefore subject to judicial interpretation throughout the late fourteenth and fifteenth centuries. Those guilty of the death of Simon of Sudbury in 1381 were indicted for murder, not treason, while one who described Henry VI as a 'natural fool' in 1456 was deemed to be guilty of the major offence.[44] It is not true to say that treason by words was unknown before 1534, but it was insecurely based upon the statutory law. However, the number of accusations reaching Cromwell's desk after 1530 indicated clearly enough that judicial discretion was no longer adequate to deal with the problem. Calling King Henry a heretic or a tyrant and Queen Anne a whore was reaching epidemic proportions, and a new treasons law was obviously called for. The Bill as presented to Parliament therefore sought to 'prohibit ... restrain and extinct all manner of shameful slanders, perils or imminent danger' which might threaten the king, the queen or their heirs.[45] It went on to decree that 'after the first day of February next coming [anyone who may] maliciously wish will or desire by word or writing ... any bodily harm to the king's most royal person, the Queen's or their heirs apparent, or to deprive them or any of them of the dignity, title or name of their royal estates', or call the king heretic, schismatic, tyrant, infidel or usurper, was to be deemed guilty of high treason.[46] The authors of all such treasons, 'their aiders, contenters, counsellors and abettors', being lawfully convicted, were to suffer the full penalty of their crime without benefit of sanctuary. This statute did not break new ground, but it laid down limits and definitions where none had existed before, and anyone calling the king a schismatic (which he was) or a heretic (which he was not) would find themselves in court on a capital charge. It was certainly perceived as introducing a new type of treason, and had a paralysing effect upon legitimate criticism of the regime, which seems to have been its main purpose. Henry did not take kindly to criticism of any kind, and, given his fragile ascendancy in the battle for hearts and minds, one can see why.[47]

Cromwell would probably have preferred to proceed by way of positive propaganda rather than the negative repression of dissent, but it was hard to judge the effectiveness of the works which he patronised. These had started with *The Glass of the Truth* in 1532, a breezy and theologically vague tract which was certainly not written by him, but whose publication bears the marks of his support.[48] Next came two works by his servant Jasper Fyllol, which read as though they were designed as part of the campaign against the clergy, and should probably be attributed to 1533. Again there is no evidence to attribute their production to Cromwell, but their content suggests that he read and approved them. The only publication which can be firmly linked to him is the translation of Melanchthon's *Apology*, of which Stephen Vaughn has provided the original, and Cromwell paid the translators.[49] Then at the end of 1533 came the *Articles devised by the whole consent of the King's most honourable Council*, which takes the Supremacy argument a stage beyond the Book of Leviticus, and indulges in an uninhibited attack on the person of the Pope, describing him as 'neither in life nor learning Christ's disciple' being both baseborn and coming to his office by simony.[50] This was probably more than Cromwell himself would have wanted to say at that stage, but he was obviously happy enough for someone to say it on his behalf, and it reflected the king's own attitude, because he had convinced himself that he was dealing with a rogue pontiff. This was followed in 1534 by two tracts, one by the evangelical Edward Foxe and the other by the conservative Richard Sampson, aimed at a clerical audience, and by the delightfully named *Little Treatise against the mutterings of some Papists in corners*.[51] This was intended for a popular audience, and can be firmly associated with Cromwell by a letter in the hand of one of his clerks ascribing it to his initiative. In so far as this dealt with the papacy, it declared the office to be one of human origin, without any warrant in scripture. This question of biblical authority was becoming characteristic of works with which the secretary was involved, and formed a part of his discreet campaign to persuade Henry to authorise a translation, although that would not come to fruition for another two years. His campaign probably had a significant impact on the literate, particularly in London, but it is hard to measure, and criticism of the regime, especially by the clergy, continued to preoccupy his servants and informers over the following years.[52] The Treasons Act of 1534 was called upon far more frequently than Thomas Cromwell would have wished.

The other Act which was called into operation at once was that which granted to the king a 10 per cent tax on all ecclesiastical property, because that necessitated an investigation into the assets of the Church, and in January 1535 Cromwell was specially commissioned to conduct such an investigation. This was a large-scale operation and the secretary, acting in the King's name as he was specifically empowered to do, set up a network of subordinate commissions to carry out the actual work, using the Privy Seal for that purpose.[53] The bishops served on these commissions *ex officio*, but the other members were drawn mainly from the sympathetic laity, and included a great many of Cromwell's friends, servants and associates. It was particularly important that these visitors should not connive at any kind of concealment, because the situation was complicated by leases and other arrangements which meant that some properties were worth very little to the Church, while others were more valuable that at first appeared. The commissioners worked fast and efficiently and before the end of the year produced a *Valor Ecclesiasticus* which showed the overall wealth of the Church at nearly £500,000 a year, a colossal sum which includes everything from the bishopric of Winchester, at £3,000 a year, to the smallest vicarage, worth only a few shillings. It was the largest and most comprehensive survey to be conducted since the Domesday Book in the eleventh century, and was a tribute to the bureaucratic capability of the Tudor state.[54] Cromwell drove it forward, and was indefatigable in dealing with the questions which inevitably arose, and which only he possessed the grasp and knowledge to answer. This was all the more remarkable because at the same time he was conducting a second enquiry into the state of the religious houses. This is also usually attributed to the king's need for money, and the investigations as a mere excuse to proceed to dissolution. However that was probably not the case, at least not at this early stage. There is plenty of evidence, going back to 1530, that both Cromwell and the king had a genuine interest in reforming the monastic establishment. Complaints of misconduct were encouraged, and unsatisfactory priors and abbots warned to mend their ways.[55] When vacancies occurred, Cromwell was often careful to ensure that suitable incumbents were put in post; and suitability included not only a willingness to accept the Royal Supremacy, but an exemplary private life and a conscientious attitude towards the rules of their order. The piety of previous generations had left a monastic establishment which was overgrown and more than little flaccid. The case for pruning was overwhelming, as Wolsey had demonstrated, and the initial policy behind the investigation appears to have been positive. The visitors were originally briefed to report on the conduct of the monks and nuns, both moral and professional, and on the existence or otherwise of dissent within the houses, but with a view to rectifying the abuses rather than closing them down. The characters of the visitors themselves has been subject to much unsympathetic scrutiny, and Dr John London in particular has been accused of inventing or exaggerating abuses.[56] In general the *Compendium Compertorum*, the commissioners' final report, presents a depressing picture of the life of the religious houses, and although this may contain individual exaggerations, on the whole other evidence supports these conclusions. Cromwell is alleged to have considered following the lead of his old master, and closing down gradually houses which were particularly prone to abuse, but the *Compertorum* was not submitted until the summer of 1536, and by then other priorities had to be taken into account. In January 1535 Cromwell had been granted the new office of Viceregent in Spirituals to enable him to carry out these multifaceted tasks, and this empowered him in effect to exercise the Supremacy on the king's behalf instead of the Archbishop of Canterbury, who would have been the natural choice for such a position. Henry seems to have been determined to appoint a layman, and since it also carried the right to preside at the convocations, to emphasise the secular superiority to which the Church was now subjected.[57] Cranmer is not known to have objected; he was Cromwell's friend and the two of them shared an ecclesiastical agenda. Time was to show that this differed in various ways from the king's, but that was not apparent at the beginning of 1535.

Meanwhile events were moving on. On 23 March 1534 Pope Clement at last pronounced a definitive sentence in favour of Catherine of Aragon. This carried a renewed threat of excommunication for Henry, but again the sentence was not fully promulgated, probably because Clement realised that neither Francis nor Charles would be willing to enforce it. England had effectively renounced papal authority by then, but it may well have been these events which prompted Henry to make his position abundantly clear by the Act of Supremacy in the autumn.[58] Consequently when Clement died in September 1534 and was succeeded by Paul III, the latter's tentative hints at renewed negotiations were not acted upon. Henry was no longer interested in reconciliation, and Cromwell, who was certainly consulted about this attitude, must have breathed a sigh of relief.

One of the reasons for this recalcitrance lay in the preamble to the Act for the Succession, which had unequivocally asserted that Catherine's marriage to Arthur had been consummated, and that therefore the papal dispensation for her second marriage was invalid:

> The Bishop of Rome and see Apostolic, contrary to the great and inviolable grants of jurisdictions given by God immediately to Emperors, Kings, and Princes in succession to their heirs, hath presumed in times past to invest who should please them to inherit in other men's kingdoms and dominions, which thing we your most humble subjects both spiritual and temporal do most abhor and detest.[59]

Such usurpation was to cease forthwith, and all the king's subjects were to swear an oath to observe the succession laid down in the Act. This should not be taken literally. There was never any intention that ploughmen and labourers should be required to swear, but by July over 7,000 clergy and gentlemen had taken the oath, which was administered by commissioners appointed for the purpose.[60] Resistance was slight but significant. Sir Thomas More was summoned from his retirement in Chelsea to swear in April, and refused to do so. He was, he professed, willing to accept the succession, but declined to set his hand to anything which implied the rejection of papal jurisdiction, as that was set out in the preamble. On 13 April John Fisher, summoned with other bishops to do his duty, likewise declined, and a few days later both of them were sent to the Tower.[61] At the same time the visitors entered the religious houses of London, and as a result four Carthusians, one Brigettine and a secular priest, John Haile, were arrested on Cromwell's orders and similarly imprisoned for refusing the oath. The Viceregent then commenced the long and frustrating task of attempting to persuade them to change their minds. In this context just about the last thing that he needed was martyrs to the Old Faith. Nevertheless that was what he got. Even before the Carthusians were arrested, in the spring of 1534, Thomas Bedyll had been sent into the Charterhouse, armed with a variety of books and 'annotations' in an effort to persuade them. He may have succeeded with the less obdurate, but not with the four who ended up in the Tower.[62] It was obviously not in Cromwell's interest that these men should be executed, and he kept up a steady pressure, using a variety of agents and methods to persuade them to recant, but without success. In April 1535 he reminded himself to ask the king what to do about them, and the answer was apparently to put them on trial, and on the 29th of that month they duly appeared before the court of King's Bench at Westminster. Once the indictment had been properly found, and perhaps with the intention of intimidating them, Cranmer visited them himself, and reminded them of the awful consequences of continued obstinacy, but had no more success than lesser agents.[63] In the course of their trial it emerged that Syon was a hotbed of treasonable gossip. One of the accused, Richard Reynolds, alleged that the king had kept a 'company of maidens' at Farnham Castle in Surrey while he was staying with the 'old lord' Bishop of Winchester (Foxe), while an anonymous layman attached to the house expressed the view that he had kept 'many matrons … in the court … almost all he has violated … and now he has taken to his wife of fornication this matron Anne not only to the highest shame and undoing of himself, but also of all this realm'.[64] With opinions like this being expressed it is not surprising that all the defendants were found guilty and sentenced to the extreme penalty of the law. Finally, Cromwell himself visited not only the imprisoned monks but also the house from which they had come. In the latter case he engaged in disputation with various of the monks on the subject of Peter's pre-eminence among the Apostles, denying vigorously that the Royal Supremacy made the king a priest, but he had no better success than Bedyll had had before. The prior submitted and so did some of the monks, but the remainder were sent off to Newgate and the house was closed. The six who had been convicted were executed at Tyburn on 4 May. They had not been degraded as was customary with clerical felons, but were hanged in their habits to make a point about the nature of their treason. According to one report which reached Paris soon after the whole city was horrified 'because they were of exemplary and holy life', but in fact opinion in London was divided, a fair proportion of the onlookers feeling that they had got what they deserved.[65] They had undoubtedly been guilty of treason as that was then defined, and so were those who had been sent to Newgate. For some unknown reason the latter were not brought to trial, but were left to rot in prison where they died of starvation and maltreatment, a fate which reflects credit on neither the king nor Cromwell.

The more exalted prisoners were not similarly neglected. Indeed in the case of Thomas More Cromwell seems to have had a great deal of sympathy with the man, if not with his opinions. They had belonged to the same humanist group as Lord Morley and Richard Pace, and had passed many congenial hours in discussing the classics before their views on the scriptures and the Royal Supremacy drove them apart. In his memoirs written during his interrogation, More describes the secretary as his 'good master', and 'one that tenderly favoureth me', not language which he would have employed about one whom he was convinced was harrying him to his death, although it is possible that More was being ironic.[66] It seems that Cromwell did his level best to save More from himself, and might have been prepared to accept an equivocal submission, which was the most that More was prepared to offer. To this he was urged by Thomas Cranmer, who shared his respect for the sage of Chelsea, and it was the king himself who scotched that scheme on the harsh but logical grounds that it would encourage others in similar evasions. Even just before his trial, Cromwell was prepared to assure him that Henry would still be a good lord to him if only he would swear the oath without dissimulation. More was prepared to insist that he was the king's good subject, but not to take the oath:

> He did no one any harm, said no harm and thought no harm, but wished everyone good. If this was not enough to keep a man alive, he longed not to live ... his poor body was at the king's pleasure, and he wished that his death might do him good.[67]

This plea (if such it was) went unheeded and he was tried in Westminster Hall on 1 July 1535. What happened then is well known, but owed nothing to Thomas Cromwell, who had parted with More in a state of some exasperation on 3 June. The chief witness for the prosecution was Sir Richard Rich, who alleged that on visiting the Tower to collect More's books on 12 June, he had become involved in a discussion with him on the powers of Parliament, in the course of which he had declared that Parliament did not have the authority to make the king Supreme Head of the Church, an opinion which Rich probably transmitted to Cromwell, who ensured that it took its place in the trial. More of course denied that he had said any such thing, making the valid point that since he had refrained from saying anything so incriminating in the course of his interrogations, he was unlikely to have made such an observation in the course of casual conversation.[68] The court, however, chose to believe Rich, and More was condemned. Following his condemnation, and in order to clear his conscience as he put it, he proceeded to confirm the substance of Rich's testimony by asserting that his indictment was grounded upon a statute 'directly repugnant to the laws of God' and invalid for that reason. This, as the Duke of Norfolk put it, confirmed his 'malice' in the terms of the Act, and Lord Chancellor Audley observed that if the statute was valid, which he did not doubt, then the indictment was good enough.[69] More was executed on Tower Hill on the morning of 6 July, and Cromwell was, as his duty bound him, present at his death. This was a consummation which was far from what he had desired and worked for while More was alive. During his sojourn in the Tower he had indeed appeared to be so solicitous for his welfare that he had attracted a series of grateful letters from his wife, Alice, saying that she was 'most deeply bound ... for your manifold goodness and loving favour, both before this time and yet daily now also showed towards my poor husband and me'.[70] In fact More's death, and the circumstances of it, was a setback for Cromwell, although he could not afford to admit it.

In a way John Fisher's execution had also been a setback, although there is much less evidence to demonstrate the fact. Fisher had originally been condemned for misprision, for not revealing the nun Elizabeth Barton's prophecies, but remained in the Tower after he had refused to take the oath. Imprisonment took its toll upon his health. He was an old man, and suffered from the cold and the poor prison diet, in spite of the supplements which he received from Antonio Bonvisi. Just before Christmas 1534 he wrote to Cromwell pleading for some relief, identifying him as the only person whom he could approach in his distress.[71] He had corresponded with Cromwell before, and although only the latter's reply survives, it is clear why he felt that he could be appealed to. Cromwell's letter, which was about the nun and her delinquencies, was crisp and theologically well informed, taking the bishop to task for misapplying texts of scripture, but it was not at all hostile, and that must have given Fisher his cue. Unfortunately we do not know what the result of his appeal may have been, although the fact that he survived to stand trial indicates that there may have been some improvement. It was not Cromwell who was after Fisher's blood – it was the king – and the key factor was probably Pope Paul's decision to confer the cardinalate upon him. This may have been done under the mistaken impression that the rank would offer him some kind of protection, although the sanctity of his life and the circumstances of his imprisonment would have constituted sufficient reasons. Henry was furious. A papal honour for his suspect traitor was an insult of the first order, and he is alleged to have remarked that he would send Fisher's head to collect his hat, 'so the twain met not'.[72] The bishop was tried by a special commission of oyer and terminer on 17 June, and inevitably found guilty. Unlike More, he probably was guilty, although the crucial evidence against him could not be produced in court. According to Chapuys, Fisher had urged Charles to intervene and 'undertake a work which must be as pleasing in the eyes of God as war upon the Turks', which was treason even by the unmodified law of 1352.[73] Cromwell was a member of the commission that condemned him, and had been involved in the interrogations which had preceded his trial, although there is no evidence about what part he played. He is alleged to have urged the bishop to confess his errors and to throw himself on the king's mercy, but this met with no response. However, it shows a good understanding of Henry's psychology, because the one thing which might have turned aside the royal wrath was the spectacle of this learned and ascetic prelate grovelling for mercy. As it was that wrath was fully expressed on 22 June 1535 when Fisher, who was too weak to walk, was borne to his death on Tower Hill. On the scaffold, after his gown was removed, men 'marvelled to see [any man] bearing life to be so far consumed, for he seemed a lean carcass; the flesh clean wasted away … as one might say death in a man's shape and using a man's voice'.[74] His body was left lying for several hours under guard, until it could be quietly interred nearby. Thomas Cromwell was left with the unenviable task of justifying both these executions (and those of the Carthusians) to the hostile courts of Europe.

The first casualty of these events was any hope of reconciliation with Paul III, who wrote to Francis I that Henry had 'exceeded his ancestors in wickedness', and sought the French king's help against this persecutor of the Church. Francis, however, absorbed by his rivalry with Charles, was not prepared to oblige.[75] Charles was similarly preoccupied, and Henry's tentative attempts to avoid isolation through an alliance with the Schmalkaldic League were not followed up. There is, however, no reason to suppose that Cromwell's attempts to justify the king's actions and to explain that the accused had been fairly tried, and were 'undoubtedly guilty' of the treasons for which they suffered, cut any ice at all, least of all in Rome. Meanwhile the French and Imperial ambassadors in London kept a watching brief and were able to report that Anne's unpopularity had been increased rather than diminished by these events. So concerned was the king by the evidences of this unpopularity that he compelled Bishop Stokesley of London to preach in support of the Supremacy in St Paul's Cathedral, and sent Cromwell along to make sure that the correct words were used.[76] Alehouse rantings, 'slips of the tongue', and more deliberate words of defiance kept the secretary busy with investigations throughout the year. Not all were as penitent as Margaret Chancellor, a Suffolk woman who blessed Catherine as 'the righteous queen', but who professed to the Suffolk justices that she had been drunk at the time and that an evil spirit had caused her to utter those treasonable words. She was let off with a caution, but not all delinquents were so fortunate. George Taylor of Newport Pagenall in Buckinghamshire appears to have paid the full price for claiming that he would play football with the Crown of England, so little did he regard it, although he also pleaded drunkenness in extenuation.[77] Meanwhile Henry's relationship with his queen had its ups and downs. In the summer of 1534 Anne miscarried, and Henry was reported to be 'much enamoured' of another lady of the court. Chapuys, who carried the story, did not name her and the chances are that it was just another bit of court gossip. Nevertheless there were periods of tension in their marriage, and the king never came to terms with her political agenda, considering such things to be inappropriate in a consort.[78] Her business was to give him a son, and towards the end of 1535, Anne was again pregnant. A lot would depend upon her safe delivery, and upon the sex of the child. Many malcontents might reconsider their positions if God gave her a son.

Then, in January 1536, Catherine died, and the political situation shifted slightly but significantly. Henry reacted with relief, declaring that he was now free from any suspicion of war, meaning conflict with the Emperor. Charles was also relieved because he now no longer had an aunt whose honour needed protection, or whose cause he felt bound to promote. The way was open for a 'normalisation' of relations between England and the Empire, and Cromwell was free to pick up the option of an Imperial alliance, which he had preferred for some time but which circumstances had appeared to render impossible.[79] He began to confer more amicably with Chapuys, and the latter's reports became less hostile. The main obstacle in the way of improved relations remained Queen Anne. Not only was her position unrecognised by the Imperialists, but her tastes and the whole logic of her position demanded a French connection. So her alliance of convenience with Cromwell broke down, and the secretary began to consider the possibility of getting rid of her. Now that the ending of his second marriage would no longer carry the threat of reviving his first, Henry's growing affection for Jane Seymour seemed to offer such an opportunity. At the end of January the king had a heavy fall in the lists, and was unconscious for more than two hours. Although he recovered completely and was none the worse apart from some bad bruising, this was a reminder of his mortality and of the urgency of the succession. Then in early February Anne miscarried for the second time. The foetus was male, and Henry became distraught at the thought of losing another son. He blamed Anne for this misfortune, and although she tried to shift the responsibility onto the Duke of Norfolk for springing the news of the king's accident on her, he was not mollified.[80] The possibility of removing her had now climbed up the agenda, and in March Henry sent a letter and a lavish gift to Jane Seymour, who rejected both with a coy profession of her virginity. The king was encouraged rather than dismayed by this demonstration of virtue, and his interest was significantly increased, which suited the Seymour family admirably. What then happened is controversial, but it seems that Cromwell's breach with Anne was finalised by a disagreement over the fate of the lesser monasteries, which were dissolved by statute in March.[81] The queen wanted the proceeds to be devoted to Church causes, such as education and the augmentation of poor livings, whereas Cromwell wished the king to have the free disposal of them, to be deployed on the defence of the realm or in the satisfaction of the demand for royal patronage. In April Anne even authorised her almoner, John Skip, to preach a sermon attacking the anticlericalism of the secretary's option, and the chips were fairly down.[82] Unfortunately for him the Emperor was also proving hard to pin down at that point and was implying conditions about Mary's right to the succession that Cromwell was in no position to satisfy and which the king was reluctant to concede. At the same time, if Anne were to be displaced, the whole Boleyn faction would need to be removed, and that necessitated an understanding at least with Mary's friends around the court, who were of course out of favour with Henry. By the end of April, Cromwell was in a cleft stick. As early as the previous July the queen had threatened to have his head if he continued to obstruct her, and that time may now have come. She was far too formidable a politician to be shunted aside as Catherine had been, and it began to look as though it was her head or his. Henry seems to have been genuinely undecided at this point, and as late as 24 April was still writing sincerely about his 'entirely beloved' wife. On the other hand, he understood the issues, and measured his favours to the Boleyns and the Seymours equally. On the 27th a special commission of oyer and terminer was established to hear treasons in London and Middlesex, and this it has been argued, was a part of Cromwell's preparations for his coup against Anne.[83] However there is no evidence to support such a supposition, and it is not even certain that the secretary was responsible. No treason was named, and it is likely to have been a mere precautionary measure taken by the Lord Chancellor. Similarly the decision to call a new parliament, which was also taken in April and was unexpected in view of the recent dissolution of the last assembly, looks like Cromwell's preparation for dealing with the queen's case. Henry, however, had still not made up his mind, and would not have consented to such a recall unless there had been other pressing business to attend to. Although he was suspicious of the queen's agenda, he was still speaking hopefully of the sons which she would bear him, and it was not until 29 or 30 April that he was finally bounced into a decision against her.

The critical event seems to have been an altercation between Anne and Sir Henry Norris, which took place on the 29th. Irritated by Norris's slowness to 'come on' to Mary Shelton, whom she had sought out for him, she accused him of waiting for herself to become available, which could only happen in the event of the king's death.[84] Appalled by the implications of this, Norris vehemently denied any such ambition, but the damage had been done. Cromwell's agents in the Privy Chamber not only made haste to inform him of the queen's treason, but also conveyed the impression of a long-standing sexual relationship between the two. This was the cue for which he had been waiting, and acting on a similar tip, on the 30th he arrested Mark Smeaton, and accused him too of an adulterous affair with Anne. He knew that Smeaton, who was a court musician, had been mooning over the queen for some time, and had been unwise enough to give voice to his obsession. He charged him accordingly. Perhaps encouraged by a promise of immunity, or perhaps indulging in wish fulfilment, the musician confessed to what was almost certainly an imaginary offence, and Cromwell hastened to inform Henry that he had been cuckolded.[85] The king quitted the tournament which he had been attending in a foul mood, and on 2 May Anne was arrested and taken to the Tower, along with Norris, Smeaton and one or two other suspects whom the secretary's informants had named. These plausible but insubstantial stories appear to have convinced Henry utterly, and from being uncertain he now became the prime agent in Anne's destruction. Cromwell was given the congenial task of assembling the case against her, and took it upon himself to make sure that their mutual friend Thomas Cranmer had no access to the king while this was under way.[86] He interrogated the ladies of her Privy Chamber, and gleaned a number of circumstantial stories which could be made to serve his purpose. Most notably he learned from Jane Rochford of the intimacy which existed between the queen and her brother, Jane's husband. This may have resulted from strained relations within the Rochfords' marriage, and the story contained no more than a hint of impropriety, but it was enough to land Lord Rochford in the Tower as well on a charge of incestuous adultery.[87] Meanwhile Anne was not helping herself. Since her arrival in the Tower she had chattered inconsequentially about the men in her life, proving nothing but giving substance to the rumours with which she was already surrounded. The trouble was that amid all this fog of innuendo, there was very little solid evidence. As Sir Edward Baynton, one of the interrogators, wrote to Sir William Fitzwilliam,

Here is much communication that no man will confess anything against her but all-only Mark of any actual thing. Whereof (in my foolish conceit) it should much touch the king's honour if it should no farther appear. And I cannot believe but that the other two [Rochford and Norris] be as fully culpable as ever he was. And I think assuredly the one keepeth the others counsel ... I hear farther that the queen standeth stiffly in her opinion ... which I think is in the trust that she [hath of the] other two.[88]

This was all very well, but it did not make Cromwell's task any easier. Norris and Rochford were two stalwarts of the Boleyn faction which he was by now determined to destroy lest it should have, in Eric Ives's words, any 'second strike capability'.[89] He built his case as best he could, not utilising Jane Rochford's testimony, nor Henry's rather wild conviction that he had been the victim of his wife's talent for witchcraft, but making heavy use of the evidence of Elizabeth, Countess of Worcester. Elizabeth was carrying a child, which the earl was convinced was not his, and she had responded to his accusations by blaming the atmosphere of the Privy Chamber, for which the queen was to blame. The other story which was central to his case was that Anne had been responsible for poisoning Catherine, and had plotted a similar fate for Mary and the king. All these rumours do not amount to much as evidence to put before a court of law, but of course in a case like this the only person who had to be convinced was the king, and he was absolutely persuaded that Anne had been guilty of adultery with a hundred men, never mind the four who were on trial.[90] A grand jury was impanelled on 9 May, not without some judicious manipulation on Cromwell's part, and a True Bill was found. Norris, along with William Brereton and Francis Weston, two other members of the Privy Chamber who had been similarly charged, was tried on the 12th and found guilty, which left Anne nowhere to go. She and Lord Rochford were tried on the 15th in the King's Hall at the Tower, with great solemnity as became her rank and the gravity of the charges which she faced. The Duke of Norfolk presided, and twenty-six peers formed the court. Anne had recovered her composure by that time, but was well aware that it was her word against her accusers; 'if any man accuse me, I can but say nay and they can bring no witnesses'. According to one observer 'she made so wise and discreet answers to all things laid against her, excusing herself with her words so clearly as though she had never been faulty in the same'.[91] It was all to no avail. The peers knew their duty well enough, and the conviction of her accomplices decided her fate. Lord Rochford put up an even more impressive performance, and the general opinion of the spectators was that he should have been acquitted. However, that would not have suited either Thomas Cromwell or the king, and the court duly convicted him as well. He was beheaded at the Tower on 17 May, making a good end in that he acknowledged the justice of the sentence against him, without confessing to his alleged crimes. By the time that Anne followed him on the 19th, she was no longer married to Henry VIII because Cranmer's court, reversing the decision of three years earlier, found the marriage to be null and void, apparently on the grounds of the king's earlier relationship with her sister, allegedly discovered since the previous verdict had been reached.[92] She had of course lost the Marquisate of Pembroke by virtue of her attainder, and thus went to block as plain Anne Boleyn. The Boleyn party had been destroyed, just as Cromwell had wished, and the Earl of Wiltshire, Anne and George's father, who had not been involved in their misdemeanours, lost his office of Lord Privy Seal and was forced to withdraw from the court. On 1 July he was replaced by Thomas Cromwell. The secretary thus emerged from what must have been a very tense and difficult time completely triumphant. He had gambled on Henry's gullibility and had been vindicated, earning the king's gratitude for the efficient way in which he had handled the case. Their relationship was consequently stronger than ever, and he could look forward with confidence to a period of Seymour ascendancy at court. Henry became espoused to Jane on the day of Anne's execution, and married her on 30 May, with what was generally regarded as indecent haste.[93] However, nobody said so, and the king entered into a period of unprecedented domestic harmony.

5

THE LORD PRIVY SEAL, 1531–1540

...whereupon the said Lords and Commons by great deliberation finally be resolved that it is and shall be much more to the pleasure of Almighty God and for the honour of this his realm that the possessions of such spiritual religious houses, now being spent, spoiled and wasted for the increase and maintenance of sin, should be used and converted to better uses...

Act for the Dissolution of the Minor Monasteries

Anne Boleyn was executed in May 1536, and Cromwell's coup against her and her family-based faction had been carried out with the co-operation of Catherine's friends at court, particularly Carew and the Courtenays, and they expected her fall, and the consequent bastardisation of Elizabeth, to be accompanied by the rehabilitation of Mary. Henry, however, did not see the connection. As far as he was concerned, it was his authority which she was flouting, and he was looking for an unequivocal submission. As he told Chapuys a few days before the crisis broke,

As to the legitimation of our daughter Mary ... if she would submit to our grace, without wrestling against the determination of our laws, we would acknowledge her and use her as our daughter, but we would not be directed or pressed therein...[1]

Anne's death changed nothing, and although there was plenty of popular support for her, and Jane Seymour herself urged Mary's unconditional restoration, there is no sign that Henry had changed his mind. Logically the deaths of Catherine and Anne should have restored the status quo in his relations with the papacy, and Pope Paul looked forward to renewed negotiations. However, Henry had no such intention, because what the conservatives did not understand, and Cromwell did, was just how deeply the king was committed to his title as Supreme Head of the Church. It was a central aspect of his special relationship with God.[2] Chapuys also noted this fact in his reports to Charles V, although he attributed it to the king's 'obstinacy'. Consequently, until Mary recognised that, there was no hope of a reconciliation. Under a similar misapprehension, several of Mary's former servants turned up at Hunsdon, expecting to be re-employed. However the status of the household there was indeterminate, because both the king's daughters were now illegitimate, and Chapuys wisely advised Lady Shelton to take on no one without the king's express authorisation.[3] Meanwhile Mary herself, who seems to have shared the common misapprehension about Anne, waited expectantly for a signal from her father that she was forgiven. None came, and the felicitations of her supporters, which arrived constantly during the latter part of May, began to have a hollow sound.

A week after the queen's execution, on 26 May, she did the obvious thing and wrote to Thomas Cromwell, asking for his intercession now that the woman who had alienated her from her father was gone. Well informed of the king's state of mind, the secretary replied that her obedience was looked for as a condition of reinstatement.[4] However Mary, whose sophisticated education seems to have given her a very naive view of the real world, did not read the signal. She wrote again on the 30th, asking to see her father and professing her willingness to be 'as obedient to the king's grace as you can reasonably require of me', not apparently realising that this reservation rendered the whole offer nugatory. The following day she wrote a disarming letter to Henry himself, acknowledging her offences in general terms 'in as humble and lowly a manner as is possible', and asking for his forgiveness and blessing.[5] She congratulated him upon his recent marriage to Jane Seymour, perhaps recognising her as a friend. Unfortunately she spoiled the effect of this dutiful submissiveness by making it clear that there were limits to her obedience. She would obey her father in all things next to God, 'beseeching your highness to consider that I am but a woman and your child, who hath committed her soul only to God, and her body to be ordered in this world as it shall stand with your pleasure'. Since her obedience to God embraced both the points at issue, the ecclesiastical supremacy and her mother's marriage, she was conceding nothing, and Henry did not bother to reply.[6] Preoccupied with Jane, he presumably saw her letter, but nevertheless went ahead with drawing up a set of articles to be presented to her which would leave no room for evasion. Chapuys, probably informed by Cromwell, was extremely worried by this development. They were allies at this point, because it did not suit either of their plans to see Mary tried, and possibly executed, for high treason. The secretary showed him the draft of a letter that he had prepared for her to sign, which the ambassador thought very dishonourable, but nevertheless agreed to go along with, realising that Henry was on the warpath. On 6 June he reported that he thought he could see an honourable way out. We do not know what this was, but it presumably did not involve the use of the letter.[7] His optimism seems to have communicated itself to Mary, although this can hardly have been by Cromwell's means, because on the 7th she wrote to the latter, full of optimism, asking for some token from the king before she paid her anticipated visit to the court. It may be that she had received the encouraging letter from Queen Jane which we know was written at about this time, because on the following day she also wrote to her father expressing her joy at the news that he had 'withdrawn his displeasure'.[8]

Unfortunately her enthusiasm was premature, and again there was no response. Anxious at this silence, Mary wrote again on 10 June, asking for his blessing, and this time copying her letter to Cromwell, asking not to be pressed further in her submission than her conscience would bear. It may be that she thought that her friends in the council would succeed in changing the king's mind, but we can imagine Cromwell's reaction on receiving this evidence of continued obstinacy. Henry's response was critical. On about the 15th he sent the Duke of Norfolk, the Earl of Sussex and Richard Sampson, the newly consecrated Bishop of Chichester, down to Hunsdon bearing his commission and two questions to which he demanded a straight answer. Would she accept her father's ecclesiastical supremacy, repudiating the Bishop of Rome? And would she accept the nullity of her mother's marriage?[9] In a stormy and emotional confrontation, she rejected both demands, and the crisis which Cromwell and Chapuys had both dreaded had broken. The judges confirmed that she could now be proceeded against for high treason, and the council went into emergency session. Ominously her known supporters, Exeter and Fitzwilliam, were excluded from these meetings; and two of her friends in the Privy Chamber, Sir Anthony Browne and Sir Francis Bryan, were arrested and interrogated 'concerning talk had of the estate of the Lady Mary', presumably of her hoped-for restoration.[10] Their testimonies make interesting reading, because what emerged was not so much treasonable words as evidence of how delicate the situation had become. Some, even in the inner circle of the court, had expressed the view that Mary would make a very satisfactory heir, if only she would submit to her father. The idea that she had been conceived in good faith by parents who believed themselves to be married (*bona fide parentum*) had also been canvassed, while others had expressed doubts about her actual submission, the latter being the acceptable majority.[11] The actual chronology of events at this time is confused, because on the 13th Mary wrote to Cromwell, saying that she could think of nothing better to do than to copy out the letter of submission which he had sent her. Either she did not do so, or Cromwell retained it, because on the 14th she was still wondering why she had received no token of forgiveness. When he received the news of her interview with the Duke of Norfolk, he exploded with exasperation, drafting a fierce letter of rebuke, in which he lamented his own foolishness for ever having attempted to help her. It is highly unlikely that he ever sent this letter, because he knew the king well enough to know that this game was by no means over, and that Henry would be very reluctant to proceed to extremes against his daughter.[12] In spite of her words to Norfolk, submission was still a possibility, because potentially she was a stabilising element in the domestic situation, and the key to improved relations with the Empire. He could not afford to give up just yet, however unpromising things looked. Consequently during the week which followed the commissioners' visit to Hunsdon and while the council was in session, Cromwell was also using all his ingenuity to find a constructive solution to the deadlock.

When it came to the point, he seems to have achieved his objective by indirect means. He convinced Chapuys that Mary faced the alternatives of surrender or death, gambling on the hope that she did not share her mother's taste for martyrdom. Chapuys in turn convinced Mary, because without Imperial support her conscience could gain no leverage, and he seems to have argued that to give way to such extreme pressure could carry no stigma of guilt, even to the most scrupulous. The pressure was indeed cruel. Apart from the troubles afflicting Browne and Bryan, her old friend Lady Hussey, the wife of her former chamberlain, had been sent to the Tower merely for speaking sympathetically of her. It gave her insomnia, toothache and neuralgia.[13] Finally, on 22 June, she gave way, signing a set of articles which had been sent by her father without reading them, according to Chapuys. However she also wrote a covering letter of unconditional surrender, remitting her whole life to his discretion, which was almost certainly a copy of the model which Cromwell had sent to her for just such a purpose.[14] It may well be that Jane had also privately urged her to follow such a course, which would explain her expressions of gratitude to her as well as to Cromwell over the days that followed. Within a few days gracious messages arrived from both the king and the queen, and the relaxation of tension was palpable. Henry was probably as relieved as anyone that the hard choice which seemed to be facing him had gone away. Mary's state of mind at this juncture is hard to assess. On the one hand her correspondence with the secretary is friendly almost to the point of warmth, and she quickly became absorbed in plans for the re-establishment of her household, which suggests that she soon began to appreciate the benefits of restored favour. On 6 July the king and queen visited Hunsdon and stayed for several days, and on the 20th she wrote to Cromwell thanking him for the gift of a riding horse and saddle. It would do her health much good, she observed, to be riding again.[15] On the other hand, Chapuys represents her as overcome with grief and remorse at having betrayed her principles, and begging him to obtain a special dispensation for her from Rome to ease her conscience. He did in fact make an unsuccessful bid of that sort, but whether it was really at her request we do not know. He had his own conscience to salve for having been a party to her surrender, and he also had her reputation to defend in the courts of Catholic Europe.[16]

There is no doubt that the real winner from all these exchanges was Thomas Cromwell. Mary's surrender had effectively drawn her teeth as the leader of the Aragonese faction, and cancelled any debt which he might have owed them for their help in bringing down Anne Boleyn. If they had been looking to him to persuade the king to wink at Mary's obstinacy, and even to include her in the succession, then they were sadly disappointed. But he would never have promised so much, knowing his own limitations. The Duke of Richmond died on 23 July, and, although Henry had never made any move to include him in succession, as his only son he would have been in a strong position, considering that both the king's daughters were equally illegitimate. The succession had in fact been rearranged by a second Act passed through Parliament in June.[17] This statute, which Cromwell had as usual drafted and pushed through both houses, declared that the king's heir would be any child born to him and his present wife, Queen Jane. Failing that, or a child born to any subsequent marriage, the king was given authority to declare the succession by his last will and testament. Neither Mary nor Elizabeth were mentioned. Nevertheless, come August Henry was offering the former's legitimation and inclusion in the succession as part of a marriage negotiation with the King of France. However, since the condition was that the Duke of Angoulême, the prospective bridegroom, should come to live in England, it is unlikely that this was a serious suggestion.[18] Mary herself certainly did not think so, but it did signal that she was back on the marriage market after a three-year absence. As she was now twenty, this was not a moment too soon. At the same time, the crowned heads of Europe were not exactly queuing up with offers, and the suggestion that she would be more attractive if she were created Duchess of York was not acted upon. She was, however, enjoying the fruits of her rehabilitation in the reconstitution of her chamber, which saw her united with a number of old friends. She no longer had need of a lady governess, so the Countess of Salisbury was not reappointed, but back came Susan Clarencius, Margery Baynton, Mary Browne and a number of others.[19] Cromwell was also reaping the rewards of his part in that operation, because within a few days he had been appointed Lord Privy Seal in succession to the disgraced Earl of Wiltshire, who was Anne Boleyn's father, and on 9 July he was raised to the peerage as Baron Cromwell of Wimbledon. On 18 July he was knighted, and had his earlier appointment as Viceregent in Spirituals confirmed and extended. Henry's confidence could not have been more fully displayed. He was now also a rich man, having been collecting stewardships and the keeperships of castles and parks, all of which carried substantial fees and could be discharged by deputy: Westminster Abbey in September 1533; Hertford Castle and Park in February 1534; the Savoy and Enfield in May 1535; the manor and park of Writtle in Essex in June 1536, and a number of others.[20] At the same time his correspondence makes it clear that he was in receipt of numerous payments in cash and kind in return for his 'kindness' to suitors and litigants. What these may have amounted to in the course of a year is hard to calculate, but we can be sure that his stables were not short of geldings, nor his table of fat partridges. Presumably what he and his household could not use or consume was sold on at a profit. We may think of such payments as bribes, but they were a part of the regular practice of petitioning the Crown, and no one thought them amiss – unless they did not get what they were after, in which case they became a grievance. Cromwell's fees for 1536 totalled seventy-eight items.

Cromwell's remembrances also indicate the huge range of business passing across his desk; memoranda as to what to do with suspects under examination, with suitors for ecclesiastical benefices, with monastic appointments and for the repair of the king's navy.[21] Very often these notes contain the phrase 'to know the king's pleasure', indicating that the secretary had to exercise a fine judgement as to what things he could process himself and what needed to be referred upwards. This was not straightforward because Henry applied no rules to himself, and was just as likely to be concerned about the disposal of a rectory in Suffolk as he was about the latest twists in Francis I's diplomacy. It depended upon what had been brought to his attention, and how it had been done, because Cromwell did not have a monopoly of access to the king. The Duke of Suffolk, or the members of the Privy Chamber might approach him via the secretary, or they might speak to him directly during their periods of attendance. A good deal depended upon whether a petitioner felt that he needed help with his suit or not; the more he felt that the king needed to be kept in mind of his request, the more likely he was to seek Cromwell's help. Miles Spencer offered to pay Cromwell £100 'to his use' for a benefice recently vacated by the death of the Bishop of Chichester. The settlement of debt was a particularly thorny issue, and several suitors wrote to the secretary repeatedly over a number of months concerning sums that were owed them by the Crown.[22] These might involve damages awarded by a court and never paid, payments due to the garrison of Calais or the wages of workmen at Westminster or Greenwich. It depended upon which pocket the sums due should be drawn from. In the case of the Exchequer or the main Chamber account, Cromwell would deal with them himself, having checked with the relevant treasurer that the sums involved were actually available. But in the case of moneys to be drawn from the Privy Purse, which would include work on the royal palaces, Henry's signature might well be required, and that could take time and patience to obtain. It also did not do to assume that the king was ignorant of other payments which had been made from other sources. It would depend on who he had been talking to, and over those conversations Cromwell had no control. It was important never to take Henry for granted, and his relationship with his secretary must have been based on many consultations which were not strictly speaking necessary, but which persuaded him that he was directly involved in the running of the country at a manageable cost in time and effort.[23]

One of the major decisions of 1536, which involved both Cromwell and the king, was the dissolution of the minor monasteries. The former had been originally of the opinion that this should proceed on an individual basis, as had been done by Wolsey, but by the beginning of 1536 had been persuaded that it would be better done by Act of Parliament. This may well have been for the purpose of demonstrating that the country was behind the king in this exercise of the Royal Supremacy, and Henry would have been easily convinced for the same reason. The reports of the commissioners, who had been visiting the religious houses since the previous year, provided an adequate excuse, and Cromwell was able to prepare a Bill stating that

> manifest sin, vicious carnal and abominable living is daily used and committed amongst the little and small abbeys, priories and other religious houses of monks canons and nuns where the congregation of such religious persons is under the number of 12 persons.[24]

Consequently all religious houses with an income of less than £200 a year were to be dissolved and their assets given to the king. This he was able to steer safely through both houses, and it received the royal assent on 14 April, coming into immediate effect. A companion statute, passed at the same time, established a Court of Augmentations to administer this property on the king's behalf, and this also bears the unmistakable marks of its origin in the secretary's office, because it formed a key element in his reorganisation of the financial administration, and because the first officers of the court all had close associations with Cromwell.[25] Queen Anne Boleyn was opposed to this secularisation of the monastic properties, arguing forcefully that the proceeds should be used for religious purposes, such as education, and it may be that the new parliament, which met in June, was called partly to resolve this disagreement. If so, it was made redundant by Anne's fall and execution in May, but was able to occupy itself fruitfully by reorganising the succession. At the same time, the accompanying convocation passed the Ten Articles, which reflected the state of Henry's thought on the reformation of the Church, and which was pushed through by Cromwell sitting as Viceregent in the upper house. The rank-and-file clergy were required to preach in support of these Articles, and the furious unpopularity of that helps to explain what happened next in Lincolnshire, because in early October the men of Louth, stirred up by a conservative parish priest, rose in rebellion.[26]

The situation in Louth was complicated by social tensions within the town, and by the arrival of Dr Frankish, the bishop's commissary, who was probably engaged in the collection of the clerical tenth which had been voted by Parliament. However, he was suspected of having come to arrange a general confiscation of church goods, and possibly the merging of parishes. Consequently he was set upon by an angry mob, and compelled to burn all the books of the 'new learning' which he had brought with him.[27] At the same time the crowd set out in pursuit of the commissioners who were currently dissolving the nearby nunnery of Legbourne, and who promptly fled the hostile demonstration. Inspired by this success, the following day the men of Louth set off for Caistor, where they succeeded in raising a sympathetic movement, and it began to seem that the whole of that part of Lincolnshire was disaffected. Egged on by their priests, the demonstrators then began to turn their attention to the local gentry, capturing a number of them and forcing them to take an oath to uphold the cause of the commons.[28] Some may not have been as reluctant as they later alleged, and as the rebels converged on Lincoln a few days later, they helped to draw up a set of articles which it was agreed should be sent to the king, outlining their grievances and suing for redress.

These articles were a mixture. The first and third dealt with the Dissolution of the Monasteries and the latest tax or 'quindene', which they complained would ruin the commons, being payable upon every beast. However the second article protested at the Statute of Uses, which was purely a gentleman's grievance, and the fourth at the king's employment of low-born councillors:

> Item, we your true subjects think that your Grace take of your council, and being about you such person as are of low birth and small reputation, which hath procured the profits [of the dissolution] most especially for their own advantage, the which we suspect to be the Lord Cromwell and Sir Richard Rich, Chancellor of Augmentations...[29]

Cromwell thus had the finger of popular disapproval pointed directly at him, and the warning was clear to see. Henry of course responded that no one had the right to tell him how to pick his council, least of all the inhabitants of one of the 'rudest' shires in the land, and because its leadership was divided, the Lincolnshire protest made no further progress. Even the more militant of the commons leaders saw themselves as a demonstration, not a rebellion, and the gentry who had been coerced into the leadership were only too anxious to escape from the trap in which they found themselves. So having, as they thought, made their point, the protesters dispersed even before the king's response arrived, which was just as well because it was less than conciliatory.[30] The king had no intention of dismissing either Cromwell or Rich, or Cranmer or Audley, his other councillors who might come within the designation of 'baseborn'. He would not be bound, he declared later, to be served by noblemen, but would choose such men as might be most suitable for the tasks he had in mind. His authority alone should be sufficient to ensure that they were obeyed.[31]

There the matter might have rested if it had not been for the fact that the disaffection had already spread across the Humber into Yorkshire. There it quickly assumed a more formidable aspect, thanks largely to the leadership provided by Robert Aske. Aske was lawyer and a dependant of the Percy Earls of Northumberland, who felt very strongly about the direction of the Crown's religious policy, and particularly about the Dissolution of the Monasteries. It was he who chose the evocative description of the movement as a 'Pilgrimage of Grace', and the badge of the five wounds of Christ under which they marched. The Pilgrim's hymn, adopted at the same time, started with the lines

> Christ crucified
> for thy woundes wide
> Us commons guide,
> That pilgrims be...[32]

Again they saw themselves as a protest rather than a rebellion, and followed the same strategy as their Lincolnshire colleagues in recruiting the local gentry to their cause. They seemed both more numerous and more purposeful than their Lincolnshire counterparts, and Henry was constrained to take them more seriously. They took York without encountering any resistance, and advanced to Pontefract, 30,000 strong, at the end of November, capturing the castle there and recruiting Lord Darcy to their cause.[33] Although the Earl of Shrewsbury remained loyal, he had only a tenth of that number under his command, and the king was unable to raise an adequate force in time to confront the 'rebels'. He therefore sent the Duke of Norfolk north with power to negotiate, and the duke was presented at Doncaster on 4 December with the so-called Pontefract Articles, embodying the Pilgrims' demands. These were more direct, and more political, than those of Lincoln, starting with demand that the Royal Supremacy be abrogated and the Lady Mary restored to her rightful place in the succession. They then proceeded to the dissolution of the abbeys, the restoration of the friars, and to the Act of First Fruits and Tenths. Article 7 read, 'To have the heretics, bishops and temporal [men] to have condign punishment by fire or otherwise', and Article 8,

> to have the Lord Cromwell, the Lord Chancellor, and Sir Richard Rich, Knight, to have condign punishment as the subvertors of the good laws of this realm, and maintainers of the false sect of those heretics, and the first inventers and bringers in of them.[34]

The last verse of the Pilgrims' hymn ran,

> Crim, Crame and Riche,
> With the ILL and the Lich,
> As some men teach
> God them amend
> And that ask may
> Without delay

> Here make a stay
> And well to end…

'Crim' is undoubtedly Cromwell. The duke may not have been altogether displeased by this fierce criticism of his successful rivals for the king's ear, but the most that he was empowered to concede was a general pardon and a parliament somewhere in the North, in Nottingham or York, to discuss the rest of their agenda. With this, Aske, mindful of his pose as a protester, professed himself satisfied, and after a sharp tussle among the Pilgrims' leaders, he was able to prevail. The rebels, many of whom were far from home and anxious to return, agreed to disperse and so lost their critical advantage.[35] Aske meanwhile accepted an invitation to go to court and discuss the Pilgrims' grievances face to face.

Throughout these events, Cromwell kept a low profile. There is no reason to suppose that he lost his place as the king's right-hand man, or even that his advice on how to deal with the Pilgrimage was ignored, but he played no part in negotiating with the rebels either in Lincolnshire or in Yorkshire. Henry was sensible enough to realise that working through him in such a context would have been unacceptable, and he was kept in the background, working through the Duke of Suffolk and other front-line noblemen. He even kept out of the way while Aske and his colleagues were at court, to avoid giving additional provocation. Had Parliament been held at York, it is difficult to see how Henry could have avoided sacrificing him, but it never was. A relatively insignificant rising in Yorkshire, led by Sir Francis Bigod in January 1537, absolved the king of all undertakings, and he found pretexts to punish all the leaders of the original Pilgrimage. Lord Darcy was beheaded in May, and Robert Aske hanged from the walls of

York in July.[36] There were minor disturbances in Cumberland and Westmorland thereafter, but nothing to cause the government the anxiety of the pre-Christmas period. So Henry escaped what was in some ways the most perilous crisis of his reign, without any obligation to dismiss his most valued servant. Indeed he was on record as saying that 'he will not forgo my Lord Privy Seal for no man living'. Cromwell was no soldier and could not have been used in the way in which the Duke of Norfolk served, but it is clear that he wrote some of Norfolk's instructions, and advised the king when it was expedient to make concessions, especially to prevent these from making any allusions to himself, or Cranmer or Rich, or any other servants who had been vilified. He even criticised Norfolk, in the king's name of course, for being soft on the monasteries that had been involved in the rising, and on papists in general; a rebuke which evoked a furious protest from the duke, who probably detected its origin, and struck back in the only way in which he was able.[37] The execution of the leaders drew a line under the events of the Pilgrimage without in any way diminishing the popular hostility towards Cromwell, or his awareness of it.

However, it was not only in internal policy that the king leaned on his Lord Privy Seal. He was equally crucial in maintaining that strict neutrality in the affairs of France and the Empire, which was the key to Henry's foreign policy during the years 1535–37. He toyed with the idea of a Lutheran alliance, both in 1533 and 1535, but in both cases drew back probably on account of the king's reluctance to commit himself. Henry on the whole leaned towards France in these diplomatic exchanges, while Cromwell leaned towards the Empire, and this tension kept the declared policy in a suitable balance.[38] When open war broke out between the rivals in the summer of 1535, it was expressed in a variety of subtle ways to keep the antagonism on the boil. Henry was always sufficiently concerned about his Continental relations to keep them in the front of his mind, and his treaty with Lübeck in 1534 was definitely a gesture against the Emperor, just at the time when he was rejecting diplomatic overtures from France over the marriage of the Lady Mary.[39]

When it came to Ireland, however, his mind was often elsewhere, and Cromwell consequently had a free hand. He was mainly concerned to extract some revenue from the country which had consistently overspent its budget for many years, and to suppress the aristocratic quarrels which had bedevilled its government. These had led the Earl of Desmond into secret negotiations with an envoy of Charles V in June and July 1533, and to bitter complaints about the partiality of the Lord Deputy, the Earl of Kildare, who was summoned to London to account for his actions in September of that year.[40] The earl appointed his son, Thomas Lord Offaly, as his stand-in, but did not eventually leave for the court until February 1534. Offaly, it quickly transpired, was opposed to Cromwell's policies, and in sympathy with the Irish chieftains who resented the whole notion of English overlordship. On 11 June 1534 he resigned his position and renounced his allegiance, thus converting a problem into a crisis. The rebellion of 'Silken Thomas', as he was known, was the most serious challenge to English rule for a generation, and seems to have been provoked by Cromwell's intrusive policies.[41] As long as Wolsey had been in charge, Ireland had been left very much to its own devices, and a balance of power had prevailed between the Anglo-Irish, the Obedient Lands and the Wild Irish. This had not been peaceful, but the strife which it engendered had been low-key and manageable. Cromwell's attempts to enforce accountability to the council in England were very much resented, almost as much by the Anglo-Irish of the Pale as they were by the Irish nobility. Silken Thomas rapidly overran most of the Pale, and seemed likely to take the whole of Ireland. The Archbishop of Dublin, John Alen, made an attempt to escape, but was caught and murdered by Thomas's followers on 28 July.[42] This overt rebellion had the effect of attracting the king's attention, and on 29 June the Earl of Kildare was arrested and sent to the Tower, a rather futile gesture but one which was inevitable in the circumstances. More to the point the experienced soldier Sir William Skeffington was appointed Lord Deputy and sent across with a substantial force on 24 October, in time to raise the siege of Dublin, which had been going on since August.[43] The appearance of this significant army, and the countervailing need to establish it, led Thomas to accept a three-week truce on 19 December. His less wholehearted followers were beginning to think twice about their commitment to his cause, and Skeffington received a number of submissions at about that time. After the expiry of the truce, he laid siege to Thomas's main stronghold at Maynooth and took it after five days.

The rebels' support was beginning to crumble, and Thomas took refuge among the Irish tribes with whom he had maintained a friendly contact. In May and June he sent envoys to Rome and to the Emperor in Spain, asking for aid and representing himself as a defender of the Catholic Church.[44] Both Paul and Charles were, however, sufficiently well informed about Irish affairs as to recognise these pleas for what they were, the appeals of a failing rebel, and responded only with encouraging words. Lord Leonard Grey, who was undoubtedly Cromwell's choice, arrived with reinforcements as marshall of the army at the end of July, and Silken Thomas surrendered in August 1535. Lord Deputy Skeffington died at the end of the year, and was replaced by Lord Grey, who fully shared the secretary's conviction that only military conquest would solve the Irish problem.[45] Unfortunately the resources were never available to make such a solution a realistic proposition, and Lord Grey had to be satisfied with the temporary ascendancy which the collapse of Thomas's rebellion had given him. This enabled him to go ahead with the commission to suppress the nunnery of Graney in County Kildare, and arrest Thomas's five uncles in February. The 9th Earl had died in the Tower in September 1534, and although Thomas was never recognised as the 10th Earl he had in a sense held the title since then. George Browne was consecrated Archbishop of Dublin at Lambeth on 19 March 1536, and the Irish Parliament met in Dublin on 1 May.[46] This was in a co-operative frame of mind, as the members were keen to display their loyalty. It passed Acts attainting Kildare and his supporters, another endorsing the reforming legislation already enacted at Westminster, and a third against absentee incumbents, always a problem in Ireland given the poverty of many benefices. Meanwhile Kildare and his uncles had been attainted by the English Parliament in July, and they were all executed at Tyburn on 3 February 1537.[47]

It would be an exaggeration to say that Ireland was pacified, but the warfare had returned to its familiar pattern of small-scale skirmishes with the native Irish, and border raids by the latter into the 'settled lands'. Cromwell's policy of repression, in which he was opposed by the Duke of Norfolk, would appear to have been vindicated, and the Royal Commission which visited Ireland in September 1537 found the same. The shock of Silken Thomas's rising, and its aftermath, had also served to curb the internecine strife between the nobles, which had been one of his principal objectives. That this was the Lord Privy Seal's policy rather than the king's was apparently confirmed in 1540, when immediately after his fall, and while the Duke of Norfolk was dominant in the council, Lord Grey was recalled from the deputyship and replaced by Sir Anthony St Leger, with an altogether different agenda.[48] The only snag with his preference for 'new English' administrators, and greater accountability to London, was the cost. In spite of the Dissolution of the Monasteries in English Ireland, and the revenues that it brought to the Crown, Cromwell never succeeded in balancing the books. Ireland was in many ways his least successful theatre of operations, because he set a precedent there for that forward policy which was to produce the Elizabethan plantations, and the long legacy of bitterness which they created. Norfolk and St Leger's approach, which involved conciliating the Irish chieftains and bringing them within the establishment by means of surrender and regrant, can be seen to have been the better long-term prospect.[49] In the case of Ireland, Cromwell's preference for the simple and logical solution seems to have betrayed him, but that only sets his success in other areas in context.

One of the more obvious of these is the measures that he took to ensure that the king's writ ran uniformly throughout his dominions. The origins of this problem lay far back in the early Middle Ages, when, in order to defend the boundaries of the realm, kings had created a number of franchises, and delegated the administration of justice, no less than the question of defence, to the noblemen who held them. Although granted originally by the Crown, these franchises had come to be seen as held by prescriptive right, and there was no obvious way of discontinuing them. Even when they escheated to the Crown through failure of heirs, or for other reasons, the jurisdictional structure of the liberties remained intact. Thus when the earldom of March was absorbed by the Crown on the accession of Edward IV in 1461, the Marcher liberties remained intact, and the king's writ ran as the holder of the franchise, not as monarch.[50] This meant that lawlessness might become a serious problem as the stewards and others who acted in his name might be rather less than zealous, and as Marcher custom protected offenders, as was the case with Welsh law. Cromwell had already partly addressed this issue in respect of the Marches of Wales by taking certain types of case into the jurisdiction of neighbouring English counties, but this proved less than satisfactory.[51] By 1536 the time had come for more drastic action, and the recently enhanced authority of Parliament offered a way forward. Consequently in the spring of that year a Bill was introduced to ensure that

> no person or persons, of what estate or degree soever, from the first day of July which shall be in the year of our Lord God 1536, shall have any power or authority to pardon or remit any treasons, murders, manslaughters or any kind of felonies,[52]

but that the king shall have the 'whole and sole' power and authority thereof 'united and knit to the Imperial crown of this realm'. In other words the rights of franchise holders were abrogated, and all writs were henceforth to run in the king's name only. Partial exceptions were then made for the Bishopric of Durham, where the bishop was to be an *ex officio* Justice of the Peace, and for the Duchy of Lancaster, which was to continue to use its existing seals and processes. However, the effect of the whole Act (as it soon became) was to remove a major jurisdictional anomaly, and to centralise the administration of the law in the manner beloved of Cromwell's tidy mind. Wales was at the same time 'reduced to shire ground', several new counties being created out of the erstwhile Marcher lordships, and endowed with sheriffs, commissions of the peace and parliamentary representation. Wales was effectively merged into England, and the language of the courts was to be English. Welsh law was thus relegated to the manorial and honour courts where it could not touch felonies, and this caused some discontent.[53] However, the Welsh gentry were on the whole in favour of the move, which gave them a new measure of local self-government as Justices of the Peace, and a doorway into national politics through Parliament. The perception of the Welsh as being second-class citizens, which had followed the Glyndŵr revolt in the early fifteenth century, was thus finally laid to rest, and Cromwell had, through Parliament, carried out a reform which had baffled generations of royal lawyers.[54]

Reginald Pole was a kinsman of the king, being the son of Margaret, Countess of Salisbury, and grandson of George, Duke of Clarence, the uncle of Henry VIII's mother, Elizabeth of York. He had been educated largely at the king's expense, and had served him in collecting the opinions of the universities in the early days of his search for an annulment of his first marriage. At the time he had been spoken of as a possible future Archbishop of York.[55] However his conscience turned him against the king's proceedings, and he begged leave to return to the Continent to continue his studies, which was granted him in 1533. In Italy his opinions soon became known to the Pope, and a prince of the English royal blood was great catch. Henry, meanwhile, had encouraged him to write, thinking perhaps that the exercise of putting his thoughts in order would convert him to the official point of view. Cromwell also appears to have corresponded with him with the same objective, but the result was an open letter to the king entitled 'Pro Ecclesiasticae Unitate Defensione', which arrived in May 1536, and was not at all what was required. Instead it was a reasoned denunciation, not only of Henry's second marriage, but of the whole drift of royal policy over the previous five years.[56] Henry was furious, declaring that he was an ungrateful subject and a self-proclaimed traitor. Shortly afterwards Pole justified this description of himself by accepting a cardinalate from Paul III, and a mission from the Pope to stimulate Charles V and Francis I into supporting the Pilgrimage of Grace. His mission failed, and Cromwell's agents dogged him every step of the way, reporting on his ill success to a gratified Lord Privy Seal. His failure, however, owed nothing to Cromwell's efforts and everything to the continuing war between Francis and Charles, which made each of them reluctant to acquire another enemy. He did, however, succeed in eluding the assassins that Henry sent out to kill him, and returned safely to Italy in the spring of 1537.[57] These agents also reported to Cromwell, but he seems to have had nothing to do with the decision to send them, murder not usually being in his line as a political weapon. If a man or a woman had to die, it must be by due process of law, however strained that process might be. Reginald's treason, however, brought his whole family under suspicion. His mother was a known supporter of the old ways in religion, and his brothers, Geoffrey and Henry, Lord Montague, were in touch with the exile, and sympathised with his point of view. They were also known friends of the Lady

Mary, who had not gone away in spite of her reticence since her surrender in July 1536. There was even talk of marrying her to Reginald, who in spite of his status was only in deacon's orders and could therefore have obtained a dispensation. However this was mere gossip as neither of the principals expressed any interest in the proposal.[58] All this was known to Cromwell's agents, and in the summer of 1538 he sent a certain Gervase Tindall down to Hampshire with a spying brief. This was about the same time that the Truce of Nice between Charles and Francis had brought a temporary end to their warfare, and raised again the spectre of papally inspired intervention in the affairs of England. It was very important to know what the conservative opposition was up to, especially those of its members, like the Countess of Salisbury and the Marquis of Exeter, who had extensive coastal estates in Cornwall and Devon that could be used as a landing place for any planned invasion.[59] The marquis was not known to have corresponded with Reginald, but he was a famous supporter of Mary, and had been kept out of the council for that reason when her fate had been under discussion in June 1536.

Gervase Tindall, who had been in Cromwell's service for several years, parked himself in a 'surgeon's house' near Warblington in Hampshire on the pretext of needing medical assistance, and became very friendly with Richard Ayer, who ran the house.[60] It was patronised by the Countess of Salisbury, and Ayer was close to the family. He was also inclined to gossip, and Tindall picked up a good deal of information as to what went on in those establishments, which he duly passed on to the Lord Privy Seal. As a result in August Sir Geoffrey Pole was arrested, and the whole neighbourhood began to buzz with rumours about the family. Ayer was alleged to have said that if Geoffrey had not been apprehended he would have sent a band of men over to Reginald in the spring of 1539, and Hugh Holland was a regular bearer of messages to and fro.[61] Under questioning John Collins, another Pole servant, corroborated this saying that he

> heard at Bockmar of Hugh Holland being beyond the seas, and that the rumour was that he should go over with letters to Cardinal Pole ... and that the disclosing of his often going beyond the seas was made by one Ayer to Tindall...[62]

Tindall was not Cromwell's only source of information in Hampshire, where he had been a considerable figure for several years, rivalling even the influence of the Bishop of Winchester. Indeed the Earl of Southampton looked on him as something of a patron at the centre of affairs, and he had taken a number of Hampshire men into his service. So the chances are that stories about the Pole family and particularly about Hugh Holland, had been circulating for some time and had reached Cromwell's ears, which would explain why he sent Gervase Tindall down to investigate. Richard Ayer seems to have been sympathetic to the New Learning, which was no doubt why he was prepared to disclose so much to Tindall, and to have been genuinely disturbed by what went on in Margaret's household. Particularly worrying was the breach of the confessional by so many local priests which caused her to know of the misdemeanours of her neighbours and servants. Even Ayer's own confession had been betrayed by the curate at Warblington, which he held fully justified his talk about the countess.[63] When Tindall set up an interview for him with Cromwell himself, he became even more revealing and Holland was arrested. By the time that this happened, Tindall had also been interviewed by Geoffrey Pole, acting as a Justice of the Peace. Geoffrey was so concerned by what he learned that he sought an interview with Cromwell himself, and came away with the impression that the Lord Privy Seal was his 'good lord'. However it appears that Tindall had only told him half a story about what he knew, and that Cromwell, who had other sources of information, was not impressed. It was not long after this that he ordered Geoffrey's arrest. He languished in the Tower for almost two months, while Cromwell's agents gathered stories about him and his associates, and on 26 October he was formally interrogated. According to the record, fifty-nine questions were asked, mostly about his relations with Reginald, but his response indicates that he was only asked about those with whom he had discussed 'a change of the world', that is of the regiment of England.[64] He named a few names, Lord La Warr and his own brother Lord Montague for instance, but stressed the innocence of the conversations. No harm was intended to the king; they were mostly concerned, he averred, with the 'plucking down of abbeys'. He was interrogated twice more on 2 and 3 November, and his brother and the Marquis of Exeter were arrested on the 4th. There was no direct connection between these events, as Cromwell already had enough on both of them from Hugh Holland's examination to justify taking action. He also had the examination of one Jerome Ragland, taken on 28 October. Ragland, described as Lord Montague's right-hand man, alone provided more than enough to incriminate his master, irrespective of anything which Geoffrey may have said.[65] The latter was by this time thoroughly intimidated, and anxious only to prove his loyalty to the king:

Now especially in my extreme necessity, I perceive ... your goodness shall not be lost on me, but surely as I found your grace always faithful unto me, so I refuse all creatures living to be faithful to you.

He ended, 'Your humble slave, Geoffrey Pole.'[66] He was examined four more times between 5 and 12 November, and each time he delivered more material against his brother, and against Sir Edward Neville, who had also been arrested. Lord Montague's own examination, by contrast, revealed little of relevance, which may explain why he was only interrogated once. Various other servants and chaplains were arrested and examined during November, and each made his contribution to the pile of evidence which Cromwell was assembling against the Poles and the Courtenays; evidence of support for Mary, of general disaffection with the king's government and of regular correspondence with the exiled Reginald. Finally, beginning on 12 November, Lady Salisbury was interrogated, being placed under house arrest at Cowdray on the 15th. She admitted nothing beyond the general conservatism of her own and her sons' religion, apparently not having been made privy to the words which passed between her sons and their servants, although she did concede that she had burned some papers before being placed under restraint.[67]

Cromwell now had more than enough to go on, and could arrange for the trials to take place. Lord Montague and the Marquis of Exeter were tried by their peers on 2 and 3 December, and were found guilty. Given the flexible nature of the treason laws, and the king's evident interest in the proceedings, there could be no other verdict. Geoffrey Pole, Edward Neville, Hugh Holland and two others were tried by special commission of oyer and terminer at the Guildhall on 4 December and likewise condemned.

Holland, Croftes and Collins were hanged, drawn and quartered at Tyburn on 9 December, and Neville, Montague and Exeter were beheaded at the Tower on the same day.[68] Geoffrey Pole was pardoned on 2 January 1539. The countess was not tried but was included in the Act of Attainder passed against all the defendants in the parliament that convened on 28 April, and was kept in prison until after Cromwell's fall. Gertrude, the Marchioness of Exeter, her son Edward, and Montague's son Henry all ended up in the Tower.

Gertrude was released shortly afterwards, but Edward remained in custody until he was released by Queen Mary in 1553, and Henry died in the Tower. It is sometimes claimed that the fall of the Poles and Courtenays was a gratuitous bloodbath engineered by Cromwell on account of their proximity to the throne.[69] However the Yorkist claim, known as the White Rose, is scarcely mentioned except in circumstantial observations by Eustace Chapuys, who reported that Henry had 'long since' threatened to exterminate its offshoots. In fact neither Henry Courtenay nor Reginald Pole had a strong claim. The former was a grandson of Edward IV through his daughter Catherine, who had married his own father, William, and the latter, as we have seen, was a grandson of George, Duke of Clarence, Edward's brother. Admittedly Henry had only one son, Prince Edward, born to Queen Jane Seymour in October 1537, and the succession was thus fragile, but there is no reason to suppose that either Henry or his Lord Privy Seal were motivated by such a consideration. The accused were all guilty of treason as that was then defined, conspiring to take away one of the king's titles, that of Supreme Head of the Church, and wishing to invite a foreign power, either the Pope or the Emperor, to intervene in English affairs. There were no overt deeds, but of 'imagining' the king's harm there was abundant evidence; and far more people were implicated than the seven who suffered.[70] Nor were the trials rigged in the way which has been alleged. The attendance of peers at the Lord Steward's court was fairly representative, and the composition of the commission which tried the commoners was unremarkable. The evidence spoke for itself, and the fact that England was threatened by an Imperial or French invasion on account of the amity between Charles and Francis added to the urgency of the situation. For the first time in years, a foreign intervention in England appeared possible, even likely, and anyone guilty of encouraging such an eventuality could expect little mercy. Instead of being blamed for arranging a bloodbath, Cromwell deserves commendation both for the thoroughness of his investigation, and for his restraint in bringing the guilty parties to the scaffold.[71]

Cromwell had been reasonably comfortable with the Seymour ascendancy at court, which had begun in the spring of 1536 and found its consummation in the marriage of the king to Jane on 30 May. Her brother, Sir Edward Seymour, whom he would have known from their days with Wolsey, was created Viscount Beauchamp the following month and was a man of talent and substance, but he was nowhere near challenging the ascendancy of the Lord Privy Seal. Nor was Jane herself a political figure of any significance, being quite unlike Anne in that respect. Sir Edward had borrowed money from the king, a deal which Cromwell had undoubtedly set up, but this created no more than an ordinary sense of obligation. There was no sense in which he was Cromwell's man, but that did not matter. As the king's brother-in-law he enjoyed a certain prestige in the Privy Chamber, but he had no political agenda. His position was enhanced on 18

October 1537 by his creation as Earl of Hertford, but this was primarily a recognition of his status as uncle of the heir to the throne, who had been born a few days earlier, rather than of any other ambition.[72] When Jane died unexpectedly on 24 October, he did not go into eclipse, but remained a substantial courtier. At that stage he was conservative in his religious preferences, as Jane had been, but not militantly so, and as time would show was open to persuasion. There is no evidence that Cromwell addressed himself to this task, and it only became apparent after his fall. Jane's death did, however, give the Lord Privy Seal a considerable problem, which had nothing to do with the Earl of Hertford. The succession, which had been an issue for so many years, had been solved in a sense by the birth of Prince Edward. However, one very young life did not represent security, and it was imperative that Henry should marry again, and quickly, as time was not on his side.[73] The king, however, was deeply affected by his wife's death, and was not inclined to consider remarriage. In this situation, Cromwell took the initiative, and raised the matter in council, which rapidly agreed that the king should be persuaded to marry again. Henry reluctantly agreed and Cromwell wrote to the ambassadors in France and the Empire, urging them to look for suitable candidates. The king, he admitted, was not personally minded to such a venture, but had agreed to undertake it for the sake of the realm, and because he needed more children.[74] The Lord Privy Seal was also mindful of the fact that Henry needed allies abroad, and that another domestic marriage might raise up formidable rivals to him for the king's favour, as had happened with the Boleyns. Cromwell's favoured candidate at this early stage was the sixteen-year-old Christina, Duchess of Milan, who was brought to his attention by John Hutton, the Governor of the Merchant Adventurers in Antwerp who doubled as an English agent in Flanders. The recently widowed Christina had just arrived at the court of Margaret of Savoy, the Emperor's Regent in the Low Countries, and Hutton was lyrical in her praise: 'A goodly personage of body and competent of beauty, of favour excellent, soft of speech and very gentle of countenance.'[75]

Christina was the daughter of the deposed King of Denmark, Christian II, and the niece of the Emperor, so a match with her would favour the Imperial alliance which, as we have seen, was Cromwell's preferred option in foreign policy. According to Chapuys he proposed a multiple settlement, in which Henry would marry Christina, Edward (still in his cradle) would be espoused to Charles's daughter Maria, and Elizabeth to a son of the Duke of Savoy.[76] However, he was running somewhat before his horse to market, because the king's preference, when he got around to thinking about it, was for a French marriage. According to the French ambassador, Castillon, he was castigated for intruding into the king's personal affairs, but the chances are that this was exaggerated, because it was Cromwell's business to look after his master's interests internationally as well as domestically.[77] In any case he was involved in both sets of negotiations from the beginning, since it was in his letter to Sir John Wallop in France announcing Jane's death that the possibility of a French marriage had been raised; either the king's sister Marguerite or the widowed Marie of Guise were mentioned. So two negotiations were launched more or less simultaneously, and Cromwell must have been at some pains not to let his left hand know what his right hand was doing. In December 1537 Henry sent Peter Mewtas, one of the gentlemen of his Privy Chamber, across to France to sound out Marie of Guise, who was the favourite, and he returned with the impression that she was available. However by the time that he returned with the king's offer in February 1538, she had been snatched from under his nose by James V of Scotland, to whom she was formally betrothed.[78] This was not only an unpleasant reminder that the Auld Alliance was in full working order, but a blow to Henry's *amour propre*. How could any woman prefer a beggarly fellow like the King of Scots to his majesty of England? Cromwell may not have been too disappointed by this denouement because it enabled him to concentrate on persuading the king of the desirability of Christina of Denmark. In this he appears to have been successful, and Sir Thomas Wyatt, with the Emperor, was instructed to raise the possibility as though it were his own idea. This it was hoped would stimulate Charles into making an offer, which would enable Henry to put forward certain demands in return for his agreement. In particular he was anxious to recruit the Emperor's support in frustrating Paul III's proposed General Council of the Church, which he feared would be used against him. As early as October 1537 he had instructed Wyatt to 'sound out' the Emperor's attitude to such a council in view of the fact that both the Lutherans and Henry had rejected it.[79] At the beginning of March he sent Philip Hoby, another gentleman of his Privy Chamber, across with Hans Holbein to secure a portrait of the lady, because he was reluctant to commit himself to one of whose very appearance he was in ignorance.[80] They returned before the end of the month, and Henry was delighted with the result, soon pretending quite wrongly that he was being wooed from all sides. This must have been self-deception because Cromwell would never have dared to give him so false an impression. Moreover the negotiations soon encountered insuperable obstacles. In the first place Christina was a kinswoman of Catherine of Aragon, and a dispensation would have been required for her marriage to Henry. A papal dispensation, favoured by the Emperor, was unacceptable to the English, and an authorisation issued by the Archbishop of Canterbury was equally unacceptable to Charles. In the second place the lady herself was reluctant, claiming that her great aunt had been poisoned, her successor executed, and the third wife lost for lack of care. She had no desire to be the fourth.[81] Although the negotiations dragged on past midsummer, there was no real prospect of success.

At the same time the French, not unaware of these difficulties thanks to their sharp-eyed ambassador, came up with two fresh offers; either Louise de Guise, Marie's sister, or the third Guise girl, Renee, reputedly the most beautiful of the three. Other ladies were mentioned, and in the summer Holbein was sent back to draw as many of them as possible. He came back with two portraits, and a third was provided by the French themselves. By this time the animosity of Francis and Charles was showing signs of coming to an end, and Henry was anxious to be included in any future treaty between them. This was undoubtedly a clause which Cromwell, ever mindful of his security, would have urged upon him, just as it was Cromwell who inserted the future of Milan into the Imperial negotiations. The suggestion was that the Emperor should confer the duchy on the Imperial candidate for Mary's hand, Dom Luis of Portugal, that discussion having run alongside the king's own bid for Christina.[82] Milan was a sensitive spot in Franco-Imperial relations, and the Lord Privy Seal was well advised to make an issue of it. Unfortunately such a consideration could not stand in the way of the need of both sovereigns for peace. To Henry's intense chagrin they met under the Pope's mediation at Nice in June 1538 and signed a ten-year truce which completely ignored him. So much for his hopes that matrimonial negotiations would keep alive the spirit of animosity between these natural rivals, and the English were left to digest failure on all fronts, because the French discussions had also come to an ignominious end when Henry tried and failed to persuade Francis to parade his beauties at Calais for an inspection. Was this how the Knights of the Round Table treated their womenfolk, he was asked by an outraged ambassador.[83] By the autumn of 1538 England was consequently isolated. Henry had been mocked by his fellow monarchs and now stood in danger of the General Council which Paul had been endeavouring to call for two years. On 17 December the Pope at last promulgated the sentence of excommunication which had been suspended over three years earlier, declaring the King of England deposed and absolving his subjects of their allegiance. The situation which Cromwell had worked so hard to avoid had now arisen, and in January 1539 Francis and Charles signed a treaty of mutual friendship at Toledo in which each agreed to enter into no relations with the English without the other's consent. The withdrawal of ambassadors, economic embargoes and even military invasion would now surely follow.[84] As if to emphasise the danger, Cardinal Reginald Pole set off on a fresh mission to mobilise the powers against Henry, and Cardinal David Beaton was sent home to stimulate James V in the same direction. The danger appeared to be acute, and musters were ordered across the south of England. In May the king reviewed his troops in London and responded to the Emperor's ban on English shipping by detaining all foreign ships in English ports. He also ordered fortifications to be built along the south coast, and Cromwell was kept busy mobilising workmen and arranging for building supplies to be delivered on site at about a dozen locations from Pendennis to Margate.[85] At the same time the defences of Berwick and Calais were also strengthened, and the fleet put on standby. The south of England resembled a warzone, as bulwarks were built, and other temporary defences put in place to withstand the expected assault.

All these precautions proved to be unnecessary as it became clear that neither Francis nor Charles, for all their belligerent talk, was willing to take any action. Ambassadors were indeed withdrawn, but the French one was quickly replaced and in March the French king privately advised Henry that the warlike preparations which Cromwell's agents had observed were not directed against him. For the time being alarms about Imperial intentions persisted. There was rumoured to be great fleet assembling at Antwerp, and an army preparing in Flanders, but it soon transpired that these reports were exaggerated, and in any case not directed against England. Pole's mission also foundered on Charles's reluctance. He was prepared, he said, to do his duty, but only if Francis moved first, which the latter was plainly unwilling to do.[86] So unwilling was Francis that he declined to see Pole, who was constrained to send an envoy to receive the discouraging tidings. The cardinal withdrew to Carpentras, and sent to Rome for fresh instructions. Since he had no money and no military resources of his own, his mission had clearly failed, and he was shortly after recalled. David Beaton had no better luck, because James was clearly waiting for the French to move, and when that showed no sign of happening he decided that he had no quarrel with his uncle which would justify an invasion. However, in spite of these failures, England still had no reliable ally on the Continent, and that was a matter of great concern to the Lord Privy Seal. There were two possible ways out of this dilemma. One was to form an alliance with the Schmalkaldic League, which had been tried before without success, though in the new circumstances Henry might be more willing to accept the Germans' conditions.[87] The second was a matrimonial link to the Duchy of Cleves, whose duke shared Henry's hostility to the Pope without being a Lutheran. Duke John had two daughters, Anne and Amelia, who might be available to seal such a treaty, and had fallen out with the Emperor. The possibility of such an alliance had been raised as early as June 1538, when it had been suggested that Mary might marry a son of the duke and the king take a kinswoman. However at that time it was lost in the welter of other proposals in hand and had not been pursued. Now in January 1539 Cromwell picked up both themes, sending Christopher Mont to the Elector of Saxony, not only to revive the proposal of a league with the Lutherans, but also to sound him out indirectly about the possibility of the Cleves marriage. The elector was the son-in-law of Duke John, so his attitude was important.[88] Towards the end of February a second mission, led by the veteran diplomat Edward Carne, was sent directly to the duke for the same purpose, and to recruit some mercenary soldiers that he was alleged to have available. In March Mont reported back. The elector was not enthusiastic about an alliance with the Schmalkaldic League, but he was supportive of the Cleves marriage. Mont had also received excellent reports of Anne's personal qualities, having heard that she excelled the Duchess of Milan 'as the golden sun [does] the silver moon'.[89] Nevertheless Carne's negotiation hung fire. Possibly William, the new duke who had succeeded his father in February, was less enthusiastic, or possibly he was holding out for a more supplicatory approach from England. Anyway the ambassador was told that Anne was promised to a son of the Duke of Lorraine, and could obtain no firm guarantee of an embassy from Cleves to England to resolve the matter. Nor could he obtain any portrait of Anne, whom he had only seen under 'monstrous habit and apparel', catching a mere glimpse of her face. By the end of June he was becoming distinctly frustrated.[90]

Meanwhile the Elector of Saxony had been persuaded to send a mission to London on behalf of the Schmalkaldic League. It was a low-key affair, headed by Francis Burckhardt, the Vice-Chancellor of the Electorate, and it is clear that nothing much was expected of it. This was because they were under strict orders to accept from Henry nothing less than a full endorsement of the Confession of Augsburg, which they knew that he would be unwilling to grant. It is probable that this embassy was set up by Cromwell with no more than a nod from the king, and more in hope than expectation, because it represented a policy to which he had been committed for a number of years. Henry had been let off this time because the hostility between Charles and Francis had surfaced again within weeks of the signing of the Treaty of Toledo, but it might not always be thus and a reliable ally against the papacy was a jewel beyond price. Particularly one so well placed to frustrate the Emperor and keep his attention focused on his own affairs. However his time was ill chosen, because in the spring of 1539 the king was becoming increasingly alarmed at the disruptive effects which evangelical preaching were having on the kingdom, and decided to act against the preachers. This did not suit Cromwell's agenda at all, and reflects the fact that Henry was always capable of taking an independent initiative. He set up a series of discussions between conservative bishops and other divines, and the result was a Bill 'abolishing diversity in opinion', otherwise known as the Six Articles.[91] This measure was introduced into the House of Lords by the Duke of Norfolk, and probably prepared by Stephen Gardiner. It was the last thing that the Schmalkaldic delegation wished to hear as they pursued their fruitless negotiation, especially as the king told them that if they did not like it, they could always go home. In fact they held on until August, perhaps in the hope that Cromwell's influence would reassert itself, but the Lord Privy Seal knew a lost cause when he saw one, and concentrated on mitigating the effects of the enforcement of the Act; so Burckhardt and his colleagues departed disappointed, as they had expected to do.

The Act of Six Articles was set back for Cromwell, but it did not mark the end of his predominant influence. It closed off one of the alliances with which he had been hoping to protect his master's supremacy, but left the other open. Realising that he must now redouble his efforts in Cleves, in early July he sent across another envoy, William Petre, to stir up the existing mission, and followed this by sending Hans Holbein to obtain the elusive portrait which the duke had been so reluctant to provide. By 11 August Holbein was back and presented the results of his efforts to the king who was at Grafton on his summer progress. Henry was impressed, but more impressed by the fact that Petre had secured a breakthrough in the negotiation. On 4 September Duke William finally commissioned an embassy to England for the purpose of arranging a marriage between his sister and the king.[92] Henry received these delegates on 24 September, but left the discussions to Cromwell and his team. They moved swiftly and by 6 October a treaty had been concluded, which provided for an alliance of mutual defence as well as for the early delivery of the lady, and both parties professed themselves well satisfied. The duke had the assurance of English aid if he should be attacked by the Emperor on account of the Duchy of Gelderland, which he had inherited the previous summer and which was a bone of contention between them; and the king was guaranteed the duke's assistance if Charles should change his mind about obeying the Pope's call to action. Anne duly set off at the end of October, accompanied by a lavish train which drastically slowed her progress, but, rather surprisingly, included no member of her family. The English expected her to sail from Antwerp, but her escort pleaded the dangers of the rather longer sea crossing, and she arrived instead at Calais on 11 December. There she was entertained by the deputy, Lord Lisle, and his wife, and made a good impression in spite of the fact that she spoke no language other than her own Low German. She would be, Lady Lisle decided, a gentle mistress to serve, which was a matter of no small concern to her since her own daughter Anne Basset was one of the ladies appointed to wait on her in England.[93] She learned some new card games, and was instructed on the etiquette of the English court. Then the weather relented, and on 27 December she was able to cross to England, landing at Deal the same day. From Deal she proceeded to Canterbury and reached Rochester on 1 January 1540. Meanwhile Henry had passed a lonely and impatient Christmas at Greenwich. At length, consumed with curiosity to see this paragon who was to share his bed, he decided on a little old-fashioned knight errantry. Confiding to Cromwell his intention to 'nourish love' he rode to Rochester to intercept her incognito. Making his way into the bishop's palace, where she was lodged, he burst into her presence unannounced, taking the poor girl completely by surprise. Not knowing the identity of the intruder, she was flummoxed, and seems to have thought that she was about to be kidnapped. Henry was profoundly and unreasonably disappointed by her lack of response, and withdrew, returning later in his own person, his companions deferring to him and making his identity plain. Then Anne found suitable words to welcome him, but the damage had been done. The New Year gifts which he had brought her were delivered the next morning by one of his servants, and he returned to Greenwich in a foul mood. 'I am ashamed that men have so praised her as they have done, and I like her not,' he confided to Cromwell, adding that if he had known the truth about her, she would never have come to England.[94] No doubt puzzled by this encounter, Anne proceeded on her scheduled way, being received two days later on Shooters Hill with splendid pageantry, and solemnly escorted to Henry at Greenwich. There on 6 January they were married.

The ceremony should have taken place two days earlier, but Henry had been looking for a way out of the commitment, which was now so distasteful to him. There was, however, no escape because he could not afford to forgo the friendship which she represented. Charles was at that very moment being entertained in Paris, having chosen to return from Spain to the Netherlands by way of France to demonstrate his confidence in Francis's friendship. There could have been no better demonstration of just how isolated England was in major European diplomacy.[95] Henry recognised this fact, and as he said to Cromwell, 'My lord, if it were not to satisfy the world and my realm I would not do that I must do this day for none earthly thing.' A less promising start to a marriage could hardly be imagined, and the Lord Privy Seal, who had done so much to bring it about, must have been regarding the future with dread.

6

VICEREGENT IN SPIRITUALS,
1536–1540

It pleaseth his majesty to use me in then lieu of a councillor, whose office is as an eye to the Prince, to forsee and in time to provide remedy for such abuses ... as might else, with a little sufferance engender more evil in his public weal than could be redubbed with much labour.

Thomas Cromwell

Thomas Cromwell was not a Lutheran. His only explicit statement about his doctrinal position was to say that it agreed with that of the king, which was the right thing to say, and accurate up to a point. However, we can only deduce his views from the actions which he took in support of the Royal Supremacy, and they suggest an independent strategy. For instance it was he, rather than Henry, who tried to recruit William Tyndale as an apologist for the king's actions, using his long-time servant Stephen Vaughn as an intermediary, only to be forced to desist when Tyndale adamantly refused to support his second marriage.[1] He agreed with Luther on the need for vernacular scriptures, but remained ambivalent on the central Lutheran doctrine of justification by faith alone. The best general description of his beliefs is that they were Erasmian or Evangelical, or alternatively of the 'new learning'. This regularly set him at odds with conservative bishops such as Stokesley and Gardiner, who saw the Supremacy in terms of the defence of the Catholic faith as they knew it, and had no time for innovations.[2] Cromwell regularly protected Evangelical preachers such as Hugh Latimer, and pressed Henry, discreetly but persistently, to accept an English translation of the Bible. He also policed the enforcement of the Act of Supremacy, and set up the commissions required to administer the oaths required by the Act of Succession. The king's confidence in his secretary's judgement in religious matters was demonstrated in January 1535, when he created him Viceregent in Spirituals for the purpose of conducting a general visitation of the Church.[3] This involved the inhibition of the visitorial powers of the bishops, resulting in the *Valor Ecclesiasticus*. It was completed by the end of the year.

This did not, however, solve the problem of preaching. Cromwell, as Viceregent, consistently licensed Evangelical preachers to spread the word of reform, but these were regularly challenged by conservatives bearing Episcopal licences, with the result that there was confusion and not a little strife. On 7 January 1536, therefore, acting in the king's name, Cromwell sent a letter to all the bishops, deploring the temerity of those who continued to defend the authority of the Bishop of Rome from the pulpit, but balancing that with an equal denunciation of those who 'treat and dispute such matters as do rather engender a contrariety' rather than edifying their audience; in other words who exceeded their brief by introducing radical notions into their sermons.[4] The king expresses his regret at the bishops' failure to suppress either sedition or extremism, and continues,

It appertains especially to our office and vocation, unto whose order, care and government it hath pleased Almighty God to commit this part of his flock ... to foresee and provide with all policy counsel wisdom and authority that the same, being educated, fed and nourished with wholesome and godly doctrine, and not seduced with filthy and corrupt abominations of the bishop of Rome or his disciples or adherents, nor yet by the setting forth of novelties ... might have their instruction tempered with such means and be taught with such discretion and judgement as little by little they may perceive the truth.

All bishops are instructed to call in and review their licences with a view to removing 'unfit persons'. This circular was enclosed with a covering letter of Cromwell's own, reminding the recipients of the 'king's highness's travails and your duties', and concluding,

I write frankly, compelled and enforced thereunto both in respect of my private duty and otherwise for my discharge, forasmuch as it pleaseth his majesty to use me in the lieu of a councillor, whose office is as an eye to the prince, to foresee and in time provide remedy for such abuses ... as might else, with a little sufferance engender more evil in his public weal than could after be redubbed with much labour...[5]

The king's signature on the main document, and this personally signed covering letter, were intended to give this instrument a unique power of persuasion and pressure. No doubt it had some effect because the problem of 'popish' dissidents could be dealt with by law, but the issue of radical innovation would not go away until some strict doctrinal parameters had been laid down. On

11 July 1536 the convocations, with the king's active assistance, produced a formulary of the faith known as the Ten Articles, 'devised by the king's highness to establish Christian quietness and unity among us, and to avoid contentious opinions'.[6]

These articles were designed, as was usually the case, to pick up on the errors and omissions noted in the visitation of the previous year. They set out the five things 'necessary to be believed', which are the 'grounds of the faith', that is the Bible, the creeds, the four ancient councils, and those patristic traditions not contrary to the scriptures: baptism; penance; the sacrament of the altar; and justification. Then follow the second five, to be retained although not necessary to salvation: the use of images; honouring of the saints; praying to the saints; rites and ceremonies; and purgatory. These articles are reformed only in the sense that they relegate prayers to the saints and belief in purgatory to the category of *adiaphora* or things indifferent, whereas the strictly orthodox would regard the denial of either as heresy. The whole document is something of a compromise, but reflects very accurately the state of the king's own thinking at that particular moment, and that argues his close oversight.[7] It is notable, for example, that the only sacraments mentioned are the Eucharist, penance and baptism, which were the three recognised by the Lutherans, although there are no signs of direct Lutheran influence. The articles were accompanied by a set of injunctions, issued in the king's name by Thomas Cromwell. They begin with a fine flourish:

I, Thomas Cromwell Knight, Lord Cromwell, Keeper of the Privy Seal of our said Sovereign Lord the King, and viceregent unto the same, for and concerning all his jurisdiction ecclesiastical within this realm, visiting by the king's highness' supreme authority ecclesiastical this deanery of [x] by my trusty commissary [y] lawfully deputed and constituted for this part, have to the glory of Almighty God, to the King's highness' honour, the public weal of this his realm, and increase of virtue in the same appointed and assigned these Injunctions ensuing to be kept and observed of the dean, parsons, vicars, curates and stipendiaries having cure of souls … within this deanery…[8]

The clergy's behaviour is then corrected by orders to instruct the people in the Christian faith, to see to the education of the young, to make proper provision for the administration of the sacraments, and to avoid scandalous activities like tavern haunting and the playing of dice. They are to study scripture, to distribute alms and to maintain scholars at the universities according to their means, on the scale specified. Naturally they are required to preach the Royal Supremacy, every Sunday for three weeks and thereafter twice a quarter, and to enforce the doctrinal position defined in the accompanying articles. They are to expound these articles regularly, and to observe and explain the recent reduction in the number of holy days and the new rules about ceremonies.[9] There is, however, no mention of the new code of canon law because although that had been drawn up in the previous year, at great cost in time and effort, it had not been implemented and remained among Cromwell's office papers.[10] He set out to conduct this secondary visitation with all his accustomed energy and efficiency, using a wide variety of sympathetic clergy as commissaries. It represented a moderate and by all accounts necessary programme of reform designed to bring about an improvement in the moral and spiritual state of the people by keeping a watchful eye upon their pastors. This represents Cromwell's best-known effort towards reform, but it was clearly not his only one. The surviving papers of his viceregential court show him issuing licences to preach, to deprive priors and abbots, to install a bishop, and to authorise irregular marriages.[11] In other words he applied himself with the same conscientiousness to this office as he did to the secretaryship or the lordship of the Privy Seal. Nothing escaped his scrutiny.

Not everyone rejoiced at this evidence of careful supervision. The traditional doctrine of purgatory, for example, constantly resurfaced in spite of all exhortations to the contrary. At Wimborne in Dorset, Edward Thorpe asserted repeatedly that the souls of the departed could be rescued from torment by the expenditure of money on intercessory prayers and ceremonies, a flagrant attack upon the whole reformed programme, which earned him at least a sequestration.[12] At the same time in Worcestershire a certain Dr Smyth luxuriated in a similar programme of prayers

for the archbishop of York, and for the bishop of Lincoln, and for our most holy father the bishop of London, a founder of the faith of Christ, and for my lord [the abbot] of Evesham, and for my lord of Hailes, and for my lord of Winchcome and for my lord of Abingdon, and for ... all the souls that are departed out of this world abiding the mercy of God that lie in the pain of purgatory.

All those he named were notorious conservatives, thus compounding his offence, but he escaped into the anonymity of Oxford, out of the jurisdiction of the Bishop of Worcester, and there he vanished.[13] Other examples could be quoted, and it is clear that the injunctions did not clean up clerical behaviour in the manner intended. John Divale was accused of continuing to devote himself to dicing, carding and bowling long after they had been issued and of calling the reading of scripture heresy in defiance of instructions. Lancelot Pocock, a curate in Kent, who can have had no excuse for his actions, declined to read the injunctions in church for eighteen months after they were published, and lodged in an alehouse although he was welcome at the parsonage.[14] In addition to following up individual cases such as these, Cromwell took one further general step in pursuit of his objective. In spite of his preoccupation with the Pilgrimage, on 16 November he issued another general circular to the bishops in the king's name. This started with a résumé of the injunctions and the benefits expected of them. However, it went on, in spite of all this care, the king understood that there was much talk against the articles, and they had featured in the recent rebellion. The bishops were therefore to declare the articles every holy day, and personally to travel up and down their dioceses, preaching from proper texts of scripture and proclaiming the Supremacy. They were (once again) to instruct their clergy in the necessary reading of the articles, and to send up to the Viceregent for punishment any that 'will not better temper' their tongues.[15] Moreover, and this is an indication that papists were not the only problem, they were also to send up to the council any who had had the temerity to marry, contrary to the injunctions and to the custom of the English Church. On the same day as Cromwell's circular, the king issued a proclamation, the original of which is corrected in his own hand, prohibiting the unlicensed printing of scripture, exiling Anabaptists, depriving married clergy, and removing Thomas Becket from the calendar. The orthodoxy of the Henrician Church was proving to be distinctly ambiguous.

By the time that this second letter was issued the Viceregent was deeply immersed in the Dissolution of the Monasteries, which was a leading issue in the Pilgrimage of Grace. Thanks to Foxe, it has been commonly supposed that this was Cromwell's innovation, and a necessary part of his programme to make Henry 'the richest prince in Christendom', but in fact the idea went back well before his rise to power. Henry had never had much time for monks, or friars, or the shrines of the saints, an attitude which may go back to his Erasmian education, or to disappointment with his pilgrimage of 1511. In January of that year he had visited the shrine of Our Lady at Walsingham to give thanks for the birth of his son, and to pray for his well-being. The child died with a matter of weeks, and the king was deeply distressed by this failure of divine intervention.[16] Unlike his father, and most of his predecessors, he was never a patron of religious orders, and had established no new foundations in the first twenty years of his reign. He had supported Wolsey's plan for a limited dissolution between 1525 and 1529, and in the latter year, with his quarrel with the Church beginning to surface, appeared willing to embrace the idea himself. In December of that year he told Chapuys that he had it in mind to reform the clergy, which the ambassador took to be a direct consequence of his frustration with the papacy, and he reported that the Duke of Suffolk was letting it be known that a selective dissolution would solve some of the Crown's financial problems.[17] In November 1530 he repeated the threat, saying that he would be 'doing God's service' to take away the temporalities of the clergy, knowing that this would be reported back to the Emperor and no doubt hoping that it would help to persuade the Pope to buy him off. The deadlock, however, persisted, and it was only the implementation of the Royal Supremacy in 1533 and 1534 that gave the king the means to carry out his threat. So that although the idea of the Dissolution was an old one, it was the arrival of Cromwell on the scene which made it a practical possibility. The secretary himself appears not to have been convinced at first, and according to Chapuys it was the dukes of Norfolk and Suffolk who first pressed the issue, in which Cromwell could see only 'great inconveniences', an attitude which irritated the king.[18] According to a later story, he had argued in council for a gradual approach to the Dissolution, taking each house on its merits (or defects), but was overruled, which could only have been done by the king personally. Whenever this decision was made, it could only have been after the visitors' reports had begun to arrive, that is sometime in the summer of 1535, and it may explain why the Bill for the dissolution of the smaller abbeys, which was introduced early in 1536, was not a very professional piece of work. It was not prepared by Cromwell, who only reluctantly agreed to its provisions.[19] This interpretation is supported by a number of references in his memoranda to the need for reform among the abbeys, both great and small. On one occasion he alludes to the 'abominations of religious persons throughout the realm, and a reformation to be devised therein' without making any distinction by size, and indicating the policy which he is known to have pursued, and which has been called 'infiltration'.

When a report suggested serious moral or professional lapses on the part of a head of house, he would take steps to secure the dismissal of the offending party and his (or her) replacement with a more satisfactory candidate.[20] The injunctions which the visitors carried with them are interesting in this respect. They demand loyalty to Henry as Supreme Head, and to the succession laid down; forbid monks from going out from their cloisters, or women to go in. At meal times the monks are to listen to a reading from the Old or New Testament, and one hour each day is to be devoted to the reading of scripture. All brethren are to observe the 'rule, statutes and laudable customs of their order', insofar as these agree with the word of God, and are to be disabused of the opinion that true religion lies in their apparel or monastic routines. True religion lies rather in 'cleanliness of mind ... Christ's faith not feigned and in brotherly charity'.[21] These were demanding requirements, especially in places where the brothers were at each other's throats for doctrinal or personal reasons, a result very often of the introduction of reformed ideas. No relics were to be displayed, or pilgrimages encouraged, and no fairs or markets were to be permitted in religious houses. In short the monasteries were to be converted into evangelical training colleges, because no house that denied the Pope's authority could properly be called a monastery at all, and if they satisfied all these requirements they would be allowed to stand. The emphasis on reformation in these injunctions suggests that they were written by Cromwell himself, and the number of houses which satisfied them was small indeed. One such was St James in Northampton, where a new abbot had been appointed in 1533, thanks to the secretary's patronage, and which received a glowing report from the commissioners.[22] Another was St Gregory's in Canterbury, where the head had also been replaced in a combined effort by Cromwell and Cranmer. As might be expected this policy became more noticeable after his appointment as Viceregent, and when the visitation was actually under way. When the Abbot of West Dereham died, Thomas Legh, who was conducting the visitation, asked whether Cromwell had anyone in mind as his replacement. On this occasion he accepted Legh's own suggestion, and that seems to have been a common reaction.[23] When the prior of St Swithin's in Winchester resigned, the visitor Thomas Parry suggested a certain William Basing, a monk of the house of the 'better sort', as his replacement, and Cromwell acted upon his advice. Basing was an educated man, a doctor of divinity 'favouring the truth' who could be expected to lead his brethren in the way they should go. Basing had also solicited the position, writing to Legh on 16 March 1536, asking him to 'move Mr Secretary' for him. Legh in turn prompted Parry's suggestion. On this occasion acceptance of the king's authority was also required, but this presented no difficulty, and Basing was soon thanking the secretary for his promotion.[24]

During the visitation Cromwell appears to have authorised his commissioners to make interim appointments on his behalf, and to have confirmed them afterwards. It was in this manner that John Vaughan appointed Joan Skydmore to be prioress of Aconbury, and Drs Layton and Legh deposed the faulty Abbot of Fountains and replaced him with a member of his house, one Marmaduke Bradley. The old abbot had neglected his house, kept prostitutes and generally violated the rules of his order; even by his own confession he ought to have been deprived, and Marmaduke was a 'right apt man', provided of course that Cromwell had not already nominated somebody else to the vacancy.[25] He had not, and their nominee was duly installed. Nor was the secretary a distant figure in respect of these activities. According to Chapuys he accompanied the king wherever he went, and conducted personal visitations of all religious houses in the vicinity. A good example of the way in which such intervention might work is provided by the Abbey of Winchcombe. About the time of his appointment as Viceregent, Cromwell had received a letter from one Hugh Coper, a Winchcombe monk, complaining of the 'papistry' of the abbot, who was endeavouring to stop the mouths of the true preachers of the gospel, and asking for release from his vows. He advised the appointment of a local priest, Anthony Saunders, to instruct the monks in the way of truth.[26] Cromwell apparently acted on this advice, and visited Winchcombe in the summer of 1535, only to be bombarded with complaints from both sides. Saunders complained that he was being obstructed in his work, and the abbot that his authority was being undermined. It was true that he was losing ground in his battle to control his abbey, but he was in no mood to resign and, in the absence of any verifiable treason, Cromwell did not have the power to dismiss him. He survived until the house was dissolved in the following year. However it was a troubled time, and Cromwell's visit produced a complaint from another reform-minded member of the community, one John Placet. Placet, who was a passionate supporter of the king's proceedings, besought the secretary to find him a benefice where he could preach the word of God uninterrupted. He was apparently successful in his quest, and wrote to Cromwell soon after promising to send him a little treatise that he had written on the Royal Supremacy, as a kind of thanks offering.[27] Winchcombe was not the only place to benefit from a personal visit. The prior of Kingswood thanked him in fulsome terms for opening his eyes to the truth, for speaking 'the Divine Word' as he put it, in his abbey. He also sent a book which he had written on the Supremacy, dedicated to Cromwell, and begged for his 'evangelical charity' to be extended to his house. In this last he was only temporarily successful, because Kingswood went the same way as the rest in 1538.

What is clear from all this is that Cromwell was not pursuing a policy of general dissolution after the passage of the Act delivering the smaller monasteries to the king in February 1536. The care with which he planted reform-minded monks in conservative institutions, and removed obstructive heads of houses, argues in favour of a genuine policy of reform. Not that this would have placated the leaders of the Pilgrimage, who were as opposed to the ideas of the evangelicals as they were to the removal of the abbeys. A number of abbeys were involved in the Pilgrimage, sometimes willingly, sometimes unwillingly, and a number of abbots suffered execution for their role. From October to December 1536 there was also a lull in the process of closure, as Cromwell kept out of the public eye, and it remained uncertain what concessions the king might make to the rebels. However, by the beginning of 1537 the Dissolution had recommenced and as the year advanced it became obvious that the greater houses, which had been so lavishly praised in the Act, were also coming under threat. This change of policy can only be attributed to the king, because it clearly ran counter to the Lord Privy Seal's advice, and raises the interesting question of who else he was listening to.[28] It would not have been Stephen Gardiner, who was unhappy with the whole process and in any case was on mission in France a lot of the time; nor would it have been Queen Jane, who had no weight in such discussions, and whose only known intervention had been in favour of their preservation. The most likely candidates are the dukes of Norfolk and Suffolk, whom Chapuys had associated with a policy of plunder towards the Church as long before as 1529. However, it is equally likely that he was listening to no one, and that the idea was his own. He knew perfectly well that the monasteries held great wealth, enough to triple his income if he could lay hands on it, and he also knew that in spite of Cromwell's efforts the great monasteries were the likeliest repositories of pro-papal sentiment. There was also the evidence of demand, because as soon as the process of dissolution began, Cromwell began to receive begging letters from noblemen and gentlemen, asking for grants or leases of former monastic property.[29] It may have been his intention to create a new landed endowment for the Crown, and to reduce the need for constant appeals to Parliament for money, but it soon began to appear that an alternative strategy was available. By releasing much of this land onto the market, Henry would be creating a vested interest in the Royal Supremacy. A vested interest which would make it much more difficult for any future ruler to renegotiate relations with the papacy, as was proved to be the case when Queen Mary undertook such a negotiation in 1554.[30] The king's determination to do away with all monasteries was therefore backed by some sound strategic considerations, both practical and religious, and Cromwell was soon converted. He began to put pressure upon the greater houses to surrender voluntarily, and they did so one by one, finishing with Waltham Abbey in Essex in February 1540. A second statute in 1539 vested the property of all these surrendered houses in the Crown, and placed it in the 'order, survey and government of our said sovereign lord the king's Court of Augmentations of the Revenues of the Crown'.[31]

This Court of Augmentations had been established by statute in 1536, as a direct result of the first round of dissolutions, and represented a critical stage in Cromwell's plans for the revenues of the Crown. He already had a foot in the Exchequer by virtue of his office as Chancellor, and a foot in the household through his office as Keeper of the Jewel House. However, although he succeeded in converting the latter into a significant spending department, neither of these personal positions represented the reform which was called for by the acquisition of the Church's wealth. John Gostwick had already been appointed treasurer of First Fruits and Tenths in the wake of the Act of 1534, but no department had been created in his support, and he seems to have remained personally responsible to Cromwell for the revenues which he collected.[32] He was the secretary's servant, and his appointment was undoubtedly arranged, but the sums which he handled were not small. Between 1535 and 1540 he collected £406,000, an average of over £60,000 a year. Of this about £130,000 was earmarked for special purposes, and was handed over directly by Gostwick or Cromwell to the intended recipients.[33] First Fruits and Tenths also administered the clerical subsidies, which had been withdrawn from the Chamber, and cash diverted to him from the Court of Augmentations. In some respects Gostwick was a paymaster rather than a treasurer, but he was nevertheless the officer responsible for handling the king's spiritual revenues. It was only after Cromwell's fall that a Court of First Fruits and Tenths was established and a proper accounting procedure introduced, which is an indication of his personal control. Augmentations did not handle spiritual revenues, but those temporalities and duties which resulted from the Dissolution. These were multifarious. The houses had to be suppressed or their surrenders accepted; surveys and valuations of their property taken; and the monks disposed of. The lands accruing to the Crown had to be administered, and their rents collected, expended and accounted for.[34] Disposal by grant, sale or lease had to be arranged and supervised, and the litigation which inevitably accompanied the possession of land had to be coped with. The departing monks had also left obligations behind them that the government was determined to honour, in the form of leases to be carried over and debts to be paid. The monks themselves had to be pensioned, or sent to Chancery to collect their 'capacities' or licences to act as secular priests. Ahead of the establishment of the court, a commission was set up to advise on how to resolve these problems, and the commissioners consulted with officials of the Duchy of Lancaster, because it was intended that the duchy should exercise similar jurisdiction over houses dissolved within its bounds.[35] A number of specific questions were identified. What was to be done with monks who wished to continue in their habit if there was no house of their order remaining nearby – or at all? How much in the way of personal possessions was each monk to be allowed to take with him? Who was to take immediate charge of the lead and bells from the dissolved houses? Who should be appointed to serve the cures of churches belonging to the houses, especially those which had been cared for by the monks themselves? And what was to be done with monks or lay brothers who were too sick or aged to be moved?[36] These questions indicate the seriousness with which the commissioners took their responsibilities, and also that no existing department had the resources to deal with them in addition to its existing duties. Hence the need for a new court, which was to be a court of record, administering both a Great and Privy Seal, and given charge of all dissolved religious houses and their property, except those within the remit of the Duchy of Lancaster and those which the king should license to continue. This last proviso was an indication that in 1536 a wholesale dissolution was not intended, and a clause that later developments swiftly rendered obsolete. Augmentations was also given control of lands acquired from other sources, notably those previously administered by the general surveyors, who were thus absorbed into the new court.[37] Its structure was closely modelled on that of the Duchy of Lancaster, governed by a council consisting of a chancellor, treasurer, attorney and solicitor, and employing ten auditors and seventeen local receivers, all of which offices were effectively within the gift of the Lord Privy Seal. Richard Rich became the first chancellor, and the other positions were filled with known Cromwell dependants. The Lord Privy Seal's control over the operations of the new court was not as direct as that over First Fruits and Tenths, but was nevertheless real, and it must be seen as an instrument of his policy.[38]

Augmentations was almost entirely independent, Exchequer interference with its processes being expressly forbidden. All grants, gifts and leases of land under its control, although authorised by warrants under the sign manual, were written by the clerk of the court and issued under its own seal. The Chancellor was authorised to make leases of up to twenty-one years on his own authority, only the granting of reversions requiring special mandate from the king or Lord Privy Seal, and the clerk was ordered to enrol all grants and leases, keeping a register of appearances before the court, decrees and orders. That is what it meant to be a court of record.[39] All the fees and expenses claimed by its officers were to be the same as for the Duchy of Lancaster. The Act of foundation specified methods of accounting both for the treasurer and for the individual receivers, but left it to the council of the court to specify how the latter should be organised, and in the event their work was divided by counties, no attempt being made to maintain the integrity of the original estates. England was divided into fifteen groups of counties, and Wales into two. Oxfordshire, for example, was linked with Buckinghamshire and Berkshire, and Middlesex with London and Kent. This was a rational and efficient system, well calculated to ensure that lands did not disappear down the cracks between jurisdictions, and a necessary precaution against the acquisitiveness of gentlemen armed with generous bribes.[40] It also meant that the whole financial organisation was on a county basis, with receivers for parliamentary taxes, duchy lands and Chamber lands, in addition to the sheriffs who accounted for the ancient demesne and the profits of justice. Nevertheless supplementary orders were soon needed, and these seem to have been issued by Cromwell as early as the summer of 1536. The foundation Act had been concerned to make Augmentations an efficient element in the financial administration, and had little to say about the legal powers of its court. This was now remedied, and it was laid down that it was to have 'authority and power to hear and determine all matters between parties anywise touching any Lordship, Lands, tenements etc. now being or that hereafter shall be within the survey and government of the same'. Apart from cases involving disputes to titles which had arisen since the lands concerned had been alienated by the Crown, which were to be resolved at the common law, the Court of Augmentations was to have full jurisdiction over all matters concerning the Crown, even disputes between party and party over property acquired at the Dissolution and not yet sold or given away.[41] Many of these points were put on a statutory basis when the law was codified in the Act setting up the Court of General Surveyors in 1542.[42]

Meanwhile, Cromwell's policy towards religious houses underwent a subtle shift of emphasis. From trying to make sure that abbots and priors of a reforming disposition were appointed, he now began to seek for those who would make no difficulty about surrendering their responsibilities. Admittedly these were often the same men, because the task of converting obstinately conservative monks and friars not only proved uncongenial but usually impossible, and those religious of a reforming turn of mind were often the first to seek escape from the 'imprisonment' of their orders. Negotiations with heads of houses began to move away from prospects of continuity to discussions of pensions and capacities, and the frequent expressions of gratitude which the Lord Privy Seal received have to be seen in this light.[43] Appeals to be good to this or that monastery meant not so much exemption from the process of dissolution as a generous deal, which it was within the commissioners' powers to grant under Cromwell's supervision. In active collaboration with Cranmer, Cromwell also continued his patronage and protection of evangelical preachers, and indeed seems to have been the senior partner because his patronage network was so extensive. His correspondence with bishops and deans, putting pressure upon them to appoint his approved men to benefices or prebends within their gift, is voluminous, and although some excused themselves on the ground that the place was already filled, on the whole he was successful. When his chosen men aroused, as they frequently did, the indignation of the other clergy in the vicinity, he proved remarkably deaf to the complaints.[44] As former monastic lands were sold or granted by Henry, Cromwell was also able to ensure that the advowsons of the churches, which were often granted with the lands, were used in the reforming interest, this being part of the understanding when the grant was brokered, as it usually was, through his intercession. At this stage the king was complaisant, being preoccupied first with clearing up the affairs of the North and then with his wife's forthcoming confinement. However, he was not theologically idle. Provoked possibly by convocation's Ten Articles of 1536, upon which he made some superficial comments, towards the end of that year he commissioned a group of bishops to produce a new definition of the faith of the Church of England which was published under their own names in September 1537. It had been completed in July, and Edward Fox, one of those involved in its production, had then written to Cromwell asking to know the king's pleasure about its printing, and most particularly whether it should go out in the king's name or not.[45] Henry did not reply, nor, apparently did he read it at that time. It was consequently printed with a humble Episcopal petition as a preface:

We knowledge and confess that we have none authority either to assemble ourselves together for any pretence or purpose, or to publish anything that might be by us agreed on and compiled...

It also asked the king to make any corrections which he thought fit.[46] This preface was accompanied by a note from Henry to the effect that he had not had time to read it, but that was the nearest it got to royal approval. It was only after Jane's death, in December, that the king got down to the task of correcting the text of the Bishops' Book, and then he was fairly drastic, implying that the saints are mediators between God and man, and adding the name of Jesus Christ to the first commandment. Where the book had stated that all men are equal in God's eyes, he added the proviso, 'Touching the soul only' and added the warning 'that there be many folk which had liever live by the graft of begging slothfully' than earn an honest living. He also deleted astrology

from the list of superstitions warned against, because he was a
keen believer in that pseudoscience.[47] In general his corrections
were in a conservative direction, and greatly annoyed Cranmer,
to whom they were communicated. Cromwell, to whom the
archbishop passed them on, was equally concerned, and was able
to make sure that as long as his influence prevailed, they never
saw the light of print. A number of them appeared eventually in
the King's Book, but that was not published until 1543.[48]

Cromwell's reform programme was not much set back by
Henry's eccentric doctrinal opinions, which remained within the
confines of the court. Publicly he inspired the destruction of the
shrines and the emergence of the English Bible. The king's views
on the saints were not entirely consistent. While he continued to
regard them as intercessors between God and man, he rejected as
superstitious the value of relics and the uses of pilgrimage. He also
endeavoured to distinguish between the acceptable appearance of
images as reminders of the Godly lives of those commemorated,
and the unacceptable worship of the same. He therefore objected
to the reformers desire to remove all images from churches,
while at the same time supporting the abolition of shrines. The
latter activity began in 1535 with the tomb of Thomas Becket
at Canterbury. Thomas had been, in the king's eyes, a traitor to
his prince and therefore in no way worthy to be regarded as a
saint.[49] Moreover his shrine was the richest in England, and several
wagons were required to take away the loot which accrued to him
from its abolition. The most celebrated destruction came two years
later in the context of the pressure building on the greater abbeys;
the exposure of the so-called 'Rood of Boxley' by Cromwell's
commissioners in 1537. This was an image which appeared to
respond to petitioners, particularly those bearing gifts, and was

revealed to be animated by a subtle system of wires and levers operated by the brother in charge. It was seized and exhibited with much derision first in Kent and then in London, where it was publicly hacked in pieces and burned.[50] Another fraud was the 'blood of Hailes', which was brought to Cromwell by the reforming abbot, who was uncertain what to do with it. He swore that it had not been tampered with during his incumbency, and a commission appointed to look into it could only decide that the phial contained 'a thick, red, sticky substance' that was certainly not blood. It was valueless, and was returned to the abbot for safekeeping until the king's pleasure respecting it should be known. What Henry decided is not known, but the treasures of the shrine went the same way as all the others – into the king's coffers. There is no doubt that the profit to be made from this destruction was a considerable motive, particularly in Cromwell's case, but it could not have been carried out without Henry's full consent and support. His sense of pastoral responsibility was also engaged by the question of an English Bible. The first attempt in this direction had been William Tyndale's New Testament of 1526, which conservative bishops hastened to assure him was full of heretical errors, and which he had banned for that reason.[51] However he was more than half-persuaded that it was his responsibility to bring the gospel of Christ to his people in their own language. Perhaps he was convinced by the value of Bible study to his own matrimonial cause, or perhaps by the words of St Paul about worshipping in a strange tongue, but in any case as early as 1530 he had promised convocation that he would authorise a new translation by 'wise and Catholic men'.

He did not, however, commission such a work, but rather, advised by Cromwell, waited for a suitable effort to emerge from the work which was already ongoing. The first candidate to appear was Cromwell's friend Miles Coverdale, who completed his translation in 1535. This was based mainly on the Vulgate, Erasmus and Luther, and Cromwell was not overly impressed, perhaps because he was looking for a version derived from the original Greek and Hebrew, and he knew that Coverdale's Hebrew was not up to the task. He would also have been aware that much of the New Testament was derived from Tyndale, and that the king would also have known that. He toyed with the idea of getting it authorised, and included in his first draft of the injunctions of 1536 a requirement that every parish should possess a copy.[52] However he then drew back, and that clause did not appear in the injunctions as issued. Coverdale thus missed out on being the first authorised version, but it was not banned and continued to circulate, being reprinted in 1537 by James Nicholson of Southwark. By the time that this happened, a rival had appeared on the scene in the form of the 'Mathew' Bible, printed in Antwerp. This claimed to be the work of Thomas Mathew, but had in fact been prepared by John Rogers, another of Cromwell's protégés and a friend of Tyndale.[53] It was derived from the Greek and the Hebrew, but the New Testament was unadulterated Tyndale, although taken from his 1534 revision, not the 1526 original. The Pentateuch was also Tyndale's work with minor revisions, and the Psalms and the Prophets were taken from Coverdale. They had probably been prepared by one of his collaborators, and the historical books may well have been Rogers' own contribution. Aware of Henry's reservations about Coverdale, Cranmer commended this version to Cromwell on 4 August 1538, and asked him to present it to the king in the hope of securing royal authority for it to be sold throughout the land.[54] In spite of its close similarity to Tyndale this rather surprisingly produced a favourable response, and Cromwell was able to insert in his second set of injunctions, sent to Cranmer on 30 September, the clause which he had omitted from the first set. Every parish was now to purchase a copy and display it in the nave of their church for everybody who was literate to read on at their will. The clergy were expressly forbidden to inhibit access to these scriptures, and were enjoined to encourage all who could do so to study them.[55] Cranmer was delighted and thanked his friend in terms which suggest that Henry's approval was by no means to be taken for granted. Cromwell's 'high and acceptable service' to God and the king 'shall so much redound to your honour that, besides God's reward, you shall obtain perpetual memory for the same within the realm'.[56] Henry's attitude towards the English Bible is a somewhat puzzling one, because within months of having approved it for general access he was worrying about the holy scriptures being 'railed on' in every alehouse instead of treated with the reverence which was their due, and in April 1539 he issued a proclamation limiting access to the educated. This did not, however, prevent him from authorising Cromwell in November of the same year to approve a new translation, the result of which was the Great Bible, which was issued with a preface by Thomas Cranmer in 1540;[57] or the issuing of a new proclamation in May 1541 repeating the order contained in the injunctions of 1538. In spite of his reservations, the king seems to have been convinced that it was his duty as a Christian prince to make the Bible available to his subjects, and it was Cromwell who persuaded him of that. In so doing he was following unintentionally the reformers' agenda, and creating a demand which proved stronger than the conservative instincts of his people, as some of his bishops ruefully acknowledged at the time.

The year 1538 was a difficult time for Henry in diplomatic terms, as the Truce of Nice brought Francis and Charles into unusual alignment, and as his marriage negotiations struggled on into the autumn. Cromwell was using Robert Barnes to keep his lines of communication with the Lutherans open, and Barnes had been in trouble for heresy over a number of years. This had never come to a head because of the Lord Privy Seal's protection, but he was undoubtedly taking a risk in using Barnes in this way as the authorised agent of a king who prided himself upon his doctrinal orthodoxy. As the Pope prepared to promulgate the sentence of excommunication issued against him three years earlier, Henry felt it to be necessary to demonstrate this orthodoxy in order to prove that Paul was acting out of malice and not for any genuine religious reason, and an opportunity was presented to him by the case of John Lambert.[58] Lambert was a sacramentary, that is to say one who denied the real presence in the Eucharist, and as such was not much more popular with the evangelicals than he was with the conservatives. In fact it had been the reformers Barnes and Rowland Taylor who had first complained about him to Cranmer. The archbishop questioned him and endeavoured to reason with him, as he was accustomed to do, but for some extraordinary reason, Lambert appealed over him to the king.[59] He must have been aware of Henry's extreme dislike of sacramentaries, and the suspicion is that he wished to make a martyr of himself in the most public possible way. It is not beyond the bounds of possibility that he may have been encouraged in this appeal by Cromwell, who would have been anxious to give Henry an occasion to demonstrate his orthodoxy in a way which did not compromise his relations with the evangelicals, who, as we have seen, were on his side in this matter. The king decided to make an exhibition of Lambert, and laid on a show trial in November 1538. At this a number of bishops and peers were in attendance, and the former played a full part in the arguments, which went on for nearly five hours, at the end of which time Lambert, who had not budged an inch in his resolution, appealed again directly to the king. Henry, who had also played a full part in the debate, is alleged to have referred him to the reserved sacrament, which was present in the room, saying, 'There is the maker of us all'; at which he doffed his bonnet.[60] But Lambert was not moved and the king called upon Cromwell, who had sat silent throughout the proceedings, to read the sentence against him. When reporting these proceedings to the ambassadors abroad, the Lord Privy Seal commended Henry's 'excellent gravity and inestimable majesty', but he might as well have commented upon his stamina. He called Lambert that 'miserable man' and there is no reason to suppose that he had any sympathy with him at all, but on the day of his execution a few days later, he was taken first to Cromwell's house where they engaged in an extended discussion. It is reasonably supposed that he had word that Lambert's death would be unusually protracted on the king's orders, and that he was endeavouring to secure a last minute recantation. If that was the case then he failed, and Lambert was burned in a slow fire a few hours later.[61] Cromwell's recorded part in Lambert's end was purely formal, but it is hard to believe that he did not derive a certain satisfaction from the fact that he and Cranmer and the king were all on the same side, because it was very important to distance the evangelicals from the radicals who were beginning to appear, and whose extreme notions gave the conservatives the opportunity to tar all reformers with the same brush, as Cromwell had pointed out to Lord Lisle in May 1538.[62]

1. Henry VIII by Holbein.

2. Anne Boleyn, Henry VIII's second and most controversial wife. Cromwell showed the king how to annul his marriage to Catherine of Aragon in order to achieve the desired union with Anne.

Above left: 3. Arthur, Henry VII's first son and Henry VIII's elder brother, from a nineteenth-century stained-glass window in St Laurence's church, Ludlow. Arthur was briefly married to Catherine of Aragon but died young.

Above right: 4. Anne of Cleves, Henry VIII's fourth wife. Cromwell advocated this short-lived marriage.

Below left: 5. Anne Boleyn's father, Thomas Boleyn, the Earl of Wiltshire. Cromwell replaced him in the office of Lord Privy Seal after Anne's fall.

Below right: 6. Henry VII.

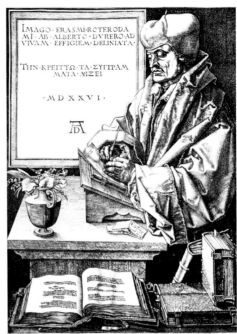

Opposite: 7. Jane Seymour, Henry's third wife, who gave Henry the son he so desired.
Top left: 8. Edward, Henry VIII's son by Jane Seymour. He would later succeed to the throne as Edward VI (r. 1547–53).
Top right: 9. Erasmus in an iconic woodcut by Dürer. Cromwell spoke French, Spanish and Italian and had a good working knowledge of Latin, which he appears to have developed by memorising chunks of the Erasmian translation of the New Testament.
Above: 10. *An Allegory of the Tudor Succession* depicting the family of Henry VIII.

11. Statue of Catherine of Aragon. By 1529 Catherine was past childbearing age and had produced only one living child, a daughter named Mary.

Right: 12. Thomas Wolsey from a drawing by Jacques le Boucq. Cromwell was Wolsey's servant from 1524 to 1530.

Below: 13. Tomb of Thomas Howard, 3rd Duke of Norfolk and uncle to both Anne Boleyn and Catherine Howard. Norfolk was a personal enemy of Cromwell.

14. Thomas Cranmer from a painting by Gerhard Flicke. As Archbishop of Canterbury, Cranmer presided over the court that finalised Henry's divorce from Catherine. He worked closely with Cromwell on religious reform following the break with Rome.

15. Thomas Wyatt, poet and friend of Cromwell. On Cromwell's death, he penned an eloquent epitaph.

Above: 16. A view of the Tudor palace at Greenwich where Henry married Anne of Cleves at Cromwell's recommendation and much to the king's distaste.

Right: 17. The Tower of London. Cromwell was arrested at three o'clock on 10 June 1540, stripped of the insignia of the Garter and taken to the Tower.

Above: 18. Following his arrest, Cromwell was conveyed by boat to the Tower and would have entered through the Traitor's Gate.
Left: 19. After his downfall, Cromwell's head was placed on a spike on London Bridge.
Opposite: 20. A plan of Westminster Palace, showing the Great Hall, the Abbey and the two Houses of Parliament. Cromwell effectively ran the House of Commons from 1532, and the House of Lords from 1536.

Great Hall,
by Wolsey, 1528

Scotland Yard

The Court Yard

The Court

Tennis court
G

Preaching
place

The

'Holbein' gate

Privy bridge

H

King St Gate

Court

F

F

Kinges streete

Channon row

B

Wesmynster Hall (the seat of the law courts)

Abby

A

E

E

E

Starre Chamber

House of Commons
(formerly chapel of St Stephen's)
from 1547 until the fire of 1834

House of Lords

Court of Requests

The Queenes bridge

Henry VII's chapel

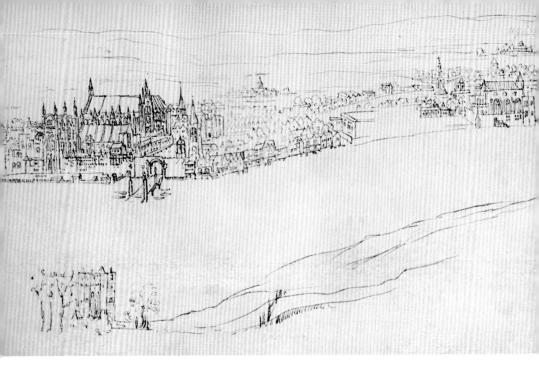

21. A view of Westminster, *c.* 1550, by Anthony van Wyngaerde. Westminster was the seat of the royal courts of justice and the meeting place of Parliament.

22. Whitehall Palace, *c.* 1550, also by van Wyngaerde. Whitehall had been extensively rebuilt by Cardinal Wolsey. It came into the king's hands on the fall of Wolsey in 1529 and was further rebuilt. It was used as a principal royal residence until largely destroyed by fire in the 1690s.

23. A drawing for the painting of Sir Thomas More and his family by Hans Holbein, *c.* 1527. Thomas More waged a fierce war on heretics while Cromwell had an increasing number of dealings with Continental Lutherans.

24. Windsor Castle, a royal palace and home of the Knights of the Garter.

Anglici Matrimonij,

Sententia diffinitiua

Lata per sanctiss.imum . Dūm Nostrum . D . Clementem . Papā . vij . in sacro Consistorio de
Reuerendiss.morum Dominorum . S . R . E . Cardinalium consilio super validitate Ma
trimonij inter Serenissimos Henricum . VIII. ꞓ Catherinam Anglie Reges contracti.

PRO.

Eadem Serenissima Catherina Angliæ Regina ,

CONTRA.

Serenissimum Henricum . VIII . Angliæ Regem.

Clemens Papa. vij.

Hristi nomine inuocato in Trono iustitiæ pro trib.nali sedentes, & solùm Deum præ oculis habentes , Per hanc
nostram diffinitiuam sententiam quam de Venerabilium Fratrum nostrorum Sanctæ Ro . Ec . Car . Consistorialiter
coram nobis congregatorum Consilio, & assensu fecimus in bis scriptis, pronunciamus, decernimus, & declaramus ,
in causa, & causis ad nos, & Sedem Apostolicam per appellationem, per charissimam in christo filiam Catherinam Angliæ Reginam Illustrem à nostris, & Sedis Apostolicæ Legatis in Regno Angliæ deputatis interposi
tam legitime deuolutis, & aduocatis , inter prædictam Catherinam Reginam, & Charissimum in christo filium Henricum . VIII .
Angliæ Regem Illustrem , super Validitate, & inualiditate matrimonij inter eosdem Reges contracti, & consumati rebusque alijs in
actis, causæ & causarum huiusmodi latius deductis , & dilecto filio Paulo Capissucho causarum sacri palatij tunc decano & pro
pter ipsius Pauli absentiam Venerabili Fratri nostro Iacobo Simoneæ Episcopo Pisaurien. vnus ex dictis palatij causarum Auditori
bus locumtenens, audiendis instruendis , & in Consistorio nostro Secreto referendis commissis, & per eos nobis, & eisdem Car
dinalibus Relatis , & mature discussis , coram nobis pendentibus , Matrimonium Inter predictos Catherinam, & Henricum An
gliæ Reges contractum , & inde secuta quecunque fuisse, & esse validum, & canonicum validaque, & Canonica , suosque debitos de
buisse, & debere sortiri effectus, prolemque exinde susceptam, & suscipiendam fuisse, & fore legitimam , & præfatum Henri
cum Angliæ Regem teneri, & obligatum fuisse , et fore ad cohabitandum cum dicta Catherina Regina eius legitima coniuge , illamque
maritali affectione , & Regio honore tractandum , & eundem Henricum Angliæ Regem ad præmissa omnia, & singula cum
effectu adimplendum condemnandum omnibusque iuris Remedijs cogendum , & compellendum fore, prout condemnamus, cogimus, &
compellimus, Molestationesque , & denegationes Per eundem Henricum Regem eidem Catherinæ Reginæ super inualiditate, ac fœ
dere dictis Matrimonij quomodolibet factas, & præstitas fuisse, & esse illicitas, & iniustas, & eidem Henrico Regi super il
lis ac inualiditate matrimonij huiusmodi perpetuum Silentium imponendum fore, & imponimus, eiusdemque Henricum Angliæ Re
gem in expensis in huiusmodi causa pro parte dictæ Catherinæ Reginæ coram nobis , & dictis omnibus legitime factis condemnandum fore, & condemnamus , quarum expensarum taxationem nobis imposterum reseruamus .

Ita, pronunciauimus .I.

Lata fuit Romæ in Palatio Apostolico publice in Consistorio die. XXIII. Martij. M . D . XXXIIII .

Blosius.

Above: 25. A copy of Pope Clement VII's 'definitive sentence' in favour of Catherine of
Aragon and against Henry VIII, issued on 23 March 1534. It was ignored in England.
Opposite: 26. Henry VIII in council. This appears to be a formal session, with the king
seated under his 'cloth of estate'. In practice, the council normally met without the king,
and attendance was usually about a dozen.

King Henry the eyght.

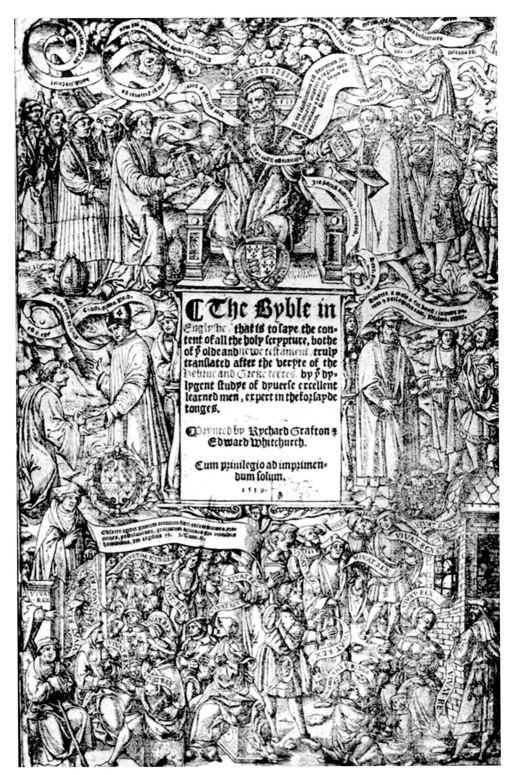

27. Title page from the Great Bible, printed by Richard Grafton and Edward Whitchurch, 1539. Enthroned as God's vicar, Henry symbolically hands out the Word of God to the spiritual and temporal hierarchies of his realm, headed by Thomas Cranmer on his right and Thomas Cromwell on his left.

As we have seen, the idea of dissolving the greater monasteries was probably the king's rather than Cromwell's, and there is some evidence that the two were at cross purposes in 1538 and 1539. The nunnery of Godstowe is a case in point because the king, on Cromwell's suggestion, had recently appointed a reforming abbess, one Katherine Bulkeley, and Katherine had named Cromwell as her steward with many expressions of gratitude. Then, in November 1538, Dr John London turned up at Godstowe, pressing for the surrender of the house. The abbess promptly appealed to Cromwell, asking him to 'continue my good lord, as you have ever been', and asking for 'the stay of Dr London'. This was apparently achieved because on 26 November she wrote again, thanking him for having sent a 'contrary commandment'. 'Be assured,' she went on,

> there is neither pope nor purgatory, image nor pilgrimage, nor praying to dead saints used or regarded among us; but all superstitious ceremonies set apart, the very honour of God and the truth of his holy words ... is most tenderly followed and regarded by us...[63]

So she and her sisters were permitted to continue with their reformed life – for a little while. By the end of the following year the house had gone down, and there was nothing further that Cromwell was able, or willing, to do about it. The prior of Malvern, faced with a similar threat, had also appealed successfully to the Lord Privy Seal, but in his case also it amounted to no more than a stay of execution. Whether Cromwell was genuinely converted to the king's view of the situation, or realised the impossibility of further resistance, we do not know. After the

Act of May 1539, vesting all the property of the dissolved houses in the Crown, his main interventions relate to the securing of generous pensions for those whom he had placed only a short while before in the hope of furthering his evangelical programme. In Katherine Bulkeley's case this was a generous £50 a year.[64] He was apparently more successful in persuading the king to devote some of the proceeds of the Dissolution to good causes than he was in checking the process. Richard Lee's appeal to convert the Abbey of Coventry into a collegiate church was heard and acted upon, and the Grey Friars church of Carmarthen was converted into a school on the petition of the mayor and aldermen. The Vice-Chancellor of Cambridge was also gratified to learn that the dissolved religious foundations within the university would be transformed into places of learning and true doctrine.[65] Six abbeys were converted into secular cathedrals to serve the new dioceses which were created, but this did not happen until after Cromwell's fall, and whether his influence can be traced there also is hard to determine. Since a plan to that effect was being actively discussed as early as May 1539, it is probable that it can.

By the time that that happened there are distinct signs that the king and the Lord Privy Seal were pursuing different agendas. Earlier in the year Cromwell had persuaded Henry to send Robert Barnes to Copenhagen to discuss Anglo–Danish relations, in particular the prospect of an anti-papal alliance, and Christopher Mont to the Duke of Saxony with a promise of England's adherence to the League of Schmalkalden. Mont was to ask for a high-level delegation to be sent to England, possibly led by Philip Melanchthon, to discuss the Confession of Augsburg, which had always been the sticking point in earlier negotiations.[66] The Germans were understandably cool, feeling that they had been this way before without success, but agreed eventually to send a low-key mission, which did not include Melanchthon, and which arrived on 23 April, to a warm welcome from Cromwell, for whom their presence represented a diplomatic success. Christian III of Denmark was more positive, and suggested a meeting in England involving Danish and Leaguer representatives to suggest a way forward. He also warmly urged Henry to accept the Confession of Augsburg and become a full member of the League.[67] Unfortunately, by the time that these tidings reached him in May, Henry was off on a different tack, and not prepared to listen to Lutheran urgings. Worried by the evidence of religious dissent, and the troubles being caused by clashes in the pulpit between old and new believers, he consulted a selection of his bishops, including Gardiner and Cranmer, and caused to be introduced into Parliament a Bill 'abolishing diversity in opinions'. This Bill, which was moved in the Lords by the Duke of Norfolk on 16 May, was a victory for Catholic orthodoxy and Cromwell was considerably disconcerted. He had, as usual, vetted the returns of members of the Commons, but that was with a view to ensuring that government measures were passed, and he had not bargained for this thumping conservative declaration. It was vigorously debated but there was never a chance that it would be rejected, and Henry, realising how strongly it would offend Cranmer's conscience, licensed his archbishop to be absent from the discussions in the Lords.[68] No similar indulgence was extended to the Lord Privy Seal, and it is not known whether or to what extent he made his opposition clear. It was, however, the last thing that the Lutheran delegation wished to hear, and even before it was passed their talks with the king became bogged down in an unseemly row over clerical celibacy. This was an issue about which Henry felt strongly, but it was not the only reason why the negotiations broke down soon afterwards. That was largely because word was received from Germany that the Lutheran princes had come to terms with the Emperor at the Diet of Frankfort. This made them useless as allies, and the king told the delegation that they might as well go home.[69] He had suspected that this might happen, which was one of the reasons why he had been reluctant to receive them in the first place, but this confirmation did nothing to sweeten his temper. Cromwell's affairs were not going well, but fortunately the Cleves negotiation was still alive, and he began to devote his whole attention to that, which was brought to a successful conclusion in August. In spite of the failure of the Schmalkaldic negotiations, Henry had an ally within the Empire, and by October was committed to a new bride.

The Act of Six Articles, which passed the Commons on 2 June, was undoubtedly a setback for Cromwell, but perhaps not as great as has sometimes been assumed. The first article ran,

In the most blessed sacrament of the altar, by the strength and efficacy of Christ's mighty word, it being spoken by the priest, is present really, under the form of bread and wine, the natural body and blood of our saviour Jesus Christ, conceived of the Virgin Mary, and that after the consecration there remaineth no substance of bread or wine, nor any other substance but the substance of Christ God and Man...[70]

This was an affirmation of transubstantiation, although the word was not used. It would have offended the Lutherans, who believed that after consecration the substance of bread and wine remained in the elements, along with the spiritual presence of Christ, but there is no reason to suppose that it distressed Cromwell. As far as we know, and in spite of the accusations later levelled against him, his Eucharistic theology was strictly orthodox. More disturbing would have been the second article, in favour of communion under one kind, but this merely stated that it was not necessary *ad salutem* by the law of God for the laity to receive the cup as well as the bread. A full Lutheran would have disagreed, and Cromwell seems to have preferred both kinds, but it was not a major issue to him. Clerical celibacy, which forms the third article, was an issue and he disagreed with it. It did not affect him personally as a layman and a widower; but it was a serious embarrassment to Cranmer, who was secretly married, and who was forced to send his wife back to Germany when the Act came into force.[71] The fourth article, on the binding nature of religious vows, was also an issue, although a strictly practical one. Cromwell could see no point in enforcing vows taken in a monastic context when that context had disappeared. It would surely be better to encourage former nuns, for instance, to marry rather than to remain dependent upon their families, because except for the heads of houses, none of them received a living wage as a pension. He did not accept the indelible nature of religious vows, but that was an issue of purely secondary importance. The fifth and sixth articles were affirmations of good Catholic practice, and ran counter to the reformed teachings that Cromwell is thought, but not known, to have embraced. The fifth affirms the validity of private masses, which Luther had set his face against, maintaining that there should always be a congregation present and receiving, to make the mass a true sacrament; and the sixth affirms that auricular confession (to a priest) is 'expedient and necessary to be retained'.[72] On neither of these matters is Cromwell known to have expressed an opinion, but his general endorsement of evangelical teaching makes it reasonable to suppose that he would have opposed these clauses also, if he had been given the chance.

The Act of Six Articles was a victory for the conservative bishops, and a defeat for Cromwell's evangelical agenda, but it was also a reflection of the king's own thinking. Together with the failure of the Schmalkaldic negotiations, it signified Henry's view of himself as a Christian prince, and his responsibility for the spiritual well-being of his subjects. He saw himself as a Catholic who had taken a stand against the jurisdictional tyranny of the papacy, not in any sense as a Protestant. It was his duty to reform the Church, but only within those Catholic parameters, and his authorisation of the English Bible, not mentioned in the Act, has to be seen in that context. He was responsible for the teaching of the English Church, and deemed it expedient that his subjects should be able to inform themselves of the contents of the holy scriptures.[73] This might be deemed anticlerical, but no more. There was no theological reason why the Bible might not be rendered into the vernacular. The only inhibition was that of Archbishop Arundel's anti-Lollard constitutions of the early fifteenth century, and they forbade unauthorised versions.[74] It was a proactive vision of the Royal Supremacy. Cromwell would have liked Henry to be more evangelical than he actually was, and was continually nudging him in that direction, realising that the more reformed the Church of England was the harder the Royal Supremacy would be to undo. His great success came over the English Bible, and his greatest failure over the Act of Six Articles. However, he accepted it, and Henry took his submission with a good grace. He remained Viceregent in Spirituals, and continued to dissolve religious houses. He was also responsible for the enforcement of the Act, and that showed some surprising features. Bishops Shaxton and Latimer resigned as soon as it came into force, and although Cromwell was undoubtedly sorry to lose the latter, whom he had supported for many years, there is some evidence that the departure of the prickly Shaxton was a relief. Barnes is alleged to have said that the king 'holds religion and the Gospel in no regard', but others more in touch with Henry thought that although he disagreed with the reformers in certain matters, he continued to be their friend, and the Act was not rigorously enforced.[75] In spite of the fierce penalties prescribed, only about thirty people suffered death in consequence of it. Over 200 were charged in the diocese of London, but only three suffered imprisonment, and of the 500 who were rounded up in the summer of 1539, a mere handful were proceeded against. The rest were released on a general pardon in July 1540. This was admittedly after Cromwell's fall, but the generally lenient treatment meted out to offenders seems to have been the consequence of his influence, which continued at least until May 1540.[76] In short, once the international crisis of 1539 was over, and Henry was apparently locked into the Cleves alliance, the Act of Six Articles became largely a matter for the clergy, and the king was satisfied to hold it in reserve. It was specific on transubstantiation, on private masses and on clerical celibacy, but there were large areas of doctrine and practice which it did not touch, so although it was a conservative measure, it was so to only a limited extent, and should not be seen as the first stage of Cromwell's decline and fall.

7

THE FALL OF THOMAS CROMWELL,
1539–1540

Master Cromwell ... you are now entered into the service of a most noble, wise and liberal prince ... you shall in your counsel given unto his grace ever tell him what he ought to do, but never what he is able to do ... for if a lion knew his strength, hard were it for any man to rule him.

Sir Thomas More

From the beginning of his service to the king, and indeed before, Cromwell had been associated with those wishing to reform the English Church. As early as 1524 he had been acting for Thomas Somer, a citizen and stockfishmonger of London. who was one of the penitents paraded in the city in November 1530 for having imported heretical books.[1] In particular Somer had brought in and sold copies of Tyndale's New Testament, which he was required to burn as a part of his penance. The unfortunate man was returned to the Tower after his penance, and died there two years later. His friendship with the up-and-coming royal councillor proved of no avail, however sympathetic Cromwell may have been to the cause of his imprisonment. This was dangerous political territory because the Lord Chancellor, Thomas More, was adamantly opposed to the translation of the scriptures, and the king was backing his campaign. It was only after More's resignation in the summer of 1532 that it began to be possible to exploit Henry's vision of himself as being responsible for the spiritual well-being of his people, to encourage him in the direction of approving an English Bible. This discreet pressure eventually paid off and by 1535 the king was prepared to authorise the Coverdale version, which as we have seen was printed in Southwark in 1537.[2] The reformers hailed Cromwell as God's special instrument and assured him that if 'for the zeal which he bore' to the truth 'the pure word of God may once go forth' then 'the whole realm ... shall have ... you more in remembrance than the name of Austen that men say brought the faith first into England'. Richard Taverner praised him for his 'godly circumspection' in promoting the true faith, and that was fair because he was extremely careful never to go beyond the parameters which Henry laid down.[3] The difficulty lay in the king's own mind, because although he came down on the side of an English Bible, in other respects he remained extremely conservative. He never abandoned his belief in transubstantiation, for example, and although he was prepared to outlaw pilgrimages, he never ceased to believe in prayers for the dead. He steered a delicate course, and the more robust reformers felt that they never quite knew where they stood with him. Tyndale was invited to return to England under safe conduct, and was then repudiated and left to his fate as a heretic in the Low Countries, having been betrayed by one Henry Philips, in whom he had confided.[4] Nor was Cromwell left in any doubt that, in encouraging the reformers, he was running many risks.

'Was not my Lord Cardinal a great man and ruled all the realm as he would,' his opponents reminded him, 'and what became of him, is he not gone?' And Thomas More also. The Lord Privy Seal 'in like manner ruleth all, and we shall see one day he shall have as great a fall as any of them'. His services to the king might appear to guarantee his safety, but his Achilles' heel was his sympathy with those whom Henry regarded as heretics, and many felt that it was only a question of time before that little weakness caught up with him.[5]

In 1536 he ventured to draft an injunction in the king's name requiring every parish to acquire a copy of the English Bible. This did not feature in the injunctions as issued because neither of the versions then available was deemed to be satisfactory. The second edition, the Mathew Bible, had been heavily criticised for being too dependent upon Luther, so Cromwell decided to arrange another translation, direct from the Greek and the Hebrew. This work he entrusted to Coverdale, Grafton and Whitchurch, and it was to be printed in Paris, where the workmanship was superior, and it would be away from critical English eyes.[6] Although this was Cromwell's project, not the king's, he managed to persuade Henry to secure Francis's approval, and by the early summer of 1538 he was receiving progress reports from Paris. These were very technical, and suggest not only a high level of engagement on his part, but also a rather unexpected expertise in the business of translation. This would seem to indicate that Henry's action had not undermined his position as much as is sometimes supposed. The king took his patronage of the Great Bible as acceptable service.[7]

Cromwell was not therefore 'tottering' in the autumn of 1539, or at least no more so than he had been on a number of occasions in the past, and his fall in June 1540 was not directly connected either with the Great Bible or with the Act of Six Articles. It was the result rather of a combination of factors which gave his enemies the critical leverage to turn the king's mind against him. One of these was the German alliance, for which Cromwell had been angling for a number of years. In 1532 he had persuaded Philip Melanchthon to dedicate his *Apology* to Henry, as a part of his campaign to soften Henry's attitude towards the Lutherans. The king was favourably impressed, and tried on a number of subsequent occasions to persuade Melanchthon to come to England with a Lutheran delegation in an attempt to sort out their theological differences.[8] One such mission, although without Melanchthon, had come in the summer of 1538, without any positive result, but in January 1539, faced with the ominous friendship between Charles and Francis, Cromwell decided to try again. He sent Christopher Mont to the Duke of Saxony, and Robert Barnes to the King of Denmark, with suggestions for an anti-papal alliance, linked with a proposal that the king should marry the daughter of the Duke of Cleves.[9] Henry must have been aware of these moves, and have approved them. They represented a break with his well-established policy of non-alignment, but one which could be easily justified by the unprecedented international situation. As we have seen, the Schmalkaldic mission came to nothing on account of the Act of Six Articles, but left the Cleves marriage on the table for further negotiation. In fact the Lutherans may have been a little hasty in judging Henry's religious attitude by the Act, because a few days after the dissolution of Parliament in June the king staged an anti-papal pageant on the Thames, wherein a boat representing Paul and his cardinals was unceremoniously overturned by another representing the king's true subjects, the message of which was clear to see.[10] The orthodoxy of Henry's doctrinal position did not imply any negotiations for the ending of the schism. At the same time an identical message was being conveyed in inn yards and private houses up and down the country by groups of players operating in the name of the Lord Privy Seal or the Archbishop of Canterbury. Cromwell had shrugged off the reverses represented by the failure of the Schmalkaldic negotiation and the Act of Six Articles. The king was still very much on his side, and the Cleves marriage, revitalised by William Petre, was proceeding satisfactorily.[11]

These favourable circumstances did not continue very long. By the end of the year Franco–Imperial hostility was beginning to reappear, and Henry was tied into a treaty which he did not really need. A lot therefore depended upon the king's marriage, because, if it worked, the link with Cleves might seem a small price to pay. Unfortunately it did not, and Cromwell found himself saddled with the responsibility for locking Henry into an unwanted treaty as the price of securing a highly unsatisfactory bride. After his disappointment at Rochester, the king had confided to Cromwell that he liked Anne 'nothing so well as she was spoken of' and that if he had known the truth about her, she would never have come to England. For two days he struggled to find a way out of his commitment, but there was none and even if there had been another twist in the international situation that would have forbidden it, Charles had decided to put his friendship with Francis to the test, and asked for safe conduct to go from Spain to the Low Countries through France. Put on the spot, Francis could not refuse, and the Emperor was being lavishly entertained in Paris even as the king contemplated his options.[12]

Reluctantly, he agreed to put his head into the yoke, saying to Cromwell (who seems to have been the recipient of a number of these confidences), 'My lord, if it were not to satisfy the world and my realm, I would not do that I must do this day, for no earthly thing.' They were quietly married in the palace at Greenwich, and the king swallowed his distaste sufficiently to behave towards his bride with most scrupulous courtesy.[13] It is hardly surprising that after such a beginning, the wedding night was a fiasco. It is not clear whether Henry attempted to consummate their union that night or not, because it was quite common for newly-weds to abstain for the first night, in order to ensure that the woman was not menstruating. However it is clear that he slept with her for many nights thereafter, entirely without success. Anne, however, was so innocent that she did not notice anything wrong. In spite of her twenty-four years she clearly did not have the faintest idea of what was supposed to happen on a wedding night. The king had kissed her and bade her 'good night'; should there be more? she asked her incredulous ladies after a few nights. Indeed there should be more, they assured her; and Lady Jane Rochford is alleged to have muttered that at this rate it would be a long time before they had a Duke of York to celebrate.[14] Henry meanwhile had confessed to his physician, William Buttes, that although he was confident of his ability to 'do the deed' with any other woman, he had left Anne as good a maid as he had found her. Shortly after Easter, in early April, the king began to have fresh scruples about his marriage. Not only did he return to the old issue of her precontract with the Duke of Lorraine's son, but he also began to allege that he had never consented to the union in the first place. The first objection was readily disposed of, and had indeed been dismissed during those fraught days between

Anne's arrival and their marriage. The documentation was missing, but Cromwell had caused Anne herself to repudiate that agreement, which was in itself sufficient discharge. It had been this news which had caused Henry to utter the ill-omened words, 'I am not well handled', and the situation had not changed since then, so there was little point in raising that scruple now.[15] The second allegation was more ominous, because it reflected directly upon the Lord Privy Seal's role in the negotiation. The evidence of lack of consent lay in the failure to consummate, which was evidently true of the first days of the marriage itself. However, for the discussions which had preceded it and for the treaty with Cleves, such a lack was largely fictitious. Reluctantly, the king had gone along with Cromwell's policy because he was desperate to avoid diplomatic isolation, but the king's memory was notoriously selective, and he remembered only what he chose to remember. So in early April Henry was remembering that his Lord Privy Seal had saddled him with an unattractive wife in pursuit of a foreign policy which was by that time again unnecessary.[16] Charles had passed through France, and was again busy with Imperial affairs, one aspect of which was a threat of military action against Cleves in pursuit of his claim to Gelderland, which Duke William had inherited in controversial circumstances in July 1538. The prospect of having to go to the aid of an ally to whom he had looked for political, but not military, support, was altogether repugnant to the King of England, and he began to show every sign that he would renege on the undertakings which Cromwell had made on his behalf only about six months before. To make matters worse, Edmund Bonner was having some success in persuading Francis that his whole policy of reconciliation with the Emperor was a mistake, and that was not good news for Cromwell either.[17]

So he had lost a couple of rounds in his constant battle to influence the king, but that was by no means decisive. Parliament reassembled on 12 April, and that gave him a fresh chance. There had been a general election in March 1539, and Cromwell had performed his usual feat of using his patronage in the Crown's interests. In Gatton, for example, which was a 'proprietary borough', the agent wrote asking for Cromwell's nomination, which enabled the owner, Sir Roger Copley, to present a suitable name to the sheriff. Norfolk was more complicated, because there the opposition of a local gentleman, Sir Edmund Knyvett, had to be overcome before the 'official' candidates could be returned, which was successfully accomplished.[18] His main problem came not from local interest groups but from rival patrons. At Farnham he came up against the Bishop of Winchester, who had already provided two members before the Lord Privy Seal's letter arrived and was unwilling to concede. A second test against Gardiner came over the county of Hampshire, and there, in spite of making a false start, Cromwell prevailed. 'I marvel not a little,' wrote one commentator, '[at] the great intended hindrance of the Bishop of Winchester', who was mightily displeased at this setback to his influence in his own backyard.[19] About a third of the membership of the House of Commons could be constructed in this fashion, which does not amount to the packing sometimes alleged. Nor was it the creation of a personal party. Although some of the members elected by this method were Cromwell's servants or dependants, more were household servants of the king and their brief was to support royal policy, which was how the Act of Six Articles came to be passed so easily.[20] Cromwell was absent from the first few days of the session because of illness, but the king was well aware that there were two conflicting parties among the members in respect of his desire for religious uniformity; one conservative and the other of the new learning. He caused a committee to be established to advise him on this vexed issue, under the chairmanship of the Viceregent in Spirituals and consisting of members of both parties. Needless to say it rapidly became bogged down in controversy, and without waiting for its report Henry decided to cut the Gordian knot. He came down on the conservative side and on 16 May the Duke of Norfolk moved the Six Articles.[21] There was no question of Cromwell opposing this move, but he used the prorogation over Whitsun to regroup, with the result that by the time the Act received the royal assent on 28 June, it had been amended in two modest but significant ways. The first put back the date by which married clergy had to repudiate their wives to 12 July, and the second limited the binding nature of religious vows to those persons who had made their vows at the age of twenty-four or older, thus freeing those who had been sworn as children and removing one of the more rational grievances against the Act.[22] Some ardent, but not very well-informed, reformers thought that Cromwell was finished and lamented the resurrected power of Gardiner, but others like Burghkardt, who knew the situation better from his recent visit to the country, contradicted them. In October Burghkardt wrote to Melanchthon to reassure him. The Six Articles had been the work of Stokesley and Gardiner, of whom the first was dead and the latter in disgrace. The king was already showing his disillusionment with the conservative religious party, and Cromwell had survived the attack. He had even succeeded in keeping Gardiner away from the court, and arranged for Edmund Bonner to take his place as ambassador to France.[23]

Although the Lord Privy Seal had not been fully in command of the agenda of Parliament in 1539, there is plenty of evidence that he had recovered that control by the time that it reassembled in 1540. The king's anxiety for unity in religion was as strong as ever, and he was now concerned to round off the basic test imposed in 1539 with an authoritative statement of doctrine and ceremonial, a full declaration of his patriarchal role as Supreme Head. Cromwell introduced this theme when he spoke in the king's name, immediately after Lord Chancellor Audley had opened the session.

> The king's majesty desires nothing more than concord ... he knows there are those who would stir up strife, and in many places in his field tares have sprung up to harm the wheat. The forwardness and carnal lust of some, the inveterate corruption and superstitious tenacity of opinion of other excite disputation and quarrels most horrible in so good Christian men; one side calls the other papists, and the other calls them heretics, both naughty and not to be borne; and that the less so because they miserably abuse the Holy Word of God and the scriptures which the same most noble prince of his gentleness, and for the salvation and consolation of his people has permitted them to read in the vulgar tongue. They twist God's sacred gift, now into heresy and now into superstition.[24]

The fact that he spoke thus is significant, but unity in religion was part of his agenda also, because with the king in his present orthodox mood, and himself associated with the reformers, continued squabbling could only damage his position. Two committees were therefore established to examine these problems, and although he remained Viceregent in Spirituals and the king's mouthpiece, it is obvious that Henry controlled the composition of these committees himself, that for doctrine being particularly dominated by conservatives, including Lee, Gardiner and Tunstall. That for ceremonies was more evenly balanced, but the traditionalists were still in a majority. However, it remained to be seen what these committees would recommend, and what the king would do with their suggestions.[25] Cromwell's own business for this session was rather different in its nature, and it has been alleged that it was only that business which caused the king to postpone his disgrace. However, if that was the case it suggests that Henry had little confidence in the other members of his council. The first such item was the dissolution of the Order of St John of Jerusalem, and the confiscation of its property. This was really a tidying-up operation after the Dissolution of the Monasteries, because the Knights of St John were not technically monks, but rather a military order based in Malta. They were thus in theory at least survivors of the old popish regiment, and held several rich preceptories. The Bill annexing all this property to the Crown was sent from the Lords to the Commons on 8 May, and passed through all its stages in time to receive the royal assent on the 11th.[26] The second item was the subsidy Bill, in which Cromwell used the unprecedented argument that Henry deserved the benefit of the tax, not because of impending war, but because of his good government. In other words it was an acknowledgement that, in spite of the wealth of the monasteries, the king could no longer even pretend to 'live of his own', and thus marked an important shift in the basis of Tudor taxation.[27] In spite of this and of the vigorous debate which it provoked, the Bill passed through all its stages by 8 May. However, when the session was prorogued for a fortnight on the 11th, the two religious committees had made no progress. They were deadlocked along predictable lines, and the brief recess was probably designed to help them to sort themselves out. It did not work, and neither had reported by the time that the Parliament was dissolved on 24 July.

That was not Cromwell's fault, because by then he had fallen victim to the king's unpredictable whims. As we have seen, his position had been precarious for some time, as he himself was the first to acknowledge, because he was so absolutely dependent upon the royal favour, and Henry seems to have been in two minds about his minister for several months. He had been a liability before, in 1536, but then there had been no doubt that his actions represented the king's intentions. Now however there was doubt, over his foreign policy and the Cleves marriage, and particularly over his patronage of religious reformers.[28] After much vacillation, in June 1540, Henry decided that he must go. It should be emphasised that this was the king's decision, very much as the fall of Wolsey had been. Faction certainly existed at Henry VIII's court, but it was always competition for influence and never for control. It also tended to be negative rather than positive in its inspiration. The faction that worked for Wolsey's overthrow was held together only by that purpose, consisting as it did of Boleyn supporters, religious reformers and others such as the Duke of Suffolk, who had personal axes to grind. It fell apart as soon as its objective had been achieved.[29] Similarly, that group which worked for the rejection of Anne Boleyn was motivated by hostility to her and to her family rather than by any enthusiasm for Mary or the Seymours. It was the same with Thomas Cromwell, because those who worked against him were driven by a multitude of private agendas, in which jealousy played a prominent part, as well as by religious conservatism. It is often said that Stephen Gardiner and the Duke of Norfolk were the leaders of the anti-Cromwell faction, but it would be more accurate to describe them as personal enemies. Nor was there a faction supporting him, any more than there had been a pro-Wolsey group in the council of 1529. In spite of his pleasant conversation, broadly ranging intellectual interests, and capacity for loyal friendship, it cannot be said that Cromwell ever succeeded in creating a party of councillors who were devoted to him, or willing to take the smallest risk on his behalf.[30] The exception to this generalisation was Thomas Cranmer, but one man, however important, does not make a faction. Sir Thomas Audley, the Lord Chancellor, acted generally as though he were Cromwell's creature, which in a sense he was, but he did nothing to support him in this crisis. Ralph Sadler and Thomas Wriothesley were the Lord Privy Seal's servants, and he had elevated them to share the secretaryship when he resigned that office in April 1540, but each of them was too concerned with his own safety to run any risks on Cromwell's behalf. Sadler has been described as 'cautious enough to give his enemies not even the shadow of an accusation against him' when Cromwell fell, which given the closeness of their relationship was quite an achievement.[31] Others who had maintained good relations with him during his years of prosperity, such as Kingston and Browne, now emerged as good conservatives, and had even been involved in a plot in 1539 to replace Cromwell as Lord Privy Seal with the impeccably orthodox Cuthbert Tunstall – a plot which failed at the time because the king was not prepared to go that far. The bishops had been divided by the Act of Six Articles, but two of the small group of reformers had since resigned their sees, and Latimer was in prison.[32] There was therefore no such thing as a pro-Cromwell faction in the council, and no one to share his misfortune when it came.

At the same time, in spite of the strong feelings which he aroused, there was no organised party opposing him either, because all the councillors were primarily interested in their own positions. They were concerned to read the king's mind, and therefore men like Southampton and Russell stood behind Cromwell when he was in favour, and turned against him when he was not. Their primary allegiance was to Henry, and as he altered his mind, so did they. This was understood by all concerned, and could even be described as a principle. It is unlikely that Cromwell was disillusioned by the failure of his friends to show up when he lost favour. It is also true that different councillors had different agendas. Southampton, for instance, was ready enough to attack the Church for its arrogance, and to seek for former monastic property, but not to favour reformed ideas in liturgy or worship.[33] Others, particularly members of the old nobility, such as the Earl of Oxford, resented the power of an upstart, just as they had with Wolsey. Oxford was prepared to be friendly enough when seeking the Lord Privy Seal's favour for himself or his servants, and even wrote in 1538 thanking him for looking after his son. However he would not let that influence him when the tide turned, and both Cromwell and Henry knew this perfectly well. It is even possible that it was a desire to maintain the support of the traditional nobility, whom he had demoted in other ways, which inspired the king to turn against Cromwell at this juncture.[34] The king knew that his minister was unpopular, not only with the nobles, but also with those old gentry families upon whom he relied for the control of the counties, and that made him willing to listen to his enemies. In the forefront of these stood his two long-standing rivals for the royal ear, the Duke of Norfolk and the Bishop of Winchester, both of whom he had outmanoeuvred repeatedly over the previous seven years and who now stood poised for revenge.

Apart from his loyalty to the king, the duke was mainly motivated by personal and family ambition. His niece, Anne Boleyn, had married Henry, which had brought him into prominence at court, but when the king turned against her he had obediently followed suit, and even presided at the trial which had condemned her. He had been ostensibly Henry's leading councillor after the fall of Wolsey, an event in which he had played a leading part, but he had been adroitly elbowed aside by Thomas Cromwell, largely because he lacked the imagination and intellectual ability to come up with a solution to the king's problems.[35] At first their relations were superficially friendly, and Norfolk made use of the secretary to secure some personal favours from the king. However late in 1534 the troubles in Ireland caused a split to develop in the council, and Norfolk became highly critical of Cromwell's methods. This had caused the latter to mount a surreptitious campaign against him, and Henry ceased to consult him on important issues. By February 1535 Norfolk had withdrawn to his estates at Kenninghall to nurse his grievances. He had effectively been driven from the council and deprived of access to the king, which was the lifeblood of all courtiers' careers. Cromwell was in no position to prevent so senior a nobleman from paying occasional visits to the court, and Henry would not have wanted to alienate him, but he came much less often and did not venture to raise personal matters with the king, because he realised that petitions needed to be cleared with the secretary first, which he was at that time unwilling to do.[36] His duchess, Elizabeth, whom he had set aside in order to live with his mistress, Bess Holland, warned Cromwell of the duke's duplicity. He could 'speak as fair to his enemy as to his friend,' she wrote, although such a warning was hardly necessary to the astute secretary.[37] Throughout his time at Kenninghall Norfolk kept up his appearance of friendship for the man whom, he was reasonably certain, had engineered his exile, reporting his doings in the country and using him as a means of access to the king. After the fall of Anne Boleyn, in spite of doing his duty as Lord Steward, as the Boleyn party collapsed he imagined that he felt the chill wind of royal disfavour. This was aggravated soon after by the death of his son-in-law, the Duke of Richmond, whom he caused to be quietly interred at Thetford Priory. Richmond was Henry's only illegitimate son, and the king apparently expected him to be buried with royal honours. On 5 August 1536 the duke wrote to his friend Thomas Cromwell, saying that he had heard from several sources

> that the king's highness should be in great displeasure with me because my lord of Richmond was not carried honourably ... A great bruit doth run that I should be in the Tower of London; when I shall deserve to be there Tottenham shall turn French...[38]

Norfolk naturally wanted to come to court and clear his name, but Cromwell did not rise to the bait, and no invitation came. He could be there in a few days, he went on, and begged to be told the truth about these rumours which were being spread about him. He would not, in any case, go to court until he had spoken with the secretary. However, he was not given the chance, and on 10 August he was writing again, still from Kenninghall, acknowledging receipt of a letter (now lost) which had obviously set his mind at rest on the subject of malicious rumours, although it contained no suggestion that he should visit the capital. This time the subject of his concern was more practical. Monastic lands were being distributed and 'every other nobleman hath already his portion'. Would Cromwell please look after his interests, since he was unable to do so himself?[39] This was obviously a task well within the secretary's power, and worth undertaking to preserve the friendship even of so slippery a customer as the Duke of Norfolk, because shortly after, Norfolk, his anxieties apparently forgotten, was writing a letter of fulsome gratitude. Thanks to the king 'for his most kind handling of me', and a million thanks to Cromwell for his pains 'taken in all my affairs'. He had got what he wanted, and was reassured of the king's favour, which was even more important.[40] How large a part the secretary had actually played in this rehabilitation is unclear. Chapuys was under the impression that Cromwell had poisoned the king's mind against the duke, but that is not consistent with what actually happened, and the ambassador was in any case far too willing to listen to gossip, which was often all he had to go on.

In early October 1536 the king sent for Norfolk, not because he wanted his company but because he had a mission for him. The Lincolnshire rebellion had broken out, and the duke was England's foremost military commander. Consequently he was summoned to London, had an amicable interview with the king, and was despatched back to Norfolk to raise troops against the rebels.[41] For the next few weeks military affairs kept him far from the court, and an understanding of what happened there depends upon which source one chooses to read. According to Chapuys, animosity lingered, with Cromwell working to keep Norfolk in the North, and the latter using his friends and agents in an attempt to exploit the rebels' grievances to discredit the secretary with the king. However, the correspondence which passed directly between them tells a different story, with Cromwell working hard to persuade the duke that he was his chief link with the life of the court, and Norfolk begging him for favours particularly in respect of his daughter the Duchess of Richmond.[42] He made Cromwell an executor of his will, and told him stories about the punishments which he had inflicted on those Northern men who had spoken hostile words against the secretary – of whom there were plenty! The early part of 1537 saw the same pattern continued. In March the duke applied for permission to come south, which was refused by the king on the ground that his mission in the North was not completed. However, the letter was drafted by Cromwell, and his hand in keeping Norfolk away from the court is clear enough.[43] The duke kept up his professions of friendship, but in July he ventured to disagree with his mentor's advice to stay where he was, because he had reason to suppose that certain 'back friends', as he put it, were damaging him with the king. In early August he was prevented from seeing Henry when the latter went north to Ampthill, and that did produce an expression of frustration, although not aimed directly at Cromwell, who was probably responsible. It was only in the latter part of the year, when his work in the North was done, and even the secretary could no longer think of plausible reason to keep him away, that Norfolk returned to the court and had an interview with the king.[44] What transpired between them we do not know, but the duke soon returned to Kenninghall and resumed his sequence of friendly letters to Cromwell. By March 1538 he was asking his advice and reassurance concerning his access to the king, and asking anxiously about the latter's attitude towards himself.[45] Neither his absence nor his presence had altered the situation in the slightest.

Cromwell was as firmly in control after the Pilgrimage as he had been before, and it became a wise man to keep on the right side of him. This was especially the case since there were unfocussed rumours of popish sympathies in circulation, which can probably be traced to the Lord Privy Seal, and Norfolk went out of his way to dissociate himself from any such inclinations. So in February 1539, when the duke undertook a three-week diplomatic mission to France, everything was ostensibly sweetness and light between them. However, that did not alter Norfolk's resentment at having to go cap in hand to a 'foul churl' like Cromwell for favours which he considered to be his right as rewards for his nobility and his service. When he returned to the council in March 1539, that resentment was still beneath the surface, but it is reasonable to suspect that the Lord Privy Seal recognised its presence, and assessed his professions of friendship for what they were worth.[46]

His relations with his other principal opponent were less complicated by duplicity. Stephen Gardiner had abandoned Wolsey's service with more haste than dignity after the latter's fall from grace in the autumn of 1529, and had seemed well on the way to power before Cromwell's arrival on the scene. However he had been out of the country, on embassy in France, early in 1532, when Cromwell was gaining the king's ear, and on his return had made the disastrous mistake of replying on behalf of convocation to the Supplication against the Ordinaries. This earned him a period of serious disfavour, in the course of which he lost his office as king's secretary to Thomas Cromwell, who had been acting on his behalf during his absence from court. By this time the two men were enemies, both in principle and in practice, and that hostility came to the surface during the first parliamentary session of 1534, an outburst which earned the bishop a period of rustication to his diocese.[47] It was during this period that Gardiner wrote his only known conciliatory letter to the man in power. On 4 July 1534 he expressed his thanks for the 'friendly handling' of his affairs during his exile, and referred to Cromwell as his 'especial friend'. For the rest his communications with the secretary were on formal matters of business. For his part, Cromwell was too wise to exult in his victory, or to imagine that a man of such evident ability would be permanently out of favour. He even advised him about the writing of *De Vera Obedientia*, which brought about his partial restoration. However, he made sure that Gardiner's employment was far from the court, and must have been at least partly responsible for his posting to the court of France where he remained from September 1535 to July 1538.[48] Away from the council, the bishop was unable to make his views known, or to exercise any influence on the conduct of policy. The letters which passed between them were cool and correct, Cromwell writing to Gardiner in December 1535, congratulating him from the king on the quality of his performance. There was only one flurry which occurred in 1536. The king had granted to Sir Francis Bryan an annuity forfeited by Henry Norris's attainder, which Gardiner thought should have gone to him. He suspected Cromwell's hand in the allocation and wrote a letter of protest to the minister, which provoked a rebuke worthy of quotation:

> Truly, my lord, though my talent be not so precious as yours, yet I trust with his help who gave it to me, to use it so as it shall do his office without gathering such suspicions upon friendship. I repeat that word again because I meant friendly in the writing of it ... And now for that advice which I took to be friendly, you take great pains to make me believe that I have neither friendship in me nor honesty...[49]

The annuity had been allocated by the king's personal wish, without any influence from Cromwell, which was probably nothing but the truth. He warned Gardiner that spending his money lavishly was not advisable while he had debts to pay, and the king had not taken kindly to the claim that it should have been his by law. The protest seems in fact to have done the bishop no harm with the king, who was minded in 1537 to bring him back to the council. However he decided to leave him in post because of the delicate state of Anglo–French relations at that time, and Cromwell may have been behind that decision.[50] Gardiner was naturally pressing for his recall, and his discontent may nave been partly responsible for the deterioration in the diplomatic situation which occurred early in 1538. He was blamed for being irritable and clumsy and the king sent him a letter of reproof in February, which Cromwell went out of his way to explain in conciliatory terms. Henry was not really displeased with him; his words were intended as a spur to greater efforts, 'nothing doubting of the continuance of his favour towards you'.[51] His efforts seem to have been wasted on the disgruntled bishop, who almost certainly blamed him for the terms of the king's letter. Gardiner was eventually recalled in July in response to his repeated requests, and this seems to have implied neither favour nor disfavour because he was allowed to retire to his see until the parliament of 1539 brought him again into the political limelight. Throughout the period from 1532 to 1539 relations between the two men seem to have been characterised by thinly veiled hostility, or at least hostility on Gardiner's part towards the man who had so clearly replaced him in the royal favour. He had no use for the Duke of Norfolk's bland assurances of friendship, and the Lord Privy Seal anticipated his opposition from the first days of the session.

As we have seen, Gardiner's thinking proved closer to the king's over the Act of Six Articles, and that was a setback to Cromwell's programme, but it did not signify any dramatic change of political fortunes. By the autumn of 1539 the Lord Privy Seal appeared to be in charge as usual, and the bishop was back in his see. Cromwell was conducting all manner of business on the king's behalf; supervising the Dissolution of the Monasteries, arranging matters of patronage and receiving reports from English agents abroad. Indeed it was obvious by the time that the parliamentary session ended on 28 June that any intention that Cromwell's enemies might have had to use the Act of Six Articles to bring about his dismissal had failed. It may have been this realisation that caused Norfolk to discard his mask of benevolence and to quarrel openly with the Lord Privy Seal on the 29th. Ironically the occasion was a 'reconciliation dinner', which the king had encouraged Cranmer to provide at Lambeth in an attempt to reduce the hard feelings created by the Act.[52] Gardiner was present, and so also was Tunstall, but they behaved themselves appropriately. Not so Norfolk, who seems deliberately to have picked a quarrel with Cromwell over the legacy of Thomas Wolsey, which resulted in high words on both sides. The archbishop pacified them to the best of his ability, but thereafter there was no longer any pretence of friendship between the two, and their subsequent correspondence was strictly on matters of business. This may have come as a relief to the Lord Privy Seal, who was now under no illusion as to the identities of his principal opponents. Although he was no doubt glad to get him out of the country, Norfolk's mission to France in February 1540 also enabled the duke to stir up anti-Cromwell sentiment at the French court. Gardiner's hostility had already rubbed off on Francis's servants, and Norfolk was able to point out that Cromwell had always been Imperialist in his foreign policy (which was true) and had been restrained from being more open about it mainly by the wishes of the king.[53] Norfolk, on the other hand, had always been pro-French, and the improvement in Anglo–French relations that resulted from this mission was an underhand blow against the Cleves alliance, which the Lord Privy Seal had arranged. With France in a friendly mood, Cleves became dispensable, and with it the Lord Cromwell. The King of France was certainly hostile to him, and it is possible that the duke brought back with him secret assurances of French support if he should be overthrown. The king certainly knew that he would not be running any risks in his foreign policy if he should decide to remove him from office.

Cromwell's fate, however, was not decided in France, but in England, and even within the king's own mind. Robert Barnes, who had been on mission to the Elector of Saxony and the King of Denmark early in 1539, had returned home when the Act of Six Articles made his efforts useless, and Henry, annoyed by his decision to return without being called, refused to see him in spite of Cromwell's intercession.[54] Ignoring this clear evidence that Barnes was no longer in favour, his patron persuaded the Bishop of St Davids to bestow upon him the Welsh prebend of Llanbedye, and thus provided clear evidence of where his sympathies lay. Should the reforming preacher commit any indiscretions in future, it would be relatively easy to hold his patron responsible, and that is precisely what Barnes did. In February 1540 the Bishop of Winchester preached at Paul's Cross, denouncing certain reformed positions in unmeasured terms. This may well have been a deliberate provocation, to tempt anyone who dared to respond, and if so it worked, because a fortnight later Robert Barnes rose to the bait. Relying perhaps on Cromwell to protect him, he denied all that Gardiner had said, and openly insulted him.[55] This was a step too far, and the Lord Privy Seal, recognising the limits of his authority, did not intervene. The Bishop of Winchester complained to the king, who was scandalised at this treatment of one of his councillors and ordered Barnes to be examined before him. Having declared him to be defeated in a theological argument, he ordered him to apologise to Gardiner and to preach a recantation sermon, which Barnes duly did at Paul's Cross on 12 March.[56] There the matter might have ended, except that the reformer's conscience smote him sore and on 30 March he publicly withdrew his recantation. Henry was enraged, not only by this act of defiance but also by the evidence which it provided that the Act Abolishing Diversity in Opinion had failed in its purpose. Barnes and two reforming colleagues, Thomas Garrett and William Jerome, ended up in the Tower, and London was full of rumours. The French ambassador reported that Cranmer and Cromwell did not know where they were, and forecast great changes within the next few days.[57] Marillac had probably been listening to the hopes of the Duke of Norfolk's friends, and those hopes proved premature. The council had indeed been recast, and Gardiner and Tunstall readmitted, which would have been little to the Lord Privy Seal's pleasure, but there is no hard evidence that his own position was under threat; except perhaps the effort which he made to repair his relations with Gardiner. This took the form of an invitation to dinner on 30 March, in the course of which they spent four hours, ostensibly restoring their damaged friendship. This constituted a strategic retreat on Cromwell's part, and protected him against any possible fallout from Barnes's behaviour.[58] It did not, however, alter the fact that Gardiner was back in favour and in contact with the king, from whom Cromwell had for so long succeeded in excluding him.

It was at about this time in March 1540, that Cromwell surrendered his office of secretary to the king. His motives for doing so are not very clear, but since he was allowed to dispose of it more or less to suit himself, it cannot have been due to hostile pressure. It was of course in Henry's gift, but it must have been Cromwell who decided to divide it into two, and to appoint two of his own servants, Ralph Sadler and Thomas Wriothesley, to discharge it, an appointment which took effect around 1 April. This may have been connected with his own forthcoming promotion, or it may have been due to his desire to increase his influence within a divided council.[59] If it was the latter, then it did not work because neither of them spoke decisively in his support, or made any move to defend him when the crunch came. What it does prove, however, is that Cromwell's influence with the king was unimpaired as late as the middle of April. This impression is confirmed by his elevation to the Earldom of Essex on the 18th of the month. This ancient and prestigious earldom had been vacated by the death of Henry Bourchier without heirs as recently as March 1540, and on the same day Cromwell was created Lord Great Chamberlain, an office vacated by the death of John de Vere, Earl of Oxford, at about the same time.[60] The earldom of Essex had escheated to the Crown on Bouchier's death, and was therefore unquestionably available, but the great chamberlainship had been hereditary in the de Vere family for several generations, and Cromwell's appointment meant disappointing the legitimate expectations of the 16th Earl. It is highly unlikely that the Duke of Norfolk would have regarded either of these promotions with any sympathy, holding as he did strong views upon the virtues of hereditary nobility. Cromwell's elevation was exclusively the king's doing, and represented the highest expression of his favour. About a month later, just after the reassembly of Parliament on 25 May, Cromwell brought off his last major coup with the arrest of Richard Sampson, Bishop of Chichester, and Dr Nicholas Wotton, staunch conservatives in religious matters.[61] Both were members of the committees which had been established in April for the examination of doctrine and ceremonies, and Sampson has been described as Gardiner's right-hand man in the struggle with the Lord Privy Seal. The charge was popish sympathies, and Cromwell was alleged to have his eye on five other bishops, who were not named but almost certainly included Gardiner and Tunstall.[62] On 11 May Lord Lisle, the Deputy of Calais, had been summoned home and placed under arrest for suspected dealings with Reginald Pole, and that also may be attributed to Cromwell's influence. However in that case the tactic backfired because the resulting investigation also revealed the activities of the sacramentary preacher Adam Damplip, which damaged both Cranmer's and Cromwell's credibility.[63] Sampson was probably arrested on Cromwell's orders alone, but if that was so then the king made haste to endorse his action, and was, according to Sadler, highly displeased with the bishop's answers to the interrogatories which had so far been administered to him. Rumours flew about; Latimer was to be released from house arrest when Henry had spoken to Cromwell about his case, and Barnes would be freed from the Tower. To all appearances the Lord Privy Seal was as much in command of the situation as he ever had been, and the only negative sign was that the king would not allow Bishop Sampson's goods to be confiscated, which indicated that he had not made up his mind about him.

There were therefore no outward indications that the king was about to turn on his Lord Privy Seal, although the reactions of his councillors indicate that they were not taken by surprise. At about noon on 10 June, Cromwell left the parliament where he had been attending to normal business and went to a Privy Council meeting. At three o'clock the door of the chamber opened to admit the Captain of the Guard and half a dozen halberdiers. The captain bore a warrant carrying the royal seal, for the arrest of the Earl of Essex on a charge of high treason. If we are to believe Marillac, Cromwell cast down his bonnet with a gesture of exasperation, and asked if this was a fair reward for all his services.[64] He appealed to his fellow councillors, but they said not a word in his defence, some reviling him and others saying that he should be judged by his own laws, by which presumably they meant the 1534 Treasons Act, which had been largely of his devising. If Marillac is correct these words were ill advised because all laws were the king's, but they passed unrebuked in the heat of the moment. The Duke of Norfolk, with opprobrious comments about his unworthiness to keep company with members of the royal family, relieved him of the insignia of the Garter, and he was hustled out by a side entrance and conveyed by boat to the Tower.[65] Cromwell had been installed as a Knight of the Garter in August 1537, when he had been at the height of his power. It was special sign of the royal favour, but had hitherto been reserved largely for those who were of the royal blood, or whose services had been of a military nature, to which Cromwell could lay no claim. The duke, in spite of his smooth professions of friendship, had been particularly incensed by this creation, and no doubt welcomed the opportunity which the Lord Privy Seal's disgrace had offered. Seeing the way in which the council had turned against him, Cromwell is alleged to have renounced all hope of pardon and asked only for a quick end.

The reasons for Henry's *volte-face* in early June 1540 have been much debated. One theory is that Cromwell was made to shoulder the blame for the failed Cleves marriage, and the king's words make that plausible, except that he had already pointed to the way out and there is no reason to suppose that he could not have arranged the annulment in the way which was eventually done.[66] Henry was very good at blaming others for his own mistakes, but there is no conclusive evidence that he did so on this occasion. Another idea is that the king was already infatuated with Catherine Howard, and that Cromwell was hanging back on annulling the Cleves marriage because he had no desire to see the Duke of Norfolk's niece installed in Anne's place. In other words he was in the same fix that Wolsey had been in 1529 when confronted with the rise to favour of Anne Boleyn, and this is true up to a point. It is certainly true that Cromwell had no desire to see the fortunes of the Howard clan in the ascendant, and regarded Catherine with distaste, but there is no evidence that he was delaying the Cleves solution for that reason.[67] He probably already knew that the Duke of Cleves would accept whatever decision Henry reached, and that the treaty would not be annulled by her rejection, because the duke's relations with the Emperor over the Duchy of Gelderland were far from resolved. The third idea is that the king was worried by the evidence of religious dissent which confronted him on all sides, and blamed Cromwell for encouraging the dissidents. This distrust was converted by interested parties, particularly the Bishop of Winchester, into the conviction that his Lord Privy Seal was a closet Lutheran, a conviction more obvious in the charges against him than in anything which he had actually done. After Cromwell's arrest, Henry sent word to Marillac to explain his action, which according to the ambassador had taken everyone by surprise.

The substance of the charge was that, while the king wished by all possible means to lead back religion to the ways of truth, Cromwell, as attached to the German Lutherans, had always favoured the doctors who preached such erroneous opinions and hindered those who preached the contrary. Recently, warned by some of his principal servants to reflect that he was working against the intention of the king and the Acts of Parliament, he betrayed himself and said he hoped to suppress the old preachers and have only the new, adding that the affair would soon be brought to such a pass that the king, with all his power, could not prevent it. But rather that his own party would be so strong that he would make the king descend to the new doctrines, even if he had to take arms against him.[68]

It was in the last part of this statement that the treason lay, and that is the least plausible. These were no doubt reported to the king as Cromwell's words, but it is very unlikely that he ever uttered them. Why should he give such hostages to fortune, knowing that any words he spoke could be turned against him? He had undoubtedly favoured those who preached reformed opinions, but that did not make him a Lutheran, let alone a sacramentary, a radical heresy of which Henry had a particular abhorrence, and of which Cromwell was also accused. Although other factors may have contributed to influence the king's mind, it seems that religion lay at the heart of his decisive change of mind, and that Gardiner rather than Norfolk was the critical agent.[69]

Meanwhile Cromwell's houses had been seized and his goods inventoried. That same afternoon, royal archers turned up at his home in Austin Friars, listed the contents and took away certain valuables to the king's treasury.[70] This was an ominous sign for the accused man, and indicated that there was unlikely to be a way back. Letters were also alleged to have been discovered, which had passed between Cromwell and the Lutheran princes of Germany, incriminating him still further. Marillac could not learn the contents, but the king was now so exasperated against him that 'he would no longer hear him spoken of ... the greatest wretch that ever was born in England'. If any letters ever existed they were almost certainly plants, because Cromwell was far too careful to leave such documents lying about, which was clearly the implication. However the king was further incensed against him, and that was the object of the exercise. Parliament and the foreign envoys were given the official version of what had happened that same afternoon, and the latter transmitted the news to their respective governments, for the most part with supporting commentary. Edward Hall recorded the reaction in London, when he wrote,

> Many lamented but more rejoiced, especially such as had been religious men for, they banqueted and triumphed that night, many wishing that day had been seven years before [but] some fearing lest he should escape ... could not be merry. Others who knew nothing but truth by him, both lamented him and heartily prayed for him. Of certain of the clergy he was detestably hated ... for he was a man ... [who] could not abide the snuffling pride of some prelates...[71]

In the circumstances it is not surprising that hardly anyone wrote in defence of the accused man, or that those who did so should have veiled their opinions in incredulity and obsequious language. Richard Pate, writing from Bruges, was appalled to learn of the treason of one who had been his benefactor and patron. He should, he went on, have eschewed the reformers and followed the king in religious matters; he who had been so patient with those of the 'adverse party'.[72] Archbishop Cranmer also wrote on the 12th, a letter full of contradictory emotions. He had not been close to Cromwell personally, but was his firmest ally in political terms, and particularly in the reform of the Church. He was also amazed that so good a servant of the king should be found to have committed treason; one who had shown such 'wisdom, diligence, faithfulness and experience as no prince in this realm ever had'. He had been so vigilant to protect the king from all treasons that he found it incredible that he should have fallen into that way himself. He had, he professed, loved Cromwell as a friend,

> but I chiefly loved him for the love which I thought I saw him bear ever towards your grace singularly above all others. But now if he be a traitor, I am sorry that ever I loved him or trusted him, and I am very glad that his treason has been discovered in time. But yet again I am very sorrowful, for whom should your grace trust hereafter...[73]

This letter came within a touch of suggesting that Henry was mistaken, and that he had been bamboozled by the conservative faction, but it did not actually say so and concluded with a plea for mercy on the grounds of Cromwell's record. Nevertheless it was a brave letter to have written, and gives a good indication as to why Crammer was kept away from Henry by his traditionalist 'minders' during the days immediately after the arrest. The reactions from abroad were predictable. Francis rejoiced, and wrote to congratulate his friend Henry on his narrow escape; the Emperor fell on his knees and thanked God; only the Lutheran princes mourned the passing of a friend, and they made little of their sympathy for fear of upsetting the king, with whom they still hoped for some kind of an understanding.[74]

It did not take Henry long to realise that the best testimony to his lack of consent to his marriage with Anne would come from his imprisoned minister, to whom he had confided each step in his mounting frustration. He therefore suggested, via Sir William Paulet, that a letter of confession would be acceptable, or as Cromwell put it in his response dated 12 June, 'that I should write to your most excellent highness such things as I thought meet to be written concerning my most miserable state and condition'. In that letter he confessed many things; on one occasion, prompted thereto by the king, he had spoken privily to her Lord Chamberlain 'and others of the queen's council, being with me in my Chamber at Westminster' to suggest that they quietly advise her to be more agreeable to her husband. He had done this without naming the king as the source of his concern, for which he humbly sought pardon. He concluded,

> For my offences to your grace which God knoweth were neither malicious nor wilful, and that I never thought treason to your highness, your realm or posterity, so God help me ... I appeal to your highness for mercy, grace and pardon...[75]

Henry received this missive without recorded comment, but he was not satisfied, and he sent Norfolk, Audley and Southampton to examine Cromwell at the Tower, and to urge him 'upon the extreme danger and damnation of [his] soul to say what [he] knew in the marriage and concerning the marriage between your highness and the queen'.[76] This provoked a second and more explicit response from the prisoner on 30 June, in which he went into all the details which Henry had confided to him about his relationship with Anne, including feeling her breasts and being sure that she was no maid, and that 'your heart could never consent to meddle with her carnally'.[77] Realising perhaps that he had no more to say, and that his usefulness to Henry was coming to an end, he finished this epistle with the words, 'Most gracious prince, I cry for mercy, mercy, mercy...' Cromwell knew perfectly well that any attempt at self-justification would be counter-productive, implying as it would that the king was mistaken in his judgement. Henry did not make mistakes, and if mistakes were made in his name, there was always someone to blame. On the other hand a confession of guilt and an abject plea for pardon might just possibly touch a responsive chord in his egotistical heart.

It was worth a try, but it did not work because others were on hand to make sure that it did not, and a Bill of Attainder was introduced into the Lords on 17 June, proceeding to the Commons on the 19th. There it seems to have stuck, not out of any sympathy for Cromwell but because a proviso was added to safeguard the property of the Deanery of Wells, which he also held and which would have been forfeit to the Crown along with the rest of his property.[78] Ten days later the amended Bill was returned to the Lords and passed through all its stages in one day – clearly it was not controversial. Why his enemies decided to proceed against him by Act of Attainder instead of by trial before the Lord High Steward is not clear. Perhaps they did not care to face the defence which he could certainly have mounted against the charges which they had prepared against him. Perhaps it was considered to be an appropriate way to deal with a man who had used that method so often himself. Perhaps they did not want to acknowledge his new-found nobility, or perhaps it was simply because the king would have it so. The Act lamented the fact that one whom the king had raised from 'very base and low degree' to be one of his most trusty councillors 'as well concerning your grace's supreme jurisdiction ecclesiastical as your most high secret affairs temporal' should have turned out to be a false and corrupt traitor.[79] It then listed the charges against him. He had, it was alleged, on his own authority, released those who had been convicted of misprision of treason, and had issued licences for his own profit for the export of coin and various other prohibited commodities. 'Elated and full of pride', he had constituted commissions without the king's knowledge or consent, and had claimed great power over Henry, 'a thing which no subject should say of his prince'. Also on his own authority, and without the king's consent, he had granted passports 'to pass without search', presumably a form of licensed smuggling. So far these charges had been of abuse of office rather than treason, but the Bill then proceeded to more serious accusations. 'Being a damnable heretic' he had caused heretical writings to be translated into English and spread abroad 'to sow sedition and variance among your true and loving subjects', and had abused his office as Viceregent in Spirituals to license other heretics to teach and preach.[80] In the same way, falsely pretending the king's consent, he had released imprisoned heretics and refused to listen to charges against them. The Bill then proceeded from the general to the specific, and Cromwell was accused of saying 'on 31 March in the parish of St

Peter Le Poor in the City of London' that the teaching of Robert Barnes was good, and that if the king should turn against reform, yet he would not turn and would if necessary fight in the field against him.[81] This was undoubtedly treason by the Act of 1534, and was the core of the charges against him, but might be difficult to prove. The remaining charge was one of *scandalum magnatum* rather than treason in that it related to his abusive reaction to those who reminded him of his humble origins.

Cromwell's defence against these accusations was circumstantial and detailed, and there is no doubt that the charges were a tissue of lies and exaggerations. However, that did not matter; Norfolk and Gardiner had succeeded in convincing the king, and he was the only person who needed to be convinced, because Parliament would follow him. Improbable as it may seem, Henry's conviction was genuine, because he was seeing traitors in all sorts of unlikely places, and heretics behind every bush.[82] He had become more than a little neurotic about Cromwell, being well aware that he had trusted him too far in the days of his favour. Being anxious to avoid the drudgery of paperwork, he had allowed his minister to manage things in his own way, and was now uneasily aware that things had happened of which he would not have approved if he had been concentrating. So he had to exaggerate Cromwell's duplicity in order to justify himself, and the Bill of Attainder was prepared with that in mind. The tactic worked and the Act received the royal assent on 24 July. It was only then, when the attainder became effective, that Thomas Cromwell ceased to be Earl of Essex. The Bill itself referred to him by that title and in all the correspondence which passed between him and the king and council, he is always so described. It was only in Marillac's imagination that he became 'Thomas Cromwell, shearman' after his arrest.[83] Perhaps the ambassador was hoping to see him executed in the manner appropriate to a treacherous shearman, by hanging, drawing and quartering, but if that was the case then he was disappointed. The former Lord Privy Seal was despatched by the axe on 28 July on Tower Green, as became his proper status. 'My prayer,' he had once said, 'is that God give me no longer life than I shall be glad to use my office in edification and not in destruction', and he seems to have come to his end with a quiet conscience. As was expected he made an address from the scaffold, although whether it was that recorded by Edward Hall is not known. 'I am come hither to die,' he is alleged to have told the crowd, 'and not to purge myself as some think peradventure that I will do.'[84] He acknowledged that he had offended God and the king, and asked forgiveness of both. 'I die,' he went on, 'in the Catholic faith, not doubting any article of my faith ... nor in any sacrament of the church.' He probably used the word 'Catholic' in the same sense as Melanchthon had used it, but his statement about the sacraments disposes of any notion that he was a radical, or even a Lutheran, because the Augsburg Confession did not acknowledge four out of the traditional seven. His final prayer, on the other hand, does raise questions about justification by faith alone.

> Of sins and evil works I see, alas, a great heap ... but through thy mercy I trust to be in the number of them to whom thou wilt not impute their sins, but will take and accept me for righteous and just, and to be the inheritor of everlasting life ... Most merciful Saviour ... Let thy blood cleanse and wash away the spots and foulness of my sins. Let thy righteousness hide and cover my unrighteousness. Let the merits of thy passion and blood shedding be satisfaction for my sins...[85]

So Cromwell departed as he had lived, with unanswered questions about his religion, and it is probably wisest to assume that his evangelical sympathies embraced some aspects of Lutheranism, but not others, and that he was certainly not a sacramentary. Edward Hall was one of those who mourned his passing, but the most eloquent epitaph was penned by his friend and protégé Sir Thomas Wyatt:

> The pillar perished is whereto I leaned,
> The strongest stay of my unquiet mind,
> The like of it no man again can find –
> From East to West still seeking though he went –
> To mine unhap, for hap away hath rent
> Of all my joy the very bark and rind...[86]

Two days later, three of Cromwell's more obvious clients, who had been in prison since Barnes retracted his recantation on 30 March – Robert Barnes himself, William Jerome and Thomas Garrett – were burned at Smithfield. Barnes was certainly a Lutheran, but that had not prevented Cromwell from using him as a diplomatic agent no further back that the beginning of 1540. None of these men was guilty of the radical heresies with which they were charged, but it was deemed necessary as part of the campaign against Cromwell to represent him as the controlling force behind a dangerous heretical conspiracy — and these were the other conspirators, or some of them. Like him they were condemned by Act of Attainder, and Barnes at least proclaimed his innocence in his last speech to the crowd.[87] He had never preached sedition or disobedience, and had used his learning against the Anabaptists. He did not know why he was condemned to die, but the true answer lay not in his own doings or beliefs, but in his association with Thomas Cromwell. At the same time three adherents of the old faith, Edward Powell. Richard Fetherstone and Thomas Abel, were executed as traitors for denying the Royal Supremacy. Their deaths must also be laid at the king's door, but the true story again relates indirectly to Cromwell's fall, because his enemies had to demonstrate that they were loyal subjects of the king, and had no sympathy with those papists against whom he had so rigorously set his face.[88] They were every bit as zealous in the cause of the ecclesiastical supremacy as he had been. Not for the first time (or the last), the machinations of Henry's servants left him with the responsibility for unnecessary and brutal executions. At the time, the king was much incensed against Cromwell, and ignored those who argued for his years of good service, but the mood did not last. In March 1541, when his leg was troubling him and he was feeling particularly sorry for himself, he berated his councillors for having deprived him of the best servant that he had ever had.[89] Whether he was missing Cromwell's expertise in affairs of state or his diligence in running the administrative machine is not clear, perhaps it was a little of both, but in any case his successors did not live up to the exacting standards which he had set. So alone among the victims of Henry's whims and policies, Thomas Cromwell received a sort of posthumous pardon. No document to that effect survives, but his son Gregory was raised to a barony, notwithstanding his father's attainder in December 1540, and so must have been restored in blood.

8

CROMWELL AND THE STATE

Who is he that can think himself to have any vein of an honest man, that feareth not God, that loveth not his country, that obeyeth not his Prince...

Sir Richard Morison

Thomas Cromwell was not an intellectual, and wrote nothing specifically directed to any theory of the state, but what he believed can be deduced from his letters and from his acts of patronage. Reginald Pole's famous description of him as a Machiavellian can be discounted, because it was written in the aftermath of his role in the destruction of Pole's family, when the cardinal's animus against him was obvious and understandable. It relates to a conversation which he had allegedly had with Cromwell several years previously in 1535, the last time when such an exchange would have been possible, and about three years after *The Prince* was published.[1] Cromwell had explained that he had told the king, in an interview which did not in fact take place, that the distinction between right and wrong did not apply to kings, and that political morality was different from the ethics which applied to ordinary people. He had also said that no realm could have two masters, and that the headship of the Church was his by right, all of which was being wise after the event. They had also discussed the proper role of a councillor, and Cromwell had declared that the first concern of such a person must be to serve the honour and advantage of his prince, and if he does his work well, his master's ambitions will be achieved without any sign of discord in his realm. However a show of moral virtue must be maintained, and only those inexperienced in the ways of the world (like Pole) would be shocked by such sentiments.[2] All this could indeed be garnered from the pages of *The Prince*, but whether Cromwell had so gathered it is not known. Pole admitted that he had met Cromwell only the once, and was not acquainted with his circle. He also confessed that the secretary never put forward his 'blasphemous' ideas in public, but rather posed as a good Christian. In fact we have the testimony of Thomas Starkey, who knew them both, that they were 'almost unacquainted and of small familiarity'.[3] So Pole's account of their alleged conversation in 1535 can be discounted as evidence of Cromwell's actual opinions; it only reflects the way in which the cardinal thought that he should have been expressing himself.

Thomas was interested in theories, however, and although he had little opinion of Plato, which he had obviously read, he thought better of other writings on the state, noticeably those of Aristotle. He also knew his Bible, as is demonstrated by his refutation of Fisher's use of Amos, and by his reproof to Shaxton for quoting the scriptures out of context, both of which citations are included in letters to the respective parties rather than in public utterances. He was sufficiently interested in legal theory to declare that the Divine Law was irrelevant to the affairs of England, an opinion again expressed in a private letter to Fisher, and not altogether consistent with his public pronouncements in Parliament.[4] The best evidence of his interest in theory comes from the testimony of Thomas Starkey, who was an ideas man by profession and well known to the secretary, who says that he had many conversations with him 'of God, of nature, and of other politic and worldly things', including the writings of Aristotle. There was no reason why Starkey should have misrepresented these exchanges, and although they also took place in private, no particular pains were taken to conceal them.[5] Taken in conjunction with his letters, they prove conclusively that Cromwell was no mere pragmatist, but made a conscience of what he did. As to his Machiavellianism, as Elton has rightly pointed out, *The Prince* is not so much a work of moral philosophy as a presentation of things as they are, and that it would be hard indeed to find any competent statesman of the sixteenth century who did not follow its advice at least to some extent.[6] Richard Morison, who was certainly a member of Cromwell's circle, knew the Florentine's works by 1535, so it is reasonable to suppose that he understood his general drift, but whether the secretary ever read *The Prince* is not known.

Cromwell was a practical man, and his letters generally stick to the point. Only occasionally do they indulge in those generalisations which give an insight into his ways of thinking. One example of such occurs in March 1538, when he wrote to the Bishop of Salisbury that his prayer was that 'God give me no longer life than I shall be glad to use my office in edification and not in destruction'. He never destroyed anything without the intention of putting something better in its place, which is interesting in view of the number of men and institutions which he swept away in the course of his reforming career.[7] He is generally reputed to have been a radical, and in so far as he disregarded obstacles in his way, that description is justified, but he was very anxious not to appear radical in his constructive work. Since innovation was a dirty word in the sixteenth century, such caution was fully justified. He preached moderation, especially to the bishops of his own way of thinking, when it came to the enforcement of reforming practices and doctrines. Intensely sensitive to the need for public order, and to the king's views on that matter, he urged them as far as possible to avoid 'contention, division and contrariety in opinion in the unlearned multitude', and to be lenient in their punishment of offenders.[8] In the debates surrounding the publication of the *Institution of a Christian Man* he made much the same point, demanding unity on a basis of moderation, and avoiding such words as 'papist' and 'sacramentary'. This debate apparently took place in an informal gathering of bishops early in 1537, where Cromwell went out of his way to be conciliatory, and of which we owe our knowledge to Alexander Alesius, whose *Of the auctorite of the word of god* was published in 1540. Cromwell apparently picked up Alesius, who was known to him, on his way to the meeting, to which he introduced him, to the consternation of some of those present. Alesius was a Scot and a known reformer.[9] In 1539 Cromwell wished to treat the Calais sacramentaries 'without rigour or extreme dealing', not because he sympathised with their point of view, but because their execution would have drawn attention to the disunion which existed in the realm. In that case he was overruled by the king, who saw such people as a dangerous menace, but his preference for relative gentleness is worth noting.

He said much the same thing in the House of Lords in 1540, when he again insisted on the need for moderation and unity in religious matters. In all his enforcement policies steady pressure rather than severity of punishment was the key. Like those who set out to suppress heresy, his aim was submission rather than execution, and on the whole, as we shall see, he was successful.[10]

He also thought a good deal about the law, which formed an important part of his own professional background. Unlike Wolsey, he had no desire to be a judge, and did not, as far as is known, ever sit in that capacity while he was Master of the Rolls. Nevertheless he cultivated a reputation for judicial fairness in his dealings with offenders, and was careful always to ensure that the formal procedures of the law were observed, telling Fisher, for example, that his private opinions were irrelevant because his case would be decided by the evidence produced in court.[11] When his own time came he wrote that 'the trial of the law only consisteth in honest and probable witness', a trial which he was to be denied by the process of attainder. Attainder was a method to which he had himself resorted when there was any doubt about the evidence available being sufficient to convince a jury, which was also, in a sense, a gesture of respect towards the common law. Cromwell, therefore, regarded the law with reverence, and the stories of his securing the condemnation of offenders on slender grounds, and of using political power to secure convictions on evidence which should not have stood up in court, are serious misrepresentations of the truth. He was also a common lawyer, and stoutly defended the king's ordinary courts against the encroachments of both equity and the civil law. About equity he could do little beyond urging potential litigants to think carefully before embarking upon suits in Star Chamber or Requests. The decisions of neither had the finality of King's Bench or Common Pleas, and this might need to be explained.[12] The procedures of both courts were relatively rapid, but their main appeal was that they offered remedies in cases where there was no relevant law, such as slander.[13] However, potential cases needed to be scrutinised to make sure that they fell into that category, and it was possibly for that reason that Requests acquired a common lawyer as a part of its permanent staff during his years in power. Requests, like the Admiralty, was otherwise a bastion of the civil lawyers. There was, however, no such thing as a reception of the civil law, and it is by no means clear who would have wanted such a thing. Wolsey, as Chancellor, may have favoured it, but his successors Thomas More and Thomas Audley were both common lawyers by training, and it never advanced much beyond the specialist courts already referred to. Several of the conservative bishops, notably Gardiner and Tunstall, were canon lawyers by background, but neither had much impact on policy in this respect, and Cromwell arranged for the canon law faculties of both universities to be closed down in 1535, as a part of his campaign against popery.[14] Several of the Crown's lesser servants were civilians, but they had no influence on official attitudes, and the stoutest protagonist of reception was Reginald Pole, who was in exile for the whole decade, and in disgrace for most of it. Before he entered the royal service, Cromwell had run a flourishing legal practice, and legal work continued to occupy a significant proportion of his time; he held powers of attorney, and acted for the Crown in cases of debt, and several other types of suit. He was a member of Gray's Inn, and knew his Bracton well enough to commend him for giving the king the title *vicarius Christi*.[15] There is no proof that he remembered that, according to the same source, *rex debet esse sub lege*, but he always acted in accordance with that principle. The common law was a remarkably tough code, especially when threatened with the Roman alternative, and much of that toughness it seems to have owed to the leadership of Thomas Cromwell. It was Stephen Gardiner, many years later, who claimed to remember Cromwell quoting to him the civil law precept *quad principi placuit, leges habet vigorem* in justification of some arbitrary action, but if Gardiner's memory was accurate it seems likely that the bishop was being twitted with a legal principle far more subversive of the king's honour than the common law to which he adhered.

It is an enduring myth that Cromwell rode roughshod over the law in pursuit of those who opposed the king's policies. Such cases were usually brought to his attention by voluntary information, not infrequently by the personal enemies of the guilty party, and his first reaction was almost invariably to order an investigation. A fairly typical example occurred in Windsor in April 1538, when the parish priest, Richard Lawson, was charged with treasonable words by Robert Guy, a singing man of the college who was obviously sympathetic to reform.[16] One afternoon in early April Guy decided to annoy two conservative citizens by quoting the king's proclamation permitting the eating of white meats during Lent, on the grounds that the prohibition was merely a 'popish superstition'. It was not to be murmured or grudged at, he added, which produced hasty disclaimers from the two worthy citizens. Warming to his task, Guy then switched his attack to Richard Lawson, accusing him of sexual improprieties in the confessional, and of warning one Agnes Wilson not to eat meat in Lent just because her husband did so, and so consequently urging her to break the king's proclamation. To Guy this was proof that the priest would not obey the king's orders and was thus a 'privy traitor'. He must then have laid his information before a local magistrate, because within two days an investigation was under way.[17] Under interrogation Guy accused Lawson of superstitious practices, which the latter denied. However, a couple of months earlier he had warned the priest to be more convincing in his prayers for the queen and the prince, and to declare the king's title to the people as he was bound to do. Lawson rebuffed him, whereupon he repeated his warning publicly in the presence of the mayor, who had seconded his urgings. The priest then turned surly and declared that he had never received instructions from his bishop about preaching the king's title, which was almost certainly untrue at this late date. The results of this examination were then communicated to Cromwell, who effectively ignored them, and nothing further happened.[18] Lawson was clearly a malcontent, but Guy was equally clearly a personal enemy and his talk of treason ridiculously exaggerated. Similar dubious denunciations came from all over England. Dr Horde, the prior of the Charterhouse at Henton in Somerset, was reported in May 1533 by a disgruntled inmate of the neighbouring house of Witham, who alleged that he had attacked Queen Anne, and claimed that he would never consent to the king's second marriage. Cromwell presumably did nothing beyond warning Dr Horde to guard his tongue. and a year later the same informant was telling him that all the Somerset Carthusians were disaffected, and would prefer death to obedience.[19] The Prior of Henton, however, was an old friend of the secretary, and in 1535 was able to write gratefully that he was pleased that their goodwill was not 'utterly extinct'. Although a number of charges were laid against him, including seeing 'seditious visions' (whatever they might have been) and running a house full of the disaffected, he survived as prior until 1539 when he reluctantly but peacefully surrendered. As he accepted his pension, he noted that the Lord Privy Seal had always been his 'especial good lord', which seems to have been nothing but the truth. Cromwell must have concluded that the charges against Horde arose out of malice on the part of his accusers, although the evidence for that is lacking.[20]

It was not always thus, and when a riot broke out at Taunton in April 1536 it was very differently handled. This was provoked by the activities of a purveyance commission, which was buying up grain at a time of dearth. The rioters were gaoled, but an armed demonstration demanded their release, threatening the magistrates. The trouble spread to Frome, where the disaffected were confronted by a local gentleman, Robert Liversiche, who was well supported. Their courage failed them and they laid down their arms without a fight.[21] However the threat had appeared to be real, and when Cromwell was informed, on 7 April he wrote ordering them to be dealt with severely. In the king's name he issued a commission of oyer and terminer, which sat in judgement before the end of the month, and sentenced twelve of them to death. They were executed in three different places over the next couple of weeks. Fifty others were also condemned, but being penitent and not ringleaders they were allowed to buy their pardons; personal recognisances of £20 and £10 in sureties being required from each of them.[22] Henry was very pleased with the prompt and severe response to this abortive riot, and in the light of what was to happen at Louth only six months later, one can see why. Cromwell was quite prepared to act ruthlessly, even when political and religious issues were not involved, but he was always concerned to use the due process of the law. At Bristol the situation was different again, because there the troubles were caused almost exclusively by religion and were stirred up by the arrival of Hugh Latimer, the reforming preacher who was favoured by the town authorities. Latimer had already been censured by convocation, but that did not prevent the mayor from appointing him to preach the Lent sermons in 1533. The Bristol conservatives struck back by importing William Hubberdyne, a popular preacher whose appeal rivalled Latimer's own, and battle royal was joined, setting the town by the ears.[23] The chancellor of the diocese then inhibited them both, and informed Cromwell of his action. The latter responded by upholding his ban on Hubberdyne because the conservatives were notorious partisans of Queen Catherine, but ordering that on Latimer to be lifted. The remaining conservatives stepped into Hubberdyne's shoes, however, and the battle continued. By 5 June the reformers were sufficiently incensed, and sufficiently sure of themselves, to send a complaint to the king's council, which was promptly referred to Cromwell. According to the protesters, Hubberdyne, before he was inhibited, had said that the Pope was above all kings, and that in matters of the faith he could not err. He had also claimed that the English Bible led men into heresy.[24] Although he swiftly presented Cromwell with his side of the case, claiming malice, the secretary was not convinced and on 4 July ordered him to the Tower. On the 10th the mayor wrote to Cromwell, thanking him for the prompt action that he had taken. At the same time the secretary ordered a commission to be appointed to examine the Bristol stirs, and carefully excluded known partisans such as the mayor, who would otherwise have been expected to serve. Instead he chose five local worthies under the chairmanship of the Abbot of St Augustine's, and they began their work on 6 July.[25] In several sessions between 9 and 11 July a large number of witnesses came forward, and although the commissioners' powers covered both parties, all the testimony was against Hubberdyne, who, it was claimed, had reviled the men of the new learning and stated that to deny the Pope's authority was heresy. In sending their report to Cromwell, the commissioners admitted that the evidence with which they had been presented was biased, but unless the king provided a remedy, 'more inconvenience' was likely to ensue.[26] Hubberdyne remained in the Tower, and Latimer, presumably on Cromwell's orders, ceased to preach in Bristol and went to work under Cranmer's direct authority in London. The situation in Bristol was pacified, at least for the time being.

Cromwell was not, therefore, concerned to harry dissidents, even those who mixed a measure of politics with their religious protest, and certainly not those whose zeal for reform outran their discretion. What he was concerned to do was to ensure the preservation of the king's peace and good order in the realm, and to punish severely those who threatened that peace. This could involve some difficult decisions. Mrs Amadas, for example, the widow of his predecessor as Master of the Jewel House, was something of a wise woman who claimed to have been in the prophesying business for twenty years. In 1533 she declared that her 'book of prophecy' had told her that the king was the moldwarp, and that he would be banished from the realm before midsummer.[27] Her sayings rambled on obscurely, but ended with some straightforward abuse of Queen Anne and Thomas Cromwell. The latter was called upon to investigate and had her to the Tower for interrogation, but decided that she was mad and took no further action. Given that shortly after Elizabeth Barton was executed for saying much the same thing under the guise of divine revelation, Mrs Amadas could consider herself fortunate, but then the king himself did not become interested in her utterances. A similar case which ended very differently was that of John Dobson, the vicar of Muston in Yorkshire. As a priest he had a certain prestige which made his prophecies the more dangerous, and when he forecast that the king would be driven from the realm and that the Emperor would restore the true faith, he was listened to. 'When Crumme is brought low, then we shall begin Christ's Cross row,' he is alleged to have said, with a clear reference to the secretary.[28] Unfortunately for Dobson, he uttered these opinions within the jurisdiction of the Council of the North and in the aftermath of the Pilgrimage of Grace, a time and a place of particular sensitivity. Tunstall reported him to Cromwell, and the latter told him to send the vicar for trial. He was convicted and executed at the Lent Assizes in York in 1538.[29] Many other examples of soothsayers and rumourmongers could be cited, but what is clear in every case is that Cromwell took the time and the trouble to examine it carefully, and based his judgement on the best evidence that was available. If he was not satisfied, then he went on investigating until he was, and came to his decision on the basis of the danger which the person or persons represented to the security of the state. In the first instance the information was almost always volunteered; only in a minority of cases did it come from his own servants or from professional informers. The fact that it was often malicious merely made his task more difficult, and led him to seek circumstantial confirmation, but what he never did was to treat accusations as proven without examination, and given the number of denunciations with which he was constrained to deal, that is a great argument for his conscientiousness.

Cromwell, however, was more than a scrupulous administrator of the law. He was a statesman with a vision of how the kingdom should be run, and this involved defending the king's honour and interests. In some respects this was relatively simple. He never, for instance, took an initiative in foreign policy without Henry's express knowledge and support.[30] This did not prevent him from having his preferences and there is plenty of evidence that he would sooner have had an Imperial alliance than a French one. He went out of his way to reassure Eustace Chapuys, Charles's ambassador in England, about the king's intentions in respect of his daughter, Mary, putting the most favourable gloss on Henry's frequently unsympathetic actions, and (with Chapuys's help) rescuing her when the crunch came over her submission to the king's will in 1536.[31] As relations with the Emperor eased after Catherine's death, he did his best to steer Henry in the direction of an Imperial alliance, but drew back when he encountered the king's obstinate refusal to go down that road. Henry preferred to see himself in the role of mediator in the perpetual conflict between France and the Empire, and did not want therefore to appear too close to either. While Anne Boleyn was queen, and Catherine was alive, he was inclined to favour France, as the only source of diplomatic support which he was likely to get against the papal/Imperial alliance, but when they were both gone he allowed Cromwell to make overtures to the Imperial camp, and encouraged his amicable relations with Chapuys.[32] The ambassador was happy to enjoy such a position, but he never really trusted the secretary, or knew quite what to make of him. His reports are full of their conversations, where apparently confidential information was passed, but Chapuys was never sure that he was not being taken for a ride, particularly where the

French were concerned, and he was right to be cautious. This was particularly the case in 1538 and 1539, when Cromwell was urging the king into an alliance with the League of Schmalkalden as an alternative to France, but was trying to stay friendly with the Emperor at the same time. This was a delicate diplomatic juggling act which was never likely to succeed, but it was the king, not Cromwell, who brought that negotiation to an end by refusing the terms which the Germans offered.[33] The alliance with Cleves was an alternative, and although the idea for that may have come from Stephen Vaughn via Cromwell, it would be fictitious to claim that Henry was not fully behind it. At the time the king welcomed the initiative, and encouraged it in every way. From 1533 until the early months of 1540, the secretary was the king's first line of defence in all diplomatic encounters. He guided the council, and frequently interviewed ambassadors ahead of their audiences with the monarch, but it would be a mistake to suppose that he controlled foreign policy. The attempt to intervene in the dispute between Lübeck and the Danes over the Danish succession in 1538 was almost certainly the king's idea, and threw his relations with the Emperor into confusion for several months as Chapuys tried to work out what he was trying to achieve.[34] With Scotland, on the other hand, Cromwell had a freer hand. Henry's intention was to assert his long-standing claim to feudal suzerainty over the northern kingdom, but there was little opportunity for that as long as James V lived, and he concentrated his efforts on attempting the persuade the Scots to follow his lead against the papacy. That was certainly in accordance with Cromwell's advice but enjoyed little success, and the day-by-day diplomacy which accompanied those efforts was left largely to the secretary. Cromwell was also responsible for managing the borders. The wardens on the spot reported to him, and badgered him for the money necessary to pay their soldiers.[35] With such details Henry had no desire to be concerned.

Cromwell's statesmanship is less obvious in his handling of foreign policy than in his dealings with Parliament, where he was responsible for a genuine revolution. As we have seen, he first sat in the House of Commons in 1523, and his ironic comment on the proceedings there led many generations of historians to believe that he held that institution in contempt. However this was no pompous or weighty judgement, but a humorous observation born of a practical man's exasperation with the long-windedness of his colleagues, and perhaps of frustration that the potentialities of Parliament were so little realised in that somewhat abortive session.[36] In 1529, at the crisis of his career, he deliberately chose to enter the House again, not with the intention of evading his enemies, but with a view to relaunching himself in public life. As he told George Cavendish later, 'he once adventured to put in his foot where he trusted shortly to be better regarded before all was done'.[37] As well as talking out the Bill of Attainder against Wolsey, he threw himself into the committee work of the House, and soon attracted a disproportionate share, because of the reluctance of other members to serve. By 1531, when he was in the royal service but not yet conspicuous, reports of his activity were spreading far and wide. Lists of things to be done dating from this time and corrected drafts of Bills survive among his papers. Entries in the Lords Journals show him bearing Bills from the Lower House on numerous occasions, indicative of his active involvement with the relevant committee, and observations in the letters of his contemporaries confirm the same impression. It would be an exaggeration to claim that this was evidence of statesmanship, but it does show him to have been an active and well thought of parliamentary politician.[38] Above all he had grasped the fact that Parliament was the highest source of law in the land. The common law was customary in origin, and derived its authority from ancient prescription. For centuries the only method of amending or adding to the law had been by judicial interpretation, but by 1485 it had been accepted that Parliament, as the representative institution of the realm, also had that right. Statute, therefore, which represented the consent of the king, Lords and Commons, was a true vehicle of legislation. The Acts of Provisors and Praemunire had established the fact that its power extended to those border lands between ecclesiastical and secular jurisdiction which were in dispute between the two, and that ecclesiastical property fell within the remit of the king's laws.[39] Statute was also the only method of approving royal taxation because it was an ancient maxim *quod omnes tetigit, ad omnibus approbetur* (that which touches all must be approved by all), and the commons were the principal taxpayers. It was generally accepted, however, that statute could not touch the spirituality, nor legislate on matters of the faith, such as the authority of the papacy. It was that boundary which Cromwell, using the undefined legislative power of Parliament, planned to cross, and did so with the Act in Restraint of Appeals.

However, it was not only the Church which felt his enthusiasm for legislation. Henry convened eight sessions in as many years while Cromwell was his chief minister, and those sessions saw the passage of 333 Acts, of which about 200 bear the unmistakable marks of his influence. This compares with 200 acts, of which 148 can be deemed public, during the twenty-two years of Henry VII's reign, and 444 during the forty-five years of Elizabeth.[40] There is no doubt that Cromwell preferred statute to any other form of lawmaking, basing royal proclamations on statute whenever possible. In 1535 for example, when Parliament was not sitting, he had an urgent need to prohibit the export of coin, and consulted the judges, who dug out an Act of the reign of Richard II which served his purpose. In spite of a judicial opinion to the effect that proclamations were 'of as good effect as any law made by Parliament', Cromwell was not reassured.[41] He enacted the new ordinances for Calais in 1535 and in 1539 caused the famous Act of Proclamations to be passed. In spite of superficial appearances, this Act was not intended to give proclamations the force of law, but only to improve their implementation, stating that the king and his council 'may set forth at all times by authority of this act his proclamations'. It was a general empowering Act, and as such subject to repeal, a fate which befell it in 1547.[42] Neither the passing of the Act nor its repeal had any noticeable effect upon the use of proclamations as executive instruments, which reached a peak under the minority government of Edward VI as conducted by Protector Somerset (1547–49). That Cromwell did not trust the interpretative power of the judges is evident from his care to include treason by words in the Act of 1534, because constructive treasons had been drawn out of the Act of 1352 in the course of the fifteenth century.[43] This statute also provided legal safeguards for the king's unprecedented position as head of the Church, declaring that

if any person or persons … do maliciously wish, will or desire by words or writing, or by craft imagine, invent, practise or attempt any bodily harm to be done to or committed to the king's most royal person, the queen's or their heirs apparent, or to deprive

them or any of them of the dignity, title or name of their royal
estate, or slanderously and maliciously publish and pronounce by
express writing or words, that the king our sovereign lord should
be heretic, schismatic, tyrant, infidel or usurper of the crown...

that then such person or persons 'being lawfully convicted' were
guilty of high treason.[44] That this form of words was Cromwell's
work can be demonstrated from the drafts surviving among his
papers, but he did not invent the concept of treason by words,
which had been applied by the judges, and indeed by Henry VII's
council.

He could perfectly well have derived this opinion from his
own observations as a practising lawyer, but there is evidence of
a more intellectual or philosophical approach, because he was
closely associated with Thomas Starkey and William Marshall.
When Starkey published his *Exhortation to the People* in 1535,
he went out of his way to stress the English *via media* between
the two extremes of popery and Protestantism, a position for
which he was much criticised, but not by his patron. Cromwell
had insisted on this line being taken before the author set pen
to paper, and found it eventually insufficiently stressed. Starkey
apologised to him because 'this mean is not put out at large which
you require', which demonstrates that he was writing to a brief,
and that the secretary, far from being the revolutionary radical
of popular legend, was rather the originator of the Anglican
middle way.[45] Whether this represented his own opinion, or was a
compromise forced on him by the king's persistent conservatism,
remains an open question but it was a position which he adopted
with apparent enthusiasm. Starkey derived some of his ideas from
Marsilius of Padua, that fourteenth-century opponent of papal

pretensions whose constitutionalist propaganda suited Cromwell's agenda admirably. So much so that he commissioned William Marshall to produce a translation of the *Defensor Pacis*, which was Marsilius's main work.[46] Not only did he provide Marshall with the money necessary for him to undertake the work, he also urged Starkey to try the Italian's ideas out on Reginald Pole, which he did without the slightest success. In his response Pole did not mention Marsilius, but he did quote Cromwell to the effect that it was monstrous that one kingdom should have two heads, which was an idea derived from the *Defensor*, so the message was getting through – only to be rejected. Marsilius was also an Aristotelian, and it is possible that some of the secretary's enthusiasm for the Greek sage originated from that source. There are also other indications that Cromwell's thought was influenced by the Italian, because Marsilius held that the state is autonomous and the church subject to it, which was the foundation doctrine of the Royal Supremacy, and an indication that he had read *Defensor Pacis* long before 1535.[47] Marsilius also maintained that the essential characteristic of the sovereign state was its ability to legislate, a function which he attributed to the *legislator humanus*, which Marshall's translation rendered as Parliament. He maintained that only the positive law was relevant to human affairs, an idea which Cromwell was swift to endorse from his practical experience, and which has been interpreted as due to the influence of Machiavelli. However, it seems more likely that the author of *The Prince* took it from his fourteenth-century predecessor. Whichever way we look at it, it seems that Cromwell as a theorist depended heavily on Marsilius of Padua.[48]

There were, however, problems with the *Defensor Pacis*, which had been based on observations of the Italian city states of his day, and which could not simply be transferred to Tudor England. In the course of translation Marshall made various amendments, which mar the accuracy of his transcript, but which were required by his patron for obvious reasons. Marsilius's preference had been for an elected head of state, but that would never do in a hereditary monarchy, and the necessary adjustment had to be made. He omitted altogether the references to the community as a whole correcting and controlling the ruler and glossed the *legislator humanus* to mean Parliament, whose consent was necessary for the making of new law, although it might not have originated it. 'In all this long tale,' he noted at one point, 'he speaketh not of the rascal multitude but of the parliament',[49] and he introduced the word into the text in a manner highly reprehensible in a translator, but significant for the purposes of Cromwell's propaganda. What he did not do, however was to remove the element of consent to legislation, or seek to transfer the rights of the legislator to the single person of the prince. The right to make law therefore continued to be vested in the community as a whole and no attempt was made to doctor Marsilius's teaching in the interest of any absolutist theory, which is a fair indication that Cromwell did not subscribe to any such view.[50] Apart from Marshall's translation, the best clue to his political thinking lies in the preambles to his Acts, and particularly the Act in Restraint of Appeals, which emphasises, not the power of Parliament to make the king Supreme Head of the Church, but the fact that he always had been such by virtue of 'divers sundry old authentic histories and chronicles'. England was an empire 'governed by one supreme head and king' whose authority both the spirituality and the temporality recognised under God.[51] The idea that the king was an emperor because he had no superior on earth was not new; it had been voiced as early as the thirteenth century by the canonist Alan. What was new was the application of that idea to a country, the creation in effect of a national sovereign state. This had first appeared in Cromwell's corrections to a draft of the Supplication against the Ordinaries in 1529, although not used in the eventual document, and the idea that all kings were emperors within their own dominions had been developed in the fourteenth century against the claims of the Holy Roman Emperor.[52] However, apart from Marsilius, no one had used it to justify a denial of the papal authority, and in no public instrument had it been used so bluntly and so fully as in the Act in Restraint of Appeals. That was the extent of Cromwell's originality, and the sovereignty of his state lay in the High Court of Parliament, not in the king. As he put it in the Act of Dispensations of 1534,

> In all and every such laws human made within this realm … your royal majesty and your lords spiritual and temporal and commons representing the whole state of your realm in this your most high Court of Parliament, have full power and authority … the said laws … to abrogate, annul, amplify or diminish…[53]

In terms of political philosophy this is a statement of limited or constitutional monarchy, and was so seen and accepted by the king. It was also a statement of the division between the legislature and the executive, because in the exercise of the latter the king's will remained supreme, which is why Cromwell's papers are so full of memoranda 'to know the king's pleasure' about everything from decisions in foreign policy to the exercise of patronage.[54]

It was the responsibility of the executive to enforce the laws, and in this respect the secretary acted very much as his master's agent, but there too he showed originality and imagination. Like Wolsey he devoted much time and energy to making the king's laws more effective, but whereas the cardinal had relied on councils to achieve that end, Cromwell preferred to change structures. The problem created by the Marches of Wales was a long-standing one because in earlier centuries the monarchy had sought to guard against the wild Welsh by creating a series of semi-autonomous lordships wherein the enforcement of the king's laws was delegated to the franchise holder.[55] The king's writ did not run, and the law in use was a mixture of the English common law and Welsh custom. Edward IV had created a Council in the Marches for the purpose of governing the lands of the Crown and the Prince of Wales, and supervising the administration of the other lordships, but it had not really worked in respect of the franchises. There were liberties in other parts of England, notably the Duchy of Lancaster and the bishopric of Durham, but the main problem was in Wales. Although they had been originally created by the Crown, by the reign of Henry VII these liberties were perceived as being held by prescriptive right ('time out of mind') and there was no obvious way of getting rid of them. Occasionally one escheated to the Crown, or came by other means. The Earldom of March came with the accession of Edward IV, and the Duchy of Lancaster with that of Henry IV, but in both cases the structure of franchisal administration was left untouched.[56] Some of these liberties carried only partial immunities, like the bishopric of Ely, or were granted by royal charter, like the City of London. In these latter cases, the charters could be revoked, in which case the rights of self-government would disappear. This was often threatened and occasionally carried out when a corporate town had caused sufficient offence.

Altogether it was a messy, decentralised system, and offended Cromwell's tidy administrative mind as well as obstructing the smooth enforcement of the king's laws. He resolved to bring it to an end, using the enhanced powers of Parliament for that purpose.

There was a precedent because the liberty of Tynedale had been merged into the county of Northumberland by statute in 1495, but nothing on the scale of the Franchises Act of 1536 had ever been attempted before. Starting with the straightforward explanation that the 'ancient prerogatives and authorities of justice appertaining to the imperial crown of this realm have been severed and taken from the same by sundry gifts of the king's most noble progenitors' it then proceeded by the authority of Parliament to redress the same.[57] The right to pardon treasons and felonies in any part of the realm, 'Wales or the marches of the same', was reserved to the king and his successors; and the creation of Justices of the Peace and of Gaol Delivery was only to be made by royal commission under the Privy Seal. All writs were to run in the king's name only, and the remaining privileges of the franchise holders were withdrawn, effectively abolishing the franchises. The Bishop of Durham and the Archbishop of York were compensated by being created *ex officio* Justices of the Peace, the first in respect of the county palatine and the latter of the liberty of Hexham.[58] At the same time, although not by the same Act, Wales was reorganised, the old Marcher lordships being converted into the counties of Denbigh, Montgomery, Radnor, Brecknock and Monmouth. The old counties of the principality and the South West were also granted commissions of the peace and parliamentary representation on the same line as the English shires. The English common law was to run uniformly throughout

Wales. Although this meant relegating the Welsh law to the commote courts, and effectively putting the bards out of business, these changes were on the whole, as we have seen, welcomed by the Welsh gentry.[59] Above all, they finally put the Welsh on the same level as their English counterparts and removed the stigma which went back to the Glyndŵr revolt in the early fifteenth century.

At the same time, in the aftermath of the Pilgrimage of Grace, Cromwell reconstructed the Council of the North. Its remit was changed and it was made more directly dependent upon the king's council in London. In this his task was eased by the death of the royal lieutenant, the Duke of Richmond, in July 1536, and the withdrawal of the Duke of Norfolk after the completion of his task in the following year. As a result of these moves, England was more centralised by 1540 than it had ever been, and this was not only conducive to the king's honour, it represented Cromwell's vision of the state. It also completed the House of Commons, adding twenty-nine seats from Wales, two from Chester, following the abolition of the liberty, and two from Calais.[60] Only county Durham remained unrepresented until the following century, except by its bishop in the House of Lords. Parliament's own authority was additionally augmented by the Franchises Act, which extended its jurisdiction into an area hitherto occupied only by the king's prerogative, a move of which Henry obviously approved.

Cromwell's other vision of the royal power was one of social responsibility. Hitherto the king had accepted this only in respect of law enforcement, and a statute of Richard II had ordered all vagabonds to be gaoled. This was modified in 1495, but only to the extent that such 'idle rogues' were to be set in the stocks for three days instead of being sent to prison, and then ordered out of the town where they had been caught begging.[61] This punitive attitude was only adjusted in respect of those unable to work, who were to be sent back to their places of origin, where they were to 'remain and abide' without begging. Presumably their communities were expected to support them, but that is not stated. In 1531, in the very early days of Cromwell's influence, this was replaced with what has been described as the first Tudor poor law. Here a clear distinction was recognised between those unable to work and those deemed to be unwilling. The first were to be licensed to beg, under certain restrictions, rather than simply expelled, and the latter were to be punished as before.[62] The burden of administering this system, and of issuing the begging licences, was thrown mainly on the Justices of the Peace, but again no provision was made for the support of the impotent other than what they could gain by soliciting alms. It was not until 1536 that any real progress was made in this direction, and in that Act the hand of Thomas Cromwell is plainly discernible. In some respects it merely strengthened the law against vagabonds and beggars, but it was mainly concerned with a new principle, the legal obligation of every parish to care for its own poor. The preamble correctly observed that the previous Act 'had not provided ... how the said poor people and sturdy vagabonds should be ordered at their repair ... into their countries', and went onto order that the officers of every administrative unit from shires down to parishes should 'succour, find and keep all and every of the same poor people' by means of voluntary alms collections.[63] The funds so collected were not only to provide charity for the impotent, but stocks of material to keep the idle and able-bodied at work 'in such wise as by their said labours they and every of them may get their own livings with the continual labour of their own hands'. Every parish was to appoint two overseers of the poor to administer and collect the money so contributed, and to ensure that none of the parties relieved then resorted to begging, which was absolutely forbidden. 'Common and open' doles were likewise prohibited, all the money contributed for poor relief being channelled through the overseers, who were given the additional onerous task of accounting for what they had received and distributed.[64]

It is sometimes said that this Act was made necessary by the Dissolution of the Monasteries, which cast many former monks and nuns, and former monastic servants, onto the street. However, with the exception of some nuns who were returned to their families, the ex-religious were catered for either by transfer to larger houses or, more commonly, by the issuing of capacities to enable them to function as secular priests. The servants were similarly employed by the new owners or lessees of the estates, so the number forced into beggary would have been very small. In any case the statute was passed in the parliamentary session before the Act dissolving even the smaller monasteries, so although some houses had gone down before the Act was passed, care was taken to place all those affected, so there is no demonstrable connection between this Act and the Dissolution. Rather it is a example of the care which Cromwell took to minimise the social disruption which he witnessed; a disruption caused by economic circumstances beyond a government's control, such as the increase in the population, which was gathering momentum in the 1530s.[65]

Thomas Cromwell therefore had a vision of the state as a sovereign nation living under a law which was controlled by Parliament. The king he saw as the head of the executive, whose pleasure and honour had always to be respected, but within the boundaries laid down by the law. Henry was also responsible for the physical and spiritual well-being of his people, which meant not only that his government had to enforce the law, but also protect the vulnerable. He had also to guide his people in the ways of religious truth, and that meant not only ruling the Church in a jurisdictional sense, but issuing articles and injunctions controlling the lives of the clergy and the practices of worship. Cromwell was committed to the English Bible, and saw the evangelicals as the best protectors of the Royal Supremacy, but on that last point he differed from the king, and that eventually led to his ruin. He was also committed to the centralisation of power and to efficiency in administration, creating new institutions to replace the somewhat ramshackle machinery of the household. The court itself he streamlined, bringing it more into line with the French model,[66] but on the whole he did not favour things French, seeing England's international security as lying rather in a working relationship with the Emperor, which he strove to build throughout his period in power. He rescued the king from the dilemma caused by his desire to annul his first marriage, showing him the way in which to use existing institutions and laws for the unprecedented task of repudiating the papal authority. Clear-thinking and uninhibited by any sense of tradition, he was able to cut through the fog of Henry's uncertainties, and to see what needed to be done to make the king's will effective. Cromwell was a ways and means man. Whether he 'invented' the Royal Supremacy is still uncertain, but he certainly showed the king the way to bring it about, and with Henry's support was able to realise the necessary legislation.[67] Although not an intellectual he was widely and deeply read and was able to promote the propaganda needed to win the hearts and minds of Englishmen in support of the king's proceedings, a task in which he was only partly successful. Above all he was a man who understood the value of information, which he collected and processed assiduously from both overseas and at home, using for that purpose not only his servants but also the innumerable friends whom he had attached to himself both through patronage and through his general amiability. He was a man who understood the value of friends, and cultivated them wisely.[68] Many a correspondent testifies to the uses of his hospitality, and the quantity of game that he received in gifts must have kept his household regularly supplied. He was a man of wit and humour, whose table conversation lingered in the mind, but above all he was a statesman and fundamentally loyal to his master. It was not long before Henry was regretting his precipitate action in getting rid of him. Policy continued to be in the king's hands, but government would never be the same again.

9

HISTORIOGRAPHY

Unlike many of his contemporaries, Thomas Cromwell left no personal works or memoirs, and the official papers, despite their bulk, do not necessarily reveal much of the inner man...

John Schofield

In a sense the historiography of Thomas Cromwell goes back to his own lifetime, in the flattering dedications of the works of such of his disciples as Richard Morison, Thomas Starkey and Sir Thomas Elyot, and to the ribald rhymes against him that circulated among his enemies.[1] However most of the comments on his worthiness, or otherwise, were delivered in the form of private correspondence, or in the works of Cavendish and Bandello, which were not published at the time. The earliest biographical references, apart from comments to his friends contained in his own letters, come in a letter by Chapuys to Granvelle dated 21 November 1535.[2] The ambassador at that time was concerned to justify his dealings with the king's chief minister, and set out a description of the latter in order to demonstrate the importance of dealing with him, and the influence which he was thought to have over Henry. It goes without saying that this was not intended for a wider audience, except perhaps for onward transmission to the Emperor. Chapuys's despatches are littered with references to Cromwell, with whom he seems to have enjoyed a special relationship. He speaks warmly of his hospitality, of his shrewdness and of his wit, but never seems to have been sure of his intentions. Usually he was convinced of his goodwill, especially in his relations with the Lady Mary, but he was sceptical of his policy of maintaining a neutral stand between the Emperor and the King of France, a policy which we now know emanated from Henry. He never knew quite where he stood with Cromwell, but his comments tend to be judicious and well informed.[3]

Neither judicious nor well informed, however, was the first comment to appear in print in Reginald Pole's *Apologia ad Carolum Quintum*, which was written in about 1539, in the aftermath of the Exeter Conspiracy, which had brought death and ruin to Pole's family.[4] This, as we have seen, was a hostile portrait, in which Pole not only misrepresented Cromwell's early life, but invented an interview between him and the king in the course of which he is supposed to have praised Machiavelli's work, and claimed that he would make Henry the richest prince in Christendom. Thereafter he became the king's evil genius, persuading him to divorce his queen, and to assume the headship of the Church. The Dissolution of the Monasteries thus became his idea also, and he invented the case against the Marquis of Exeter and Lord Montague, which had brought them both to the scaffold. The whole of Henry's misguided policy after about 1530 was laid at Cromwell's door. This may have been intended to exonerate the king from every offence except that of taking bad advice, but it did not have that effect, and Henry's reputation in Catholic Europe remained that of a lascivious tyrant who executed anyone who displeased him. Cromwell was dismissed as a mere toady.[5] From 1540 onwards, until the twentieth century, he was viewed primarily as the executive force behind the English Reformation, and accounts of his career were coloured by the religious allegiance of the narrator. Edward Hall, who served in the Reformation Parliament, and must have known him personally, alleged that his fall was welcomed by 'religious persons', and all those who tended to the conservative side in the conflicts which were then ongoing. He went on:

> Others who knew nothing but truth by him both lamented him and heartily prayed for him. But this is true that of certain of the clergy he was detestably hated, and especially of such as had born swing, and by his means were put from it; for indeed he was a man that in all his doings seemed not to favour any kind of Popery, nor could not abide the snuffling pride of some prelates, which undoubtedly, whatever else was the cause of his death, did shorten his life and procured the end that he was brought unto...[6]

As a description of his role as Viceregent in Spirituals, this is accurate as far as it goes, but there is no hard evidence to suggest that any conspiracy of conservative bishops was behind his fall, welcome as it may have been to them. The king alone was responsible for his execution, but that could hardly be admitted in 1542, when the first edition of Hall's *Chronicle* appeared. Hall significantly did not mention the English Bible, because Henry regarded that as a master stroke of his own, and one which remained in place after the Lord Privy Seal's fall. He would not have wanted to share the credit for that with anyone, least of all with a minister disgraced partly on the grounds of heresy. So Hall's cautious praise was designed to avoid offending the king, and as it happened corresponded well enough with Henry's own regrets about his precipitate action.[7]

Others were less circumspect, and after Cromwell's execution a propaganda war of ballads and broadsides broke out in London, reflecting a deep division at the popular level. 'A Ballad of Thomas Cromwell' did not mince words:

> Both man and child is glad to tell
> Of that false traitor Thomas Cromwell
> Now that he is set to learn to spell
> Sing troll on a way.

It ends with a patriotic flourish:

> God save King Henry with all his power
> And Prince Edward that goodly flower
> With all his lords of great honour
> Sing troll on a way.[8]

There is no indication as to who the author may have been, and the suspicion that it may have been officially inspired is probably unworthy. In any case it was quickly responded to in 'A Ballad against Malicious Slanderers', written, interestingly enough, by a humble servant of the court, a sewer by the name of Thomas Smyth. Smyth was extremely careful not to criticise the king, and concentrated his fire upon his anonymous opponent.

> Although Lord Cromwell a traitor was
> Yet dare I say the king of his grace

Has forgiven him that great trespass.

To rail on dead men thou art to blame,

Troll now into the way again for shame.[9]

And so on for eighteen verses. These were not the only contributions to this conflict, and many must have been written which do not now survive, but they indicate the lively debate which went on in London over the pints of ale or the washtubs. Thomas Cromwell was a popular figure in certain quarters of the city. Not only did he keep a large household, which provided a livelihood for numerous tradesmen, but he was also extremely generous with doles. As many as 200 poor men and women were fed at his door every day, so he practised what he preached in terms of charity, which was more than could be said for most of the bishops who kept houses in the city.[10] Admittedly he was a wealthy man who could well afford such largesse, but that was not the point. When his injunctions sought to ensure that well-endowed clergy kept hospitality and supported scholars at the universities, he could justly point to his own example. When his house was closed down on 10 June 1540, and his goods confiscated to the king's use, not only were his servants put out of work, but the numerous beneficiaries of his generosity would have been forced to seek their sustenance elsewhere. He had been a reformer who had taken the biblical injunctions seriously, and that was not soon forgotten. Outside of London, and beyond the reach of his generosity, there was less debate, and the evidence suggests that only committed reformers lamented his fall. The gentry of the shires, who had benefited most from the efficiency of his government, tended to remember only his taxes, unless they had been on the receiving end of his distribution of monastic lands, in which case they would have been looking to the legal security of their tenures.[11]

After Hall, the next historian to make an issue out of Cromwell's career was John Foxe. Foxe did not know quite what to make of Henry, and explained his apparent waverings in pursuit of true religion by the proposition that he was easily led.

> Thus while [good] council was about him, and could be heard, he did much good, so again when sinister and wicked councillors under subtle and crafty pretences had gotten ever the foot in, thrusting truth and verity out of the prince's ears, how much religion and all good things went prosperously forward before, so much on the contrary side all revoked backward again...[12]

Foxe was of course a Protestant, and 'much good' involved the creation of the Royal Supremacy, the destruction of 'superstitious' shrines, the Dissolution of the Monasteries and the authorisation of the English Bible. By 'revoking backwards' he meant particularly the Act of Six Articles and Henry's persistent loyalty to the mass. Cromwell was thus the good councillor and his fall the ultimate expression of the factious spirit and fundamental disloyalty of his enemies. Modern research has indicated that the king was much less suggestible than Foxe believed, but for him Cromwell was the great hero of the English Reformation, and he began his account of his career with the heading, 'The history concerning the life, acts and death of the famous and worthy councillor Lord Thomas Cromwell, Earl of Essex.' No praise was too high for the subject which he had thus invented:

> Thomas Cromwell although born of a simple parentage and house obscure, through the singular excellency of wisdom and dexterity of wit wrought in him by God, coupled with like industry of mind and

deserts of life, rose to high preferment and authority, in so much that by steps and stays of office and honour, he ascended at length to that, that not only was he made Earl of Essex, but also most secret and dear counsellor to King Henry, and Viceregent unto his person, which office hath not commonly been supplied, at least not so fruitfully discharged within this realm.[13]

Although handicapped by his obscure origins, and lacking a patron in the court, he nevertheless caught the king's eye by his 'pregnant wit' and discreet judgement, 'in tongue eloquent and in service faithful' he earned every step of his promotion and in the course of his rise gathered to himself faithful friends who helped him on his way. Foxe then proceeds at some length to give an account of Cromwell's early life, and particularly of his visits to Rome in company with his friends from Boston, which he probably derived from local witnesses since Boston was his own town of origin, and he must have known the sons and daughters of those involved.[14] After giving a brief account of how Cromwell dissolved monasteries for Wolsey, he describes how he entered the royal service, being commended by Sir Christopher Hales to the king as being a man 'most fit for his purpose, having then to do against the Pope'. Foxe then follows Pole in depicting Cromwell as having a crucial interview with the king, only in this case the main thrust of their conversation was directed to persuading Henry that he should properly be head of the English Church, advice which he was soon in a position to implement. Having negotiated that hurdle, the account then proceeds to the Dissolution of the Monasteries, with considerable exaggeration of the secretary's hostility to those 'synagogues of Satan' and many details about the closing of particular houses, which Foxe no doubt received from the survivors of that process, of whom there were still a fair number around in the early 1560s.[15]

He no doubt derived his extended account of the disputation in convocation in 1537 from a similar source, Alexander Alesius still being alive when he was writing. Alesius's oration on that occasion is quoted at length, along with similar speeches by Cranmer, Stokesley and Cromwell himself, all designed to emphasise the Lord Privy Seal's godly credentials. 'How desirous and studious this good Cromwell was,' he comments, 'in the cause of Christ's religion, examples need not to be brought. His whole life was nothing else but a continual care and travail how to advance and favour the right knowledge of the Gospel and reform the House of God, as by his many proclamations, above specified by his means set forth, may well appear.'[16]

He then proceeded at some length to give examples of the ways in which Cromwell had used his position to protect those sympathetic to reform, particularly Thomas Freebarne and his wife, who, being pregnant, had craved meat during Lent, thus getting herself into trouble with the bishop, and Ralph Morice, Cranmer's secretary, who had lost his master's representations against the Act of Six Articles. To this last he added authenticity with the marginal note that Morice was 'yet alive'. Nor was it only the Lord Privy Seal's godliness which Foxe praised. In an extended account derived from Bandello, he describes how the aged Frescobaldi arrived in London in pursuit of moneys which were owed to him, and being spotted by Cromwell in the street, was welcomed by him with open arms for old times' sake.

'This is he,' he told the lords of the court, 'by whose means I have achieved the degree of this my present calling, and because ye shall not be ignorant of his courtesy when I greatly needed, I shall tell it to you' ... [and] holding him by the hand, entered his house, and coming to his chamber, where his dinner was prepared, he sat him down to the table...[17]

Frescobaldi's creditors were soon persuaded by his means to settle their debts, and the Italian returned to his country a happy man. Foxe then proceeded by means of other examples to demonstrate the 'fruits full of gratitude and courtesy' which his subject displayed, and his zeal for peace, both domestic and international. Throughout all the time of Cromwell's prosperity the king 'never had war with any foreign nations', notwithstanding that the Pope, the Emperor and the kings of France and Scotland were 'mightily bent and incensed against him', an outcome which he attributes to the secretary's irenic influence. Inevitably much is made of the destruction of those monuments of superstition, the shrines of the saints, particularly the Rood of Boxley and the blood of Hailes, the 'idolatrous forgery' of these being disclosed by Cromwell's means. Finally he came to the minister's fall, which he attributed not to the king but to a conspiracy of certain 'religious persons', in the description of which he largely followed Hall. He ended his account with the patient sufferings of Cromwell in prison, and with his 'true Christian confession' at his death, giving what purports to be a verbatim rendering of his final prayer, and his quiet submission to the stroke of the axe.[18]

Foxe's narrative proved to be normative for the next generation of historians who dealt with the subject, and for long after. Raphael Holinshed for example, comments, 'If we consider his coming up to such high degree as he attained, we may doubt whether there be cause to marvel at his good fortune or at his worthy and industrious demeanour...'[19]

Other Protestant authors, such as Gilbert Burnet and John Strype, also followed Foxe in making Cromwell the hero of the English Reformation, but stressed his influence on the king rather than his independent policy. To such writers the key developments of the period were the break with Rome, the Dissolution of the Monasteries and the authorisation of the English Bible, in each of which they had no difficulty in tracing the hand of the secretary. The only biography, Michael Drayton's *History of the Life and Death of the Lord Cromwell* (1609) followed the same line, largely ignoring the alternative tradition which derived from Pole.[20] The latter was followed, however, by Catholic authors such as 'Charles Dodds', whose *Church History of England* was published, ostensibly in Brussels, in 1742.[21] It was not until the nineteenth century that this sectarian approach to the minister was abandoned in favour of a more secular interpretation. From about 1850 onwards the Renaissance took the place of the Reformation as defining the beginning of 'modern times', and the emphasis shifted from the Church to the State. The crucial date became 1485, and Henry VIII the central figure in this transformation. William Stubbs, the constitutional historian, identified Henry as the central figure in the creation of a 'Tudor despotism'.

'I am inclined,' he wrote, 'to regard Henry himself as the main originator of the greatest and most critical changes of his reign; and I am sure that, after the fall of Wolsey, there is no minister great or small, who can claim anything like an original share in determining the royal policy.'[22]

Not everyone agreed with him. J. A. Froude, writing in 1856, regarded Henry as the interpreter of a popular will and allowed Cromwell a leading part in the transmission of that will. 'For eight years his influence had been supreme with the king ... the nation

... was absolutely controlled by him, and he left the print of his individual genius stamped indelibly ... into the constitution of the country.' The debate was hot, and occasionally bad-tempered. Writing in 1874, J. R. Green agreed with Stubbs. 'Parliament,' he wrote 'assembled only to sanction acts of unscrupulous tyranny, or to build up by its own statutes the great fabric of absolute rule.' To this view of Cromwell's role as essentially subservient, Pole's near-contemporary portrayal of him as a Machiavellian was central, and led to a revival of interest in the cardinal's opinions, and a corresponding diminution of the influence of Foxe, in spite of the appearance of two new editions of the *Acts and Monuments* during these years.[23]

The most influential, as well as the most exhaustive study of Cromwell to appear during these years was undoubtedly R. A. Merriman's *Life and Letters of Thomas Cromwell*, which was published in 1902. Merriman was inclined to agree with Green, and portrayed the minister as an unscrupulous secularist, whose priority was consistently his own position. He was not convinced that the policies involved in the break with Rome were Cromwell's idea, nevertheless 'he was the man who planned and carried through the various measures which have rendered famous the period of his ministry'. He was effectively the man who showed the king how to do what he wanted, but did not necessarily tell Henry what he ought to want.[24] Merriman believed that Cromwell was totally dedicated to the business in hand, and did not allow morality or justice to stand in his path. He showed a complete lack of emotion, 'ticking off in his memoranda the lives of human beings as if they were items in an account'. The morality of any action which he planned lay in its utility for his desired purpose, and that created its own justification. 'Whether his desires were obtained by fair means or foul mattered little to him; he kept his eyes steadily fixed upon the goal.' This being so, his enthusiasm for religious reform was a mere pose.[25] Committed as he was to the idea of the Royal Supremacy, the reformers were his natural allies, and his protection of them has to be seen in that light. It was part of his constant campaign to retain the king's favour. His patronage of the English Bible should be viewed in the same way. He did not care a jot for the scriptures, but the translation formed a useful way of maintaining the reforming initiative upon which he depended for purely secular reasons. Merriman was prepared to concede that his subject had an agreeable social manner. 'Of his charm as a host,' he wrote, 'there is no room to doubt.' But this also had its utility, and he quotes Chapuys to the effect that even the most experienced politicians (himself included) were often completely disarmed by Cromwell's pleasing manner, uttering in the course of casual conversation things which they would have been better advised to keep to themselves.[26]

Cromwell was also incurably venal. He allegedly wrote to the Prior of St Faith's on 23 September 1536, informing him that although his house was scheduled for closure, through the Lord Privy Seal's diligence it had been redeemed, and suggesting that a reward would be acceptable. A similar letter, written shortly after to the Prior of Coxford, is also reproduced by Merriman. Both these letters were probably forgeries, and their appearance in the Cromwell archive is something of a mystery, unless they were planted.[27] Cromwell certainly took rewards for similar services, but these were freely offered and only occasionally took the form of cash. More often they were preferential leases of abbey properties, either for himself or for one of his clients. On those occasions when he asked for leases, they were often refused on the grounds that the property concerned was already granted. Cromwell clearly received fees in return for services rendered, and these could be represented as bribes by those unfamiliar with sixteenth-century practices, but they would not have been seen in that way at the time. He did not see any reason why he should not enjoy the fruits, official and unofficial, of the offices which he held, and these included a number of stewardships and receiverships for noblemen and corporate towns as well as for abbeys.[28] Although he enjoyed a handsome lifestyle, he never sought to emulate the opulence of Wolsey, or indeed the Duke of Norfolk. Merriman's accusation that Cromwell took bribes, and allowed his actions to be influenced by the inducements which he received, therefore rests upon a very selective use of evidence, and on a mistaken conception of what those inducements represented. Similarly his statement that 'Catholicism and Protestantism passed over his head. He was not touched by either of them' now seems a serious misreading of the facts. Merriman did not like Cromwell, whom he regarded as an amoral upstart, but he was prepared to concede his diligence, and his efficiency.[29]

A. F. Pollard's *Henry VIII* was published only shortly after Merriman (1905), but presented a very different view of the situation. Henry was Pollard's hero, and the events of the 1530s were almost entirely due to his management. Parliament was an instrument of royal absolutism, and the Royal Supremacy was his idea, building on the position which had been established as long before as the fourteenth century, and reiterated by Henry himself in 1516.[30] Cromwell was a useful functionary, but special only in the efficient manner in which he carried out the king's decisions. His influence compared unfavourably with that of Wolsey, and was in any case brought to a crunching halt by his fall in June 1540. He was the instrument used for the destruction of Anne Boleyn, which again owed nothing to his initiative, and was used as a scapegoat when the Cleves marriage ended in tears. Only in his dismissal of any serious content in Cromwell's religious programme did Pollard agree with Merriman. The English Bible was the king's idea, and the minister got caught out badly when Henry decided that a reforming agenda no longer served his purposes, and turned back to the conservative party in 1539. Pollard's secular and rather small-scale Cromwell was the orthodox view of the middle years of the twentieth century, until the monumental researches of G. R. Elton turned the situation around in 1953 with the appearance of *The Tudor Revolution in Government*. This had begun its life as a PhD thesis for the University of London, submitted in 1948, but had been substantially reworked in the interval. Elton's hero was a secular Thomas Cromwell, and the main theme of his study was the transformation of a medieval household government into a recognisably modem bureaucracy by his means.[31] The essentially personal office of king's secretary was turned by him into an office of state, controlling all kinds of business which he ensured passed over his desk; the affairs of Ireland and the workings of royal commissions no less than the minutiae of royal patronage. The realm was centralised in a manner never before contemplated, Wales was aligned with England and the old franchises were abolished. Above all, the Church was turned into a department of state, with full authority vested in the king. For the first time the papacy and its courts had no place in the English polity, a situation which went far beyond that envisaged by the praemunire laws of 1394. All this was done through the medium of Parliament, and it is in Cromwell's use of that institution that Elton's thesis goes furthest.[32] Admittedly the secretary's main aim was the augmentation of royal power, which was completely consistent with the king's wishes, and has left the way open for controversy over responsibility for the strategy.

But Elton was in no doubt that the initiative lay with Cromwell, whom he portrayed as having a vision of constitutional monarchy in which the king and his parliament were equal partners. The king was the head of the executive, spiritual as well as temporal, and of the judiciary; but only Parliament could make the laws which the king enforced.[33] This in itself did not involve a revolutionary change in the functions of Parliament, which had long been recognised as a representative assembly with an exclusive right to make new laws and to vote on taxes. However, the extension of its jurisdiction to the Church gave it a competence recognisable as modern sovereignty, and that elevated it to a different plane. In addition, Cromwell transformed the revenue administration of the Crown, moving the main spending department from the Chamber, which was part of the household, to the Court of Augmentations, which he had created himself and staffed with like-minded colleagues.[34] In other words he transformed the medieval constitution, court-centred and personal, into that of a bureaucratic and sovereign state. Of course that state depended heavily upon its head, but his power was in no sense absolute. It was circumscribed by the law and by the will of the nation represented by Parliament. It was as a constituent element of Parliament that the king stood 'highest in his estate royal', as he himself expressed it in 1545.[35]

Needless to say, Elton's thesis came under immediate attack. Medievalists like Gerald Harriss stressed the continuities which ran through the period, and would not admit that any very revolutionary changes had taken place in the 1530s, while Tudor specialists of a different persuasion, such as Penry Williams, tended to place the responsibility for the changes on Henry himself. Cromwell was undeniably a good minister, even a great one, but they denied him the constitutional vision which Elton had proposed.[36] The latter's thesis was nevertheless a compelling one, and excellently presented, especially when set in context, as the author himself did in his *England under the Tudors*, first published in 1955. This traced the whole history of the dynasty, and pointed out that Henry had never shown any originality of thought on political issues either before or after Cromwell's time, and that the developments which took place later in the sixteenth century can be traced largely to those who had been trained by Cromwell, or consciously modelled themselves on him. The century as a whole saw the transformation of a medieval monarchy into a modern sovereign state, and the epicentre of that revolution was the 1530s. The polemical balance on the whole lay with Elton, and in 1973 he extended his interpretation in the published version of his Wiles lectures, given at the Queen's University of Belfast in 1972. In this work, called *Reform and Renewal*, he proposed a rather different Thomas Cromwell; not only an intellectual, persuaded by the *Defensor Pacis* of Marsilius of Padua, but a man who added a vision of the commonweal to his concept of the state.[37] Again proceeding largely by statute, he sought to revitalise the economy by encouraging the trade in unfinished cloth, and created the first poor law worthy of the name. This not only distinguished the impotent poor from the 'sturdy vagabonds', which earlier legislation had been designed to punish, but provided a system of local relief for them. This was set up on a parish basis, and involved the appointment of collectors and distributors of the relief payments, operating under the supervision of those favourite workhorses of Tudor government, the Justices of the Peace. This Act of 1536 created the model for all subsequent poor law legislation down to the seventeenth century, and Elton argued that it reflected Cromwell's sensitivity and compassion as well as a willingness for the state to assume a degree of responsibility for the well-being of all its subjects.[38] Law enforcement was no longer his primary concern.

This thesis proved equally controversial. David Starkey pointed out that, far from creating a kind of impersonal bureaucracy, Cromwell had actually created a highly personal ascendancy, the main difference from the medieval system being that it was not centred on the court. Nevertheless, he argued, the court, and particularly the Privy Chamber, not only retained but actually increased its importance during these years, as the king sought agents and means of communication that did not depend upon his ubiquitous chief minister.[39] He was inclined to agree with Penry Williams and with Pollard that Henry had himself been responsible for the Royal Supremacy, although he did not deny that Cromwell had shown him the best way to realise his ambitions. Altogether Starkey regarded the whole Elton thesis of the visionary Cromwell with scepticism, pointing out that many of his actions can be explained just as plausibly by the minister's need to respond to immediate and urgent situations which had developed, as to any vision, whether political or social. John Guy showed a similar scepticism, although with a narrower focus, when he challenged Elton's view that the development of the Privy Council, which the latter had attributed to the Lord Privy Seal and dated to 1536–38, was actually the result of his fall and did not occur before 1540.[40] Was it likely, he asked, that a man who had spent his public career building up a highly personalised administration, would have surrendered a large part of his control to an institution over which not he, but the king had ultimate authority? Guy and Starkey between them created another orthodoxy, which did not deny the revolutionary nature of the changes which had taken place during the 1530s, but were inclined to emphasise contingency in the actions which were taken, thus diminishing Cromwell's role from that of a visionary statesman to that of an inspired opportunist. At the same time, they did not really address that other aspect of the Elton portrait, the generous and compassionate Cromwell, who could always be appealed to by the unfortunate with a reasonable chance of success. In place of the harsh and avaricious minister of Merriman's biography, Elton had portrayed a man with a highly developed sense of justice, careful to investigate every case which was brought before him, and scrupulous in the administration of the law.[41] He was also a man of faith, or at least of the Bible, which he regarded as an infallible guide to life and morality. So devoted was he to the promulgation of the scriptures that he risked falling out with his master over them, and although not a heretic in any obvious sense of that word was nevertheless a Protestant in certain aspects of his beliefs.[42] There is no room here for the cynical scepticism of Merriman, whose Cromwell treated religion merely as a means of his own personal advancement. He was a man who took his faith seriously. He was also a man of charm and humour, some of whose more lapidary utterances can be attributed to the quality of his hospitality, which not even his worst enemies denied.

Faced with this criticism, Elton reiterated his interpretation, only slightly modified, in *Reform and Reformation* in 1977. He might, he admitted, have been overly dismissive of the court. The Privy Chamber retained an independent role, and although Cromwell succeeded in placing some of his own men in it, they did not dominate. It was predominantly the king's own context, and he alone appointed its members. He also conceded that the financial reorganisation could be interpreted as a personal bid by Cromwell to control the royal money, because Augmentations did not endure as a separate institution. It was absorbed into a reformed

Exchequer in 1554.[43] On the centralisation and bureaucratisation of government, however, he retained his position, pointing out that although the secretaryship lost some of its power when Cromwell surrendered it, it did not return to its earlier household status. It remained central to the administration of the state, to be picked up and augmented further by Sir William Cecil. Above all, he held his ground over the relative importance of Parliament, re-emphasising that the ecclesiastical supremacy, although personal to the king, made it a sovereign legislative body. This was new, and in accordance with Cromwell's vision of the state. These views he also defended in a series of trenchant papers, most notably 'The Political Creed of Thomas Cromwell', which appeared originally in 1956 and was reprinted in his *Studies in Tudor and Stuart Government and Politics* in 1974.[44] Others meanwhile had entered the fray on his side. In *Thomas Cromwell and the English Reformation* (1959), Geoffrey Dickens went further in the direction which Elton had indicated, arguing that the secretary was indeed a covert Protestant, and the success of the reformation after Henry's death owed a great deal to the foundations which he had been able to lay. Henry had accepted his concept of a 'middle way' for the English Church, but differed from him in where to draw the line, a difference which was exploited by his enemies in order to destroy him in 1540. It was, however, above all in his patronage of the English Bible that Cromwell had laid the foundations for ultimate Protestant success, creating a taste for Bible reading which remained popular throughout the changes which took place in 1547–58. It was he who had facilitated the shift in reform from a Lollard base to a Lutheran one, and thus laid the doctrinal foundations which were to be developed after 1547.[45] He had not been a sacramentary, but he had been close to being a Lutheran; far too close for

Henry's comfort as he never relaxed his hostility to the German reformer. In 1978 B. W. Beckingsale summed up the debate as it had developed by that time, expressing a cautious support for Elton's interpretation. His *Thomas Cromwell, Tudor Minister*, based largely on published works, was judicious but added little that was original. He was inclined to believe that his subject had indeed been the brains behind the Henrician Reformation, both in its political and its religious aspects, although admitting that the evidence was not altogether clear, being based mainly on Cromwell's own archive, which had been confiscated at the time of his fall. In 1990 Glyn Redworth, in his study of Stephen Gardiner, denied that Gardiner had been a party to any conspiracy against the minister at the time of his fall, thus removing a minor plank from Elton's platform and placing the responsibility firmly and only on the king.[46] This had the effect of reviving the debate of King or Minister, but only in respect of the end of Cromwell's career.

In 1991, just three years before his death, Geoffrey Elton expressed his final thoughts on the man who had dominated so much of his academic career:

These issues are here important because they must be fundamental to any assessment of Thomas Cromwell's role and achievement. He exercised at least a great measure of authority for not more than eight years; if ever he was influential it was between 1532 and 1540. Now it is plain that that period coincided with the main unfolding of dramatic change, even if much of that change had signalled its coming before 1532 and continued to work itself out after 1540. On these grounds I long ago concluded that the peculiar character of the years in question must be ascribed to the particular work of the man who operated in high office at that time and no other, while the reign of Henry VIII before Cromwell's arrival and after his departure bore noticeably different features.[47]

Much evidence had emerged since he originally wrote, but he remained convinced that the 1530s were Cromwell's decade. That did not necessarily justify the extreme respect which he had once bestowed upon him as the creative statesman who was single-handedly responsible for the transformation. The only view which he continued to regard as wholly mistaken was that nothing of great significance happened in the 1530s at all.

The creation of a national church under a layman as Supreme Head, the insertion into the system of a sovereign law-making Parliament, the consolidation of diverse members of the commonwealth into a unitary state, and indeed the recasting of the central administration which replaced government by the king by government under the king – all these, with their tenuous prehistory and their shaky aftermaths characterise the age of Thomas Cromwell and make it an age of change sufficient to permit thoughts of revolution.[48]

So Elton stood by his original thesis, although without the thumping affirmatives which had originally characterised it. The emerging evidence had undermined certain aspects of his proposition, but had confirmed others. Perhaps Cromwell had not been wholly responsible for the emergence of the Privy Council, and perhaps his regime had been highly personal. He had, on the other hand, reformed the household, streamlining it and making it more effective for the king's service, and nothing had touched his idea that Cromwell's initiatives had transformed the role of Parliament in the government of a centralised state. Henry's principal minister thus remains supreme. A man ruthless in pursuit of his chosen objectives, but extremely careful of the niceties of the law, and a humane man even to those who stood in his way, like Thomas More.[49] A *bon viveur*, and a man of humour and wit, who impressed his contemporaries with the quality and quantity of his hospitality. Above all, a man of faith, who may not have been always certain where his doctrinal sympathies lay but who honestly professed himself to be a Christian and a follower of scriptural precepts.

The biographies which have emerged since Elton wrote, Robert Hutchinson's in 2007, John Schofield's in 2008 and J. P. Coby's in 2012, although carefully researched, have not significantly modified his last considered opinion. Hutchinson is relatively unsympathetic to his subject, following Merriman in portraying him as a harsh man and incurably avaricious, but the others are more judicious, accepting Elton's revised judgement of the man and of his achievements.[50] A word should also be said about the fictitious Cromwell portrayed in Hilary Mantel's prize-winning novels, *Wolf Hall* and *Bring up the Bodies*. These are naturally concerned with him as a man rather than as a public figure, portraying his relationships with his son, his servants and his friends in a lively and realistic fashion. They are careful to respect the known facts about his career, and steer carefully between the conflicting theories about his role, operating (as it were) in the interstices of the established evidence. Together they constitute a fictional tour de force, but do not amount to a biography. The Cromwell they present is humane, intelligent and devout, closer to the man portrayed by Elton than to Merriman's austere and corrupt figure, but they are essentially concerned with his private life, about which the authentic record is usually and infuriatingly silent.

NOTES

1 The Making of a Man, *c.* 1485–1522

1. Bodley MS Dods, xxvi, p. 97. R. B. Merriman, *Life and Letters of Thomas Cromwell* (1902/68), p. 2.

2. John Cromwell's wife was the sister of one William Smyth, described as an armourer. There is no tangible evidence that Walter ever practised the trade of blacksmith. Merriman, *Life and Letters*, p. 3.

3. Court Rolls of the Manor of Wimbledon, cited by Merriman, pp. 3–4, n. 3.

4. There is no record of the death of Walter Cromwell.

5. This story originated in a conversation with Chapuys in 1534, apropos of the age of Catherine of Aragon, who was forty-nine at that point. *Calendar of State Papers, Spanish, 1534–5*, p. 468.

6. Robert Hutchinson, *Thomas Cromwell* (2007), p. 268.

7. Neither the exact date nor the method of his flight are recorded. Bandello later wrote that he was 'fleeing from his father'. M. Bandello, *Novella XXIV*, p. 251. It was possible for a father to have his son imprisoned at that time without legal process.

8. Bandello, *loc. cit.*

9. It was not until 1539 that Lord Morley sent Cromwell a copy of *The History of Florence* in Italian, although Reginald Pole claimed that he had read *The Prince* ten years earlier (before it was published). John Schofield, *Thomas Cromwell* (2008), pp. 265–6. Machiavelli was a senior servant of the republican government at the time of Cromwell's stay in Florence.

10. Cromwell's service in the English house in Antwerp is something of a mystery. Merriman supposes that he was 'either a merchant or a clerk to a merchant', and the latter is probably more likely. As such he would have needed knowledge of Flemish law rather than English, and that he could have picked up on the spot.

11. He is supposed to have passed the time on his second visit to Rome in this

fashion. During his years in power he was to be a great promoter of the English Bible.

12. According to Foxe, 'Cromwell, observing his time accordingly, as the Pope was newly come from hunting into his pavilion, he with his companion approached with his presents brought in with a three man song (as we call it) in the English tongue and after the English fashion ...', J. Foxe, *Acts and Monuments* (1583).

13. Elyot's letter was written in June 1536, and related to the 'honour of God', suggesting that Cromwell's reforming qualities had been manifest as early as 1512. However, there is no contemporary evidence for that. *Letters and Papers of the Reign of Henry VIII*, X, no. 1218.

14. Merriman, *Life and Letters*, pp. 12, 17–18.

15. *Letters and Papers*, III, no. 2447; a power of attorney granted 18 August 1522.

16. A 'Mistress Prior' and a 'Master Prior' both had rooms in Cromwell's house at Austin Friars in 1527. Mr Prior presumably died at some point between then and 1529. *L and P*, IV, no. 3157.

17. Wolsey had been translated from Lincoln to York in August 1514, and appointed Lord Chancellor in succession to Warham on 24 December 1515. Peter Gwyn, *The King's Cardinal* (1990). He had been the king's chief minister since 1512.

18. There is a large grey area relating to Cromwell's service to Wolsey, but it presumably relates to his work as an attorney. The evidence is circumstantial, and relies mainly on later memories. The first record evidence is in a letter dated 18 October 1520, but by then the connection was obviously well established. *L & P*, III, no. 1026.

19. *L & P*, III, no. 1026.

20. *Ibid.*, no. 2447. Power granted by Perpetuus Deonantur in a suit against George Byrom of Salford. The document names several members of Wolsey's household.

21. Creke to Cromwell, 17 July 1522. *L & P*, III, no. 2394. The messenger who delivered the letter presumably had more precise directions!

22. 14 August 1522, *L & P*, III, no. 2437. For Wolsey's earlier relationship with the Marquis, see Gwyn, *The King's Cardinal*, pp. 2–3, and J. P. Coby, *Thomas Cromwell* (2012), p. 33.

23. Cromwell appears to have been frequently absent from London on the cardinal's business, but these journeys seldom occupied more than a few days. Chawffer to Cromwell, 15 August 1522. *L & P*, III, no. 2441. For Wolsey's itinerary during these years, see N. Samman, *The Court of Henry VIII, 1509–1530* (forthcoming).

24. Lacy to Cromwell, 18 August 1522. *L & P*, III, no. 2445. In June the king had asked London for £20,000, and the mayor 'sent for none but men of substance'. Mr Ellderton was one such, and although 'the crafts sold much of their plate ... the sum was paid'. Edward Hall, *Chronicle* (1809), I, p. 258.

25. Hutchinson, *Cromwell*, p. 12. ODNB.

26. 23 August 1522. *L & P*, III, no. 2461.

27. *Ibid.*, no. 2577.

28. The nature of the commission requested is unclear; it was probably one of

investigation. *L & P*, III, no. 2557.

29. That Cromwell made a conscious decision to give up the clothing business is a supposition, but it was almost certainly the result of the death of his father-in-law, which seems to have occurred in 1524. Twesell's letter is dated 20 October 1522. *L & P*, III, no. 2624.

30. Merriman says that 'the spirit of the Italy of Machiavelli and Cesare Borgia stamped itself deeply upon his youthful character', but there is no indication that any of his contemporaries noticed.

31. Robert ap Reynolds of Calais claimed that he owed him 47 angels (£17 13s), 'with opprobrious words'. Hutchinson, p. 12. This might have been an attempt to blackmail one who by then stood high in the king's favour.

32. Schofield, *Thomas Cromwell*, p. 22.

2 The Cardinal's Servant, 1523–1530

1. S. T. Bindoff, *The House of Commons, 1509–1558* (1982).

2. *Letters and Papers*, III, no. 2958. The speech is printed in full in Merriman, *Life and Letters*, I, pp. 30–44. There is no conclusive evidence that it was ever delivered.

3. Merriman, p. 30

4. *Ibid.*, p. 43.

5. F. C. Dietz, *English Government Finance* (1964), pp. 94–5. P. Gwyn, *The King's Cardinal* (1990), p. 370.

6. *Ibid.* Surrey's raiding on the Scottish borders ran the risk of provoking war, but did not in fact do so. M. C. Fissel, *English Warfare, 1511–1642* (2001), p. 22.

7. P. Gwyn, *The King's Cardinal*, pp. 369–70. Ellis Griffiths was not alone in expressing the opinion that this was a 'gentleman's war', in which ordinary people had no interest. G. W. Bernard, *War, Taxation and Rebellion in Early Tudor England* (1986), p. 5.

8. For the manner in which Wolsey extracted this peace from the complexities of Henry's foreign policy, see J. J. Scarisbrick, *Henry VIII*, pp. 138–41.

9. *L & P*, IV, Appendix, no. 238. The letter is printed in full in Merriman, pp. 67–8.

10. *L & P*, III, no. 3249.

11. It was a sign of his coming eclipse that Henry was persuaded to call what would be known as the 'Reformation Parliament' on 9 August 1529.

12. *L & P*, III, no. 3015. That Robinson was a friend of Cromwell's is evident from other letters which passed between them.

13. *Ibid.*, no. 3530.

14. The passages were closed to all normal merchandise, and this concession must have been due to the fact that Hanseatic goods were involved.

15. *L & P*, IV, nos 106, 695.

16. *Ibid.*, no. 3157.

17. Checkyng was very defensive of his reputation as a tutor, although it does not seem to have been intended that Gregory should take any degree. Hilary Mantel is of the opinion that Gregory was much brighter than he is represented

as being, pointing to his successful career at court. I do not necessarily agree with her (though I do in part), because intellectual ability was no particular advantage at court, and the evidence for his dullness at this stage seems conclusive. (Hilary Mantel, personal communication.)

18. It would have been normal at that time for the sons of a gentleman to have spent a year or two at either Oxford or Cambridge to improve their cultural awareness. *L & P*, IV, no. 5757. Checkyng was claiming 40s for the bedding which Christopher had destroyed, and Cromwell may well have thought this excessive.

19. It does not seem that Cromwell carried out his threat, because Checkyng wrote again in November 1530 in terms which make it clear that the boys were still with him, although one of Gregory's companions had departed. He declares that Gregory will be 'loaded with Latin' before he sees his father again, and refers to a visit which Cromwell had paid to Cambridge six weeks earlier. The tone of the letter is friendly, and it seems that their financial disagreements had been resolved.

20. *L & P*, IV, no. 1732. Schofield, *Thomas Cromwell*, p. 23.

21. According to Foxe, Cromwell was 'in the wars of the Duke of Bourbon at the siege of Rome'. This would have been at the sack of Rome in May 1527, but there is no supporting evidence for such a presence, and it is difficult to fit in with his other known commitments. Schofield, p. 26.

22. See, for example, *L & P*, IV, nos 1833–4, 2365, 5117, 5145.

23. Gwyn, *The King's Cardinal*, p. 481.

24. Schofield, p. 24.

25. Reginald Pole, *Apologia ad Carolum Quintum Ceasarem*. Epistolarum pars I (1744).

26. *L & P*, IV, nos 990, 1137.

27. *Ibid.*, nos 1409, 1834.

28. Merriman, *Life and Letters*, p. 51. This story also comes from Pole.

29. Henry Lacy to Cromwell, 30 April 1527. *L & P*, IV, no. 3079.

30. *Ibid.*, nos 2538, 2738. Wolsey's total income at this point has been calculated at approximately £30,000 a year.

31. *Ibid.*, nos 3461, 3676.

32. *Ibid.*, no. 3536. Wolsey was to regret importing scholars from Cambridge, because by the following year several of them were in trouble for heresy. Gwyn, *King's Cardinal*, pp. 495–6.

33. Dated at Orvieto, 12 June 1528. *L & P*, IV, no. 4365.

34. *Ibid.*, no. 4778.

35. *Ibid.*, no. 5186.

36. For example on 12 April 1529 he was written to by the Guild of Our Lady, thanking him for letters which he had written on their behalf. *L & P*, IV, no. 5460.

37. *Ibid.*, no. 5330.

38. *Ibid.*, no. 5772. The document is printed in full by Merriman in *Life and Letters*, I, pp. 56–63. The date is altered from 1528 in the clerk's hand. All the other amendments (including the deletion of his daughters) were made subsequently by Cromwell, so we do not know exactly when they died.

39. Merriman, p. 56.

40. *Ibid.*, p. 61. Foxe is mainly responsible for the image of Cromwell as the patron of the Reformation, and he did not know of the existence of this document.

41. *Ibid.*, p. 59. It is not known how long Mercy Prior lived after this, but commendations were still being sent to her in 1531.

42. Bernard, *War, Taxation and Rebellion*, pp. 60–66.

43. D. Loades, *The Boleyns* (2011), pp. 82–3.

44. For the full story of this deteriorating relationship see E. W. Ives, *The Life and Death of Anne Boleyn* (2004), pp. 102–4.

45. *Ibid.*, pp. 118–9. Gwyn, *The King's Cardinal*, p. 525. Wolsey may have had his suspicions of Campeggio's intentions, but he had no option but to proceed with the trial.

46. Scarisbrick, *Henry VIII*, pp. 228–30. Wolsey was under attack both from above and below.

47. The charge was absurd because, far from wielding his ecclesiastical jurisdiction without the king's consent, his status, both as cardinal and legate, had been actively sought by Henry.

48. Cavendish's 'Life and Death of Cardinal Wolsey', in *Two Early Tudor Lives*, ed. R. S. Sylvester and D. P. Harding (1962), p. 108.

49. *Ibid.*

50. *Ibid.*, pp. 109–13.

51. *L & P*, IV, Appendix 238. Merriman, pp. 57–8.

52. Bindoff, *House of Commons, 1509–1558*.

53. *L & P*, IV, no. 6076.

54. Wolsey never in fact forfeited York, because the praemunire was suspended before it was pardoned. He was, however, deprived of some of its properties which were restored with his reinstatement.

55. *L & P*, IV no. 6061.

56. See for example, *ibid.*, nos 6076, 6080.

57. *Ibid.*, no. 6335.

58. *Ibid.*, nos 6226, 6263.

59. *Ibid.*, nos 6196, 6326.

60. *Ibid.*, no. 6185.

61. It is impossible at this distance to tell what that illness was, but sickness and diarrhoea were among the symptoms. He also predicted the time of his death with great accuracy, which gives rise to the suspicion that he hastened his end by self-poisoning. Gwyn, *The King's Cardinal*, p. 637.

62. Cromwell to Wolsey, 18 August 1530. *L & P*, IV, no. 6571.

63. For a full discussion of these manoeuvres, see Gwyn, pp. 607–10.

64. Schofield, *Thomas Cromwell*, p. 43.

65. *L & P*, IV, no. 3149.

66. For instance, the letter of Edward Johns, the rector of Northrewly, to Cromwell on 18 May 1529, complaining of a non-payment by the Bishop of Bangor (Thomas Skevington), who had not been in his diocese for fourteen years. *L & P*, IV, no. 3533.

67. *Ibid.*, no. 6420. Russell's hint was not wasted.

68. *Ibid.*, no. 6748.

3 The King's Servant, 1533–1536

1. G. R. Elton, 'The Commons' Supplication of 1532: Parliamentary Manoeuvres in the Reign of Henry VIII', *Studies in Tudor and Stuart Politics and Government*, II, 1974, pp. 107–36. The original version of this paper was published in the *English Historical Review* for 1951, and attacked by J. P. Cooper in the *EHR* for 1957. This version is Elton's response.

2. Schofield, *Thomas Cromwell*, p. 44.

3. Elton, *The Tudor Revolution in Government* (1953), pp. 90–91.

4. Graham Nicholson, 'The Act of Appeals and the English Reformation', *Law and Government under the Tudors*, ed. Cross, Loades and Scarisbrick (1988), pp. 19–30.

5. On the use of the *privilegium regni*, see Nicholson, p. 20.

6. In a document entitled 'Quaedem pertinencia ad Regis officium', TNA SP1/236, f. 204.

7. The relevant text is 2 Chronicles, 19. Nicholson, 'Act of Appeals', p. 22.

8. *Ibid.*, p. 23.

9. *Calendar of State Papers, Spanish*, IV, p. 460.

10. Merriman, *Life and Letters*, I, p. 334. Cromwell to Wolsey, 21 October 1530. Cromwell expressed his scepticism of this praemunire, writing that 'the prelates shall not appear in the praemunire ... there is another way devised...'

11. Elton, *The Tudor Constitution* (1982), p. 330.

12. 'An act concerning the pardon granted to the king's spiritual subjects', 22 Henry VIII, c. 15. *Statutes of the Realm*, III, pp. 334–8.

13. D. Wilkins, *Concilia Magnae Britanniae et Hiberniae* (1737), III, p. 756.

14. Schofield, *Thomas Cromwell*, pp. 47–50.

15. P. L. Hughes and J. F. Larkin, *Tudor Royal Proclamations* (1964), I, pp. 181–6, 193–7.

16. Elton, *Tudor Revolution*, pp. 94–5.

17. David Daniell, *William Tyndale: a Biography* (1994), p. 201. *L & P*, IV, no. 5823.

18. Vaughn to Cromwell, 26 January 1531, *L & P*, V, no. 65. Amended copy of a letter also sent to Henry VIII.

19. *L & P*, V, no. 153.

20. Schofield, p. 50, Scarisbrick, Henry VIII, p. 299.

21. Wilkins, *Concilia*, III, pp. 725, 746–7. Lehmberg, *Reformation Parliament*, p. 117.

22. Cromwell to Stephen Vaughn, 20 May 1531. *L & P*, V, no. 248.

23. *Ibid.*, no. 247.

24. Daniell, *Tyndale*, pp. 206–7. Schofield, p. 51.

25. *L & P*, V, Appendix, no. 18. Daniell, *Tyndale*, pp. 184–5.

26. Korey D. Maas, *The Reformation and Robert Barnes* (2010).

27. Vaughn to Cromwell, 9 December 1531, *L & P*, V, no. 574.

28. Schofield, pp. 52–3.

29. According to Scarisbrick, 'Henry was never a Catholic in any but a conventional way', but this does rather less than justice to his tenacious adherence to the mass. *Henry VIII*, p. 248. For a full examination of Henry's doctrinal convictions, see G. W. Bernard, *The King's Reformation* (2005).

30. The supplication is printed in full in Merriman, *Life and Letters*, I, pp. 104–11.
31. Elton, 'The Commons Supplication', pp. 109–14, where the processing of the various drafts is discussed.
32. Merriman, *Life and Letters*, p. 105
33. *Ibid.*, p. 106.
34. Glyn Redworth, *In Defence of the Church Catholic: the Life of Stephen Gardiner* (1990).
35. Elton, 'The Commons Supplication', p. 135. *ODNB*.
36. D. Loades, *The Tudors* (2012), p. 27.
37. For a full discussion of this meeting and its significance, see Scarisbrick, *Henry VIII*, pp. 305–8.
38. *Calendar of State Papers, Venetian*, IV, nos 820, 824. Schofield, p. 74.
39. Scarisbrick, p. 309 and note.
40. Nicholson, 'The Act of Repeals', pp. 29–30. In January 1531, acting on the king's behalf, he gave Eustace Chapuys a lesson in church history. *Cal. Span.*, 1531–33, no. 598.
41. Cranmer and Chapuys both accepted the date of 25 January, but Cranmer by his own confession was not present, and Chapuys was relying on court gossip. D. MacCulloch, *Thomas Cranmer*, pp. 637–8. Edward Hall accepted the November date. Hall, *Chronicle*, p. 794.
42. MacCulloch, *Thomas Cranmer*, pp. 55–60. Guy Bedouelle, 'Le recours aux Universités et ses implications' in Bedouelle and Le Gal, *Le 'Divorce' du Roi Henry VIII* (1987), p. 49.
43. Henry in fact found out about Cranmer's marriage, but never let it trouble him in spite of his general insistence upon a celibate clergy. MacCulloch, *Cranmer*, pp. 320–22.
44. *Ibid.*, pp. 88–9.
45. 'An Act that the appeals in such cases as have been used to be pursued to the see of Rome shall not from henceforth [be] used but within this realm.' Statute 24 Henry VIII, c. 12. *Statutes of the Realm*, III, pp. 427–9.
46. *Ibid.*
47. That being the day upon which the session ended.
48. 'The Noble Triumphant Coronation of Queen Anne, wife to the most noble King Henry VIII' (1533). Reprinted in A. F. Pollard, *Tudor Tracts* (1903), p. 15.
49. J. E. Paul, *Catherine of Aragon and her Friends* (1966), p. 123.
50. Robert Hutchinson, *Thomas Cromwell* (2007), p. 60.
51. *L &P*, V, nos 458, 1185. The latter shows him handling council business on the king's behalf.
52. *Ibid.*, no. 773.
53. *Ibid.*, nos 38, 86, 168, 181, 182.
54. *Ibid.*, nos 323, 371.
55. *Ibid.*, nos 621, 708.
56. It was Kildare's unsatisfactory performance as deputy that led to his summons to London, and subsequently to the revolt of his son, Thomas, Lord Offaly. S. G. Ellis, *Tudor Ireland* (1985), pp. 123–6.
57. *L & P*, V, nos 840, 926.
58. *Ibid.*, nos 1040, 1100.

59. Hutchinson, *Thomas Cromwell*, p. 53. Cromwell's first inventory of Jewel House holdings is TNA E36/85.

60. *Ibid*.

61. Cromwell's holding of the office of the Wards is something of a mystery, because William Paulet held that position. Perhaps he only held it for a short while. For Cromwell's reputation as a taker of bribes, see Merriman, *Life and Letters*, I, passim. This interpretation is now largely discredited, see G. R. Elton, *Thomas Cromwell* (ed. 2008).

62. For an interpretation of that strategy, which had subsequently been challenged in general terms, see Elton, *The Tudor Revolution in Government*, Chapter three, 'The reform of the agencies of finance', pp. 160–258.

63. *L & P*, V, nos 359, 496.

64. *Ibid.*, no. 1136

65. Various letters of Margaret Vernon are calendared in *L & P*, V, nos 15–23.

4 The Royal Supremacy, 1533–1536

1. Garrett Mattingly, *Catherine of Aragon*, pp. 206–7.

2. For example the statute of 1497, 12 Henry VII, c. 7, which prohibited those not in major orders from claiming benefit for misprision of treason.

3. G. R. Elton, *The Tudor Constitution*, pp. 236–7.

4. Statute 24 Henry VIII, c. 12. *Statutes of the Realm*, III, pp. 427–9.

5. Scarisbrick, *Henry VIII*, pp. 250–52.

6. Schofield, *Thomas Cromwell*, pp. 88–90. A. Neame, *The Holy Maid of Kent; the Life of Elizabeth Barton, 1506–1534* (1975).

7. Schofield, *loc. cit.*

8. BL Cotton MS Cleopatra E iv, f. 75.

9. Hutchinson, *Thomas Cromwell*, p. 62. Neame, *The Holy Maid*.

10. Christopher Hales to Cromwell, 25 September 1533, *L & P*, VI, no. 1149. Thomas Wright, *Three Chapters relating to the Suppression of the Monasteries* (Camden Society, 1843), p. 29.

11. The text of his sermon is printed in L. E. Whatmore, 'The sermon against the Holy Maid of Kent and her Adherents...', *English Historical Review*, 58, 1943, pp. 463–75.

12. Sir Henry Ellis, *Original Letters Illustrative of English History* (1846), II, pp. 315–8.

13. Unless it was a matter of extreme urgency, all Acts received the royal assent at the close of the session.

14. G. Burnet, *The History of the Reformation of the Church of England*, (1841), I, ii, p. 115.

15. BL Cotton MS Cleopatra E iv, f. 85. Hutchinson, *Thomas Cromwell*, p. 64.

16. Elton, *Policy and Police*, p. 58.

17. *Ibid.*, p. 60. Less fortunate was John Dobson, the vicar of Marston in Yorkshire who was executed in Lent 1538 at York for possessing an incriminating roll of such prophecies. Elton, *Policy and Police*, p. 61.

18. Statute 25 Henry VIII, c. 6. Homosexual acts were frequently alleged against the occupants of male religious houses, and some may well have been true, but

there is no suggestion that Cromwell was fiercer on this type of immorality than on ordinary fornication.

19. Statute 25 Henry VIII, c. 19, 'And for lack of justice at or in any of the courts of the Archbishops of this realm ... it shall be lawful to the parties grieved to appeal to the King's Majesty in the King's court of Chancery...'

20. Statute 25 Henry VIII, c. 20, iii. *Statutes of the Realm*, III, pp. 462–4.

21. Statute 25 Henry VIII, c. 21. *Statutes of the Realm*, III, pp. 464–71.

22. For a full discussion of the king's consistency in respect of heresy, see G. Bernard, *The King's Reformation* (2005).

23. On Wingfield, see S. T. Bindoff, *The House of Commons, 1509–1558* (1982).

24. Henry Brandon, Earl of Lincoln, was a mere child who was to die in 1534, while James V was a foreigner, born 'out of the realm' whose father had been James IV, killed at Flodden in 1513.

25. Statute 25 Henry VIII, c. 22. *Statutes of the Realm*, III, pp. 471–4.

26. *Ibid.*

27. Elton, *Tudor Revolution in Government*, p. 120. Schofield, *Thomas Cromwell*, p. 90.

28. For a full discussion of Gardiner's difficult temperament, see Glyn Redworth, *In Defence of the Church Catholic; the life of Stephen Gardiner* (1990).

29. Elton, *Tudor Revolution*, pp. 298–315.

30. Elton, *Policy and Police*, passim. *L & P*, VI, nos 711, 717, 724, 742, 746 etc.

31. E. W. Ives, *The Life and Death of Anne Boleyn* (2004), pp. 291–318.

32. For instance Thomas Wriothesley undertook several missions to Calais, and one or two to France on Cromwell's behalf. *L & P*, VI, nos 1306, 1400.

33. Elton, *Tudor Revolution*, pp. 259–60. *Ibid.*, *Tudor Constitution*, pp. 117–28.

34. Statute 27 Henry VIII, c. 21. Elton, *Tudor Revolution*, p. 270.

35. *Ibid.*, pp. 276–97.

36. Elton, *Tudor Constitution*, p. 118.

37. Statute 26 Henry VIII, c. 1. *Statutes of the Realm*, III, p. 492.

38. John Foxe, *Acts and Monuments* (1583) p. 1122.

39. Statute 26 Henry VIII, c. 3. *Statutes of the Realm*, III, pp. 493–9. Lehmberg, *Reformation Parliament*, pp. 206–7.

40. *Ibid.*, p. 207.

41. Statute 26 Henry VIII, c. 6. Elton, *Tudor Constitution*, pp. 202–3. P. Williams, *The Council in the Marches of Wales under Elizabeth* (1958) also covers this earlier period.

42. The Marcher Lordships were abolished and the whole area reduced to 'shire ground' by the Franchises Act of 1536 (27 Henry VIII, c. 24).

43. J. G. Bellamy, *The Law of Treason in the Later Middle Ages* (1970).

44. D. Loades, *Politics and the Nation, 1450–1660* (1999), p. 24.

45. Statute 26 Henry VIII, c. 13. *Statutes of the Realm*, III, pp. 508–9.

46. *Ibid.*

47. Brad C. Pardue, *Printing, Power and Piety; appeals to the Public during the early years of the English Reformation* (2012), pp. 1–15.

48. *The Glasse of the Truth* was published anonymously, but Henry is suspected of having had a hand in it himself, *ibid.*, p. 122.

49. Merriman, *Life and Letters*, I, p. 226. Schofield, *Thomas Cromwell*, p. 110.

50. *Ibid.*, pp. 96–7.

51. By Thomas Swinnerton, *RSTC* 23551.5.

52. For a very full account of the activities of his servants and informers, see Elton, *Policy and Police*, which contains a large number of relevant stories.

53. TNA E 344/1 – 21/8. Hutchinson, *Thomas Cromwell*, pp. 92–3.

54. John Caley and Josiah Hunter (eds), *Valor Ecclesiasticus*, 6 vols., (1810–34).

55. In December 1535 a canon of St Osythe wrote to Cromwell claiming profession at the age of thirteen, and saying that he would rather die than live in such misery. His petition was granted. D. Knowles, *The Religious Orders in England, Vol. 3: The Tudor Age* (1959).

56. A. G. Dickens, *The English Reformation* (1964), pp. 141–2.

57. D. MacCulloch, *Thomas Cranmer* (1996), p. 130. Cromwell was originally appointed to conduct a royal visitation, during which the powers of all bishops were suspended.

58. Statute 26 Henry VIII, c. 1. *Statutes of the Realm*, III, p. 492.

59. Statute 25 Henry VIII, c. 22. *Statutes of the Realm*, III, pp. 471–4.

60. Hutchinson, *Thomas Cromwell*, p. 69.

61. J. Scarisbrick, 'Fisher, Henry VIII, and the Reformation Crisis' in B. Bradshaw and E. Duffy, *Humanism, Reform and the Reformation: the Career of Bishop John Fisher* (1989), pp. 155–68.

62. Schofield, *Thomas Cromwell*, pp. 105–7.

63. MacCulloch, *Cranmer*, p. 130.

64. *L & P*, VIII, no. 750 (p. 280).

65. BL Add. MS 8715, f. 53. Scarisbrick, *Henry VIII*, pp. 332–3.

66. It is possible that More's whole correspondence with Cromwell is a kind of jest, designed to secure his favour, just as he mock-commended Henry VIII. E. F. Rogers (ed.), *Correspondence of Thomas More* (1947), pp. 506, 517, 541, 552, 554–5.

67. BL Arundel MS 152, f. 294.

68. *L & P*, VIII, p. 385. Nicholas Harpesfield, *Life and Death of Sir Thomas More*, ed. Elsie Hitchcock and R. W. Chambers (Early English Text Society, 186, 1932), p. 189.

69. Scarisbrick, *Henry VIII*, p. 332.

70. W. Roper, *Life of Thomas More*, ed. E. V. Hitchcock (EETS, 1935), p. 97.

71. C. A. Hart (ed.), *The English Works of John Fisher, Bishop of Rochester* (2002), pp. 12, 350. Schofield, *Thomas Cromwell*, p. 104.

72. *Ibid.*, pp. 104–5.

73. Scarisbrick, 'Fisher, Henry VIII, and the Reformation Crisis', p. 157.

74. Harpesfield, *Life and Death of Sir Thomas More*, pp. 243–4.

75. R. J. Knecht, *Francis I* (1982) p. 275. *L & P*, VIII, no. 837.

76. Hutchinson, *Thomas Cromwell*, p. 78.

77. *L & P*, VIII, no. 196. Elton, *Policy and Police*, p. 137. Hutchinson, *Thomas Cromwell*, p. 79.

78. D. Loades, *The Boleyns* (2011), pp. 134–5.

79. Loades, *Henry VIII* (2011), pp. 262–3.

80. *L & P*, X, no. 282. Ives, *Life and Death of Anne Boleyn*, p. 296.

81. Statute 27 Henry VIII, c. 28. Elton, *Tudor Constitution*, pp. 379–81.

82. Ives, *Life and Death*, pp. 307–10.

83. Charles Wriothesley, *A Chronicle of England, 1485–1559*, ed. W. D.

Hamilton (Camden Society, 1875), I, pp. 189–91. Ives, *Life and Death*, pp. 319–20.

84. Thus 'imagining' the king's death. *Ibid.*, p. 325.

85. *Ibid.*, p. 326.

86. Loades, *The Boleyns*, pp. 162–3.

87. G. W. Bernard, *Anne Boleyn, Fatal Attractions* (2010)

88. *The Life of Cardinal Wolsey, by George Cavendish*, ed. S. W. Singer (1827), pp. 458–9.

89. Ives, *Life and Death*, p. 328.

90. *Ibid.*, p. 327.

91. Wriothesley, *Chronicle*, I, pp. 37–8.

92. MacCulloch, *Cranmer*, pp. 158–9.

93. Loades, *Jane Seymour* (2013).

5 The Lord Privy Seal, 1531–1540

1. D. Loades, *Mary Tudor; a Life* (1989), pp. 98–9.

2. *Ibid.*, p. 99. On Henry's special relationship with God, see Scarisbrick, *Henry VIII*, esp. pp. 278–80.

3. *L & P*, XI, no. 7. Loades, *Mary Tudor, loc. cit.*

4. BL Cotton MS Otho C.x, f. 283. *L & P*, X, no. 968.

5. Loades, *Mary Tudor*, p. 100.

6. BL Cotton MS Otho C.x, f. 278. *L & P*, X. no. 1022.

7. Chapuys's surviving correspondence does not make this point clear. None of the documents immediately connected with this crisis are dated.

8. *L & P*, X, no.

9. *Cal. Span.*, V, ii, p. 70.

10. BL Cotton MS Otho C.x, ff. 172, 174. *L & P*, X, no. 1134.

11. *L & P*, X, nos 429, 1150.

12. Loades, *The Reign of Mary Tudor* (1979), p. 19.

13. Chapuys to the Emperor, 1 July 1536. *L & P*, XI, no. 7.

14. Mary merely dated the letter 'Thursday', but since she received her first intimation of forgiveness on the 26th that day must have been the 22nd. *Royal Historical Society, Handbook of Dates* (1978), p. 135.

15. *L & P*, XI, no. 334. Loades, *Mary Tudor*, p. 103.

16. *Cal. Span.*, V, ii, p. 70.

17. *L & P*, XI, no. 163. B. Murphy, *Bastard Prince* (2001), p. 176. Statute 28 Henry VIII, c. 7.

18. Henry VIII to Gardiner and Wallop. *L & P*, XI, no. 445. The reference is to Charles, Francis's third son, who became Duke of Orléans following the death of the Dauphin, Francis, in August 1536.

19. Mary to Cromwell, probably 30 June 1536. *L & P*, X, no. 1186.

20. He was made Warden and Chief Justice of all forests north of the Trent in December 1537, with a fee of £100 a year. *L & P*, XII, ii, no. 1311. Hutchinson, *Thomas Cromwell*, p. 273. For Cromwell's acquisition of the manor of Wimbledon, see *Ibid.*, p. 124.

21. *L & P*, XI, no. 1355. Memoranda for the King's Council, 2 December 1533,

L & P, VI, no. 1486.

22. *L & P*, XI, no. 629. For repeated petitions over the settlement of debt, see Christopher, Lord Conyers to Cromwell, 13 October 1533. *L & P*, VI, no. 1366.

23. G. R. Elton, 'King or Minister? The man behind the Henrician Reformation', *History*, 39, 1954, pp. 216–32. *Ibid., Thomas Cromwell* (ed. 2008), pp. 8–11.

24. Statute 27 Henry VIII, c. 28. *Statutes of the Realm*, III, pp. 575–8.

25. Elton, *Tudor Revolution in Government*, pp. 208–9.

26. R. W. Hoyle, *The Pilgrimage of Grace and the Politics of the 1530s* (2001), p. 93.

27. *L & P*, XII, no. 380.

28. TNA SP1/110, f. 162. *L & P*, XI, no. 968. Hoyle, *Pilgrimage*, p. 109.

29. *L & P*, XI, no. 705.

30. Hoyle, *Pilgrimage*, pp. 149–50.

31. D. Loades, *Politics and the Nation*, p. 148.

32. *L & P*, XI, no. 786 (iii). Merriman, *Life and Letters*, I, p. 181.

33. TNA SP1/119, f. 4. *L & P*, XII, i, no. 1022. Hoyle, *Pilgrimage of Grace*, pp. 265–81.

34. TNA SP1/112, ff. 118–211. *L & P*, XI, no. 1246 (1–2). Hoyle, *Pilgrimage*, pp. 460–63.

35. *Ibid.*, p. 302.

36. Suffolk to Cromwell, 27 November 1536, *L & P*, XI, no. 1180. Hoyle, *Pilgrimage*, pp. 409–10. On Bigod's revolt, and his bid to capture Scarborough, see J. Binns, 'Scarborough and the Pilgrimage of Grace', *Scarborough Archaeological and History Society*, 33, 1997, pp. 23–39.

37. Gervase Clyfton to Mr Banks, 11 November 1536. *L & P*, XI, no. 1042. *L & P*, XII, i, no. 698.

38. Scarisbrick, *Henry VIII*, pp. 355–60.

39. Merriman, *Life and Letters*, p. 221. T. Rymer, *Foedera, Conventiones etc.* (1704–35), XIV, p. 539.

40. S. G. Ellis, *Tudor Ireland* (1985), p. 123.

41. B. Bradshaw, 'Cromwellian Reforms and the Origins of the Kildare Rebellion', *Transactions of the Royal Historical Society*, 5th series, 1977, pp. 69–94. S. G. Ellis, 'The Kildare Rebellion and the Early Henrician Reformation', *Historical Journal*, 19, 1976, pp. 807–30.

42. Ellis, *Tudor Ireland*, p. 125.

43. *Ibid.*, pp. 127–8. Skeffington brought 2,300 men with him, the largest force to be seen in Ireland since 1399.

44. Ellis, 'The Kildare Rebellion...', pp. 812–16, 822–30. *Ibid.*, 'Tudor Policy and the Kildare ascendancy in the Lordship of Ireland', *Irish Historical Studies*, 20.

45. Ellis, *Tudor Ireland*, pp. 130–31. B. Bradshaw, *The Irish Constitutional Revolution of the Sixteenth Century* (1979), p. 141.

46. Bradshaw, 'George Browne, the first Reformation Archbishop of Dublin', *Journal of Ecclesiastical History*, 21, 1970, pp. 310–12.

47. Ellis, 'Thomas Cromwell and Ireland, 1532–1540', *Historical Journal*, 21, 1980, p. 510.

48. Ellis, *Tudor Ireland*, p. 133. Bradshaw, *Irish Constitutional Revolution*, pp. 193–6.

49. The policy of surrender and regrant involved the Irish chieftains surrendering

their tribal land to the Crown, and receiving them back as fiefs, together with appropriate English titles. These titles then gave them seats in the Irish House of Lords, and integrated them fully into the government of English Ireland. The take-up was patchy, but disappointing. Ellis, *Tudor Ireland*, pp. 137–42.

50. Elton, *Tudor Constitution*, p. 202.

51. By the statute of 26 Henry VIII, c. 6.

52. Statute 27 Henry VIII, c. 24. *Statutes of the Realm*, III, pp. 555–8.

53. W. S. K. Thomas, *Tudor Wales* (1983), pp. 49–65.

54. David Rees, *The Son of Prophecy; Henry Tudor's Road to Bosworth* (1997), pp. 15–21.

55. W. Schenk, *Reginald Pole, Cardinal of England* (1950), pp. 21–3.

56. Reginald Pole to Cromwell, 2 May 1537. *L & P*, XII, i, no. 1123. Tunstall to Pole, 14 July 1536. T. F. Mayer, *Reginald Pole, Prince and Prophet* (2000), pp. 13–33. Mayer, *The Correspondence of Reginald Pole, I, A Calendar, 1518–1546* (2002), pp. 100–01.

57. *L & P*, XII, i, no 270. Hutchinson, *Thomas Cromwell*, p. 175. Cromwell did not normally resort to assassination as a political weapon, but see his letter to Michael Throgmorton in September 1537: 'There may be ways found enough in Italy, to rid a traitorous subject.' Merriman, *Life and Letters*, p. 218.

58. Mayer, *Reginald Pole*. Loades, *Mary Tudor*, pp. 110–11.

59. Hazel Pierce, *Margaret Pole, Countess of Salisbury, 1473–1541* (2003), pp. 164–5.

60. *Ibid.*, pp. 117–20.

61. Confessions of John Wissdome and Joan Tristlelowe, 13 September 1538. TNA SP1/136, ff. 202–3. *L & P*, XIII, ii, no. 392.

62. Examination of John Collins. TNA SP1/139, f. 23. *L & P*, XIII, ii, no. 829.

63. According to what Richard Ayers told John Ansard. *L & P*, XIII, ii, no. 817, f. 84. Pierce, *Margaret Pole*, p. 119.

64. *Ibid.*, p. 127.

65. Examination of Jerome Ragland, 28 October 1538. TNA SP1/138, f. 37. *L & P*, XIII, ii, no. 702.

66. *L & P*, XIII, ii, no. 743.

67. The Countess of Salisbury's examination, 12 and 13 November 1538. TNA SP1/138, f. 243. *L & P*, XIII, ii, no. 818.

68. Scarisbrick, *Henry VIII*, pp. 364–5. Pierce, *Margaret Pole*, p. 139.

69. For a full discussion of this issue, see *Ibid.*, pp. 141–5.

70. *Ibid.*, pp. 149–53. See also Christopher Hollger, 'Reginald Pole and the legations of 1537 and 1539; diplomatic and polemical responses to the break with Rome'. (Unpublished D.Phil. thesis, University of Oxford, 1989).

71. It seems to have been Henry, enraged by Reginald's actions, both in his letter and in his legation, who was after blood. Cromwell kept his revenge within the boundaries of the law. At least a dozen other people could have suffered.

72. Loades, *Jane Seymour*, p. 91. *ODNB* sub Edward Seymour.

73. Henry was forty-six by this time, and not in the best of health. Even before Edward's conception he had expressed doubts about his ability to beget more children.

74. Cromwell to Lord William Howard and Stephen Gardiner (ambassadors in France), announcing the king's intention to marry again. *L & P*, XII, no. 1004,

printed in full by Merriman in *Life and Letters*, II, pp. 96–9.

75. Schofield, *Thomas Cromwell*, p. 337.

76. *L & P*, XIII, i, no. 241.

77. *Ibid.*, no. 995.

78. *Ibid.*, XIII, i, nos 56, 203. Scarisbrick, *Henry VIII*, p. 356.

79. Cromwell to Sir Thomas Wyatt, 10 October 1537. *L & P*, XII, ii, no. 870.

80. John Hutton to Thomas Wriothesley, 2 June 1538. *L & P*, XII, i, no. 1126. Cromwell's instructions to Philip Hoby, BL Add. MS 5498, ff. 1–2. *L & P*, XIII, i, no. 380. Merriman, *Life and Letters*, II, p. 121.

81. *L & P*, XIV, ii, no. 400. This report came from the reformer George Constantine.

82. *L & P*, XII, i, no. 1277. Hutton to Wriothesley, 28 June 1538. *L & P*, XIII, i, no. 241.

83. *Ibid.*, ii, no. 77. Francis offered to send one of the girls to Calais to be inspected, but that was all. *Ibid.*, no. 277.

84. *L & P*, XIV, i, no. 62. Chapuys was not withdrawn until his replacement (Mendoza) arrived, which rather destroyed the point of the gesture. *Ibid*, nos 345, 365.

85. For a full examination of these defensive works, see H. M. Colvin. *The History of the King's Works, IV, 1485–1660* (1982).

86. Mayer, *Reginald Pole*, p. 93. Scarisbrick, *Henry VIII*, p. 363.

87. Henry had been totally unwilling to accept the Confession of Augsburg, which the Germans made their minimum condition for admission to the League. Rory McEntegart, *Henry VIII, the League of Schmalkalden, and the English Reformation* (2002), pp. 131–68.

88. Retha M. Warnicke, *The Marrying of Anne of Cleves* (2000), pp. 71, 75.

89. *State Papers of the Reign of Henry VIII*, I, p. 605. L & P, XIV, i, no. 552.

90. *Ibid.*, no. 920. Warnicke, *The Marrying*, p. 64.

91. 31 Henry VIII, c. 14, *Statutes of the Realm*, III, pp. 739–43.

92. Warnicke, *The Marrying*, p. 98.

93. *Lisle Letters*, 5, nos 1574, 1620. Warnicke, *The Marrying*, p. 112.

94. *L & P*, XV, nos 822–3, 850.

95. Scarisbrick, *Henry VIII*, pp. 370–1.

6   Viceregent in Spirituals, 1536–1540

1. David Daniell, *William Tyndale: a biography* (2001), pp. 208–20. William Tyndale, *Practice of Prelates* in *The whole workes of W Tyndall, John Frith and Doct. Barnes...* (1573), RSTC 24436, in which he denounces the king's use of Leviticus.

2. Redworth, *In Defence of the Church Catholic*, pp. 103–5.

3. *L & P*, VIII, nos 75, 76. Merriman, *Life and Letters*, I, p. 166. Logan, 'Thomas Cromwell and the Viceregency in Spirituals; a revisitation', *English Historical Review*, 103, 1988, pp. 658–67.

4. TNA SP1/101, ff. 33–4. *L & P*, X, no. 45.

5. *Ibid.* Elton, *Policy and Police*, p. 245. The letter is printed by Merriman (II, pp. 111–13), where it is wrongly dated to 1538.

6. Burnet, *History of the Reformation of the Church of England* (1865), IV, pp. 272–90. Merriman, *Life and Letters*, II, pp. 25–9.

7. Elton, *Policy and Police*, p. 247.

8. W. H. Frere and W. M. Kennedy, *Visitation Articles and Injunctions of the period of the Reformation* (1910), II, p. 2.

9. *Ibid.*, p. 5.

10. Gerald Bray, *Tudor Church Reform: The Henrician Canons* (2000) pp. xxvi–xxx.

11. Elton, *Policy and Police*, p. 248. The Register was kept by William Saye, and was copied in part by Robert Beale, the Elizabethan Clerk of the Privy Council, BL Add. MS 48022, ff. 83–96.

12. TNA SP1/109, f. 196. *L & P*, XI, no. 876.

13. TNA SP1/124, f. 56. *L & P*, XII, ii, no. 534.

14. *L & P*, XIII, i, no. 942.

15. Burnet, *History of the Reformation*, IV, pp. 396–9. For Henry's proclamation, see Hughes and Larkin, *Tudor Royal Proclamations*, I, pp. 270–6.

16. Scarisbrick, *Henry VIII*, p. 27.

17. Schofield, *Thomas Cromwell*, p. 111. *Cal. Span. 1529–30*, no. 211. *Ibid.*, no. 492.

18. *Cal. Span., 1536–8*, no. 43.

19. Statute 27 Henry VIII, c. 28. *Statutes of the Realm*, III, pp. 575–8. Elton, *Tudor Constitution*, p. 379.

20. For the working of the Viceregential court, see BL Add. MS 48022, ff. 83–96. *L & P*, X, nos 372, 774.

21. Schofield, *Thomas Cromwell*, p. 115. The injunctions are printed in J. Youings, *The Dissolution of the Monasteries* (1971), pp. 149–52.

22. *L & P*, V, no. 1428.

23. *Ibid.*, IX, no. 808.

24. *L & P*, XIII, i, no. 778, ii, 1121.

25. *Ibid.*, no 1164. *L & P*, X, no. 424.

26. Schofield, *Thomas Cromwell*, pp. 119–20. For Kingswood, see *L & P*, VIII, no. 73.

27. TNA SP1/96, f. 127–8. *L & P*, IX, nos 321–2.

28. It was a myth propagated by John Foxe that Henry always followed the last advice he had been given. He was perfectly capable of making up his own mind on issues of this level of importance. Loades, *Henry VIII*, pp. 214–5. For a typical plea by a nobleman see Thomas, Earl of Rutland, to Wriothesley, 12 September 1538. *L & P*, XIII, ii, no. 332.

29. Youings, *Dissolution of the Monasteries*. *L & P*, X, no. 1152.

30. Loades, *The Reign of Mary Tudor*, pp. 96–128.

31. Statute 27 Henry VIII, c. 27. *Statutes of the Realm*, III, pp. 569–74.

32. *L & P*, IX, nos 65, 279, 301. Elton, *Tudor Revolution in Government*, pp. 192–3.

33. BL Lansdowne MS 156, ff. 146–9.

34. Elton, *Tudor Revolution*, pp. 203–5. Memorandum to the Chancellor of Augmentations to send to the Exchequer a list of sequestered properties, 11 February 1538. *L & P*, XIII, i, no. 253.

35. TNA DL 5/6, ff. 204–5.

36. TNA DL 12/7, no. 39. Elton, *Tudor Revolution*, pp. 209–10.

37. *Ibid.*, p. 212. W. C. Richardson, *A History of the Court of Augmentations* (1962).

38. *L & P*, XIV, ii, no. 13.

39. Elton, *Tudor Revolution*, p. 208. Richardson, *Augmentations*.

40. *Ibid.*, p. 206. For a list of the counties and how they were divided, see TNA E323/2B, pt l.

41. TNA E361/11/49.

42. Statute 33 Henry VIII, c. 39.

43. For example the abbot of Whitby's letter to the Lord Privy Seal in May 1538. *L & P*, XIII, i, no. 1113.

44. Cranmer to Cromwell, 7 February 1538, asking him to write to the Bishop of London, *L & P*, XIV, i, no. 744. Schofield, *Thomas Cromwell*, pp. 118–9.

45. *State Papers,* I, p. 555. *L & P*, XII, ii, no. 289.

46. C. Lloyd, *Formularies of the Faith put forth by Authority during the reign of Henry VIII* p. 26 et seq.

47. Scarisbrick, *Henry VIII*, p. 406.

48. *The Necessary Doctrine and Erudition for any Christian Man* (1543), RSTC 5168.

49. For a full discussion of the Becket situation, see Elton, *Policy and Police*, p. 257, n. 1. J. F. Davis, 'Lollards, Reformers and St.Thomas of Canterbury', *University of Birmingham Historical Journal*, 9, 1963, pp. 1–15.

50. *L & P*, XIII, i, no. 231. S. Anglo, *Spectacle, Pageantry and Early Tudor Policy* (1969), p. 273. B. W. Beckinsale, *Thomas Cromwell, Tudor Minister* (1978), p. 126.

51. David Daniell, *William Tyndale: a Biography* (1994), pp. 174–81.

52. Frere and Kennedy, *Visitation Articles*, p. 1.

53. D. Daniell, *The Bible in English: Its History and Influence* (2003), pp. 193–7.

54. Schofield, *Thomas Cromwell*, p. 227. For a comparison of the Mathew, Tyndale and Coverdale editions, see Daniell, *William Tyndale*, pp. 335–57.

55. Clauses 2 and 3 of the Royal Injunctions. Frere and Kennedy, *Visitation Articles*, pp. 35–6.

56. Schofield, *Thomas Cromwell*, p. 227.

57. Hughes and Larkin, Tudor Royal Proclamations, I, pp. 284–7, RSTC 2068. Daniell, *The Bible in English*, pp. 204–9.

58. John Foxe, *Acts and Monuments* (1583) pp. 1102–24.

59. *Ibid.*, p. 1122. John Lambert to Cromwell, 16 November 1538. *L & P*, XIII, ii, no. 849.

60. *Ibid.*, p. 1123

61. Cromwell to Sir Thomas Wyatt, 28 November 1538. BL Harley MS 282, f. 217. *L & P*, XIII, ii, no. 924. Merriman, *Life and Letters*, II, pp. 161–3. Foxe, *Acts and Monuments*, p. 1124.

62. Cromwell to Lord Lisle, 14 May 1538. *L & P*, XIII, i, no. 396.

63. H. Ellis, *Original Letters Illustrative of English History* (1846), II, pp. 233–4.

64. T. Wright (ed.), *Three Chapters of Letters Relating to the Dissolution of the Monasteries* (Camden Society, 26, 1843), p. 227.

65. *Ibid.*, pp. 238–9. *L & P*, XIII, ii, nos 593, 677, 866. *Ibid.*, XIV, i, no. 1191, no. 787.

66. *L & P*, XIV, i, nos 441–3, 955, 981.
67. Schofield, *Thomas Cromwell*, p. 351.
68. MacCulloch, *Thomas Cranmer*, pp. 266–8.
69. Scarisbrick, *Henry VIII*, p. 367. In fact they lingered on until August.
70. Statute 31 Henry VIII, c. 14. *Statutes of the Realm*, III, pp. 739–43.
71. MacCulloch, *Thomas Cranmer*, pp. 249–51.
72. Statute 31 Henry VIII, c. 14. Elton, *Tudor Constitution*, p. 400.
73. A proclamation appointing Thomas Cromwell to approve a new translation of the Bible. Hughes and Larkin, *Tudor Royal Proclamations*, I, no. 192.
74. M. Deansley, *The Lollard Bible* (1920), p. 295.
75. Elton, *Policy and Police*, p. 41. Alex Ryrie, *The Gospel and Henry VIII*, pp. 281–5.
76. Elton, *Thomas Cromwell*, pp. 20–22.

7   The Fall of Thomas Cromwell, 1539–1540

1. Daniell, *Tyndale*, pp. 189–95. This was in response to a proclamation against heretical books, dated by Hughes and Larkin 'before 6 March 1529' but in fact issued early in 1530. Elton, *Policy and Police*, p. 218, n. 5.
2. Daniell, *The Bible in English*, p. 199.
3. Richard Taverner, *The Confession of the Faith of the Germans* (1536), *RSTC* 909. Prefatory letter.
4. Philips was allegedly employed by someone in London who may have been Stephen Gardiner. For his subsequent career, see the correspondence of various English agents on the Continent. Daniell, *Tyndale*, pp. 361–73.
5. Treasonable words, spoken 17 January 1538, *L & P*, XIII, i, no. 35. Schofield, *Thomas Cromwell*. The fragility of his position is demonstrated in a proclamation issued on 16 November 1538, which Cromwell drafted and the king corrected. All the king's additions are in the direction of severity. J. Strype, *Memorials of Cranmer*, Appendix, document VIII, where the king's corrections are shown.
6. Daniell, *The Bible in English*, pp. 200–1. Hutchinson, *Thomas Cromwell*, p. 190.
7. Hughes and Larkin, *Tudor Royal Proclamations*, I, pp. 286–7.
8. Schofield, *Thomas Cromwell*, pp. 46–62.
9. *L & P*, XIV, i, no. 103 (2). Merriman, *Life and Letters*, II, pp. 174–5.
10. *L & P*, XIV, i, no. 1137.
11. *Ibid.*, no. 1193. Retha Warnicke, *The Marrying of Anne of Cleves* (2000), pp. 84–5.
12. R. J. Knecht, *Francis I*, pp. 295–7.
13. Warnicke, *The Marrying of Anne of Cleves*, pp. 155–7.
14. Patricia Crawford, *Blood, Bodies and Families in Early Modern England* (2004), pp. 29–30. J. Strype, *Ecclesiastical Memorials* (1822), II, p. 462. Loades, *The Tudor Queens of England* (2009), p. 110.
15. Warnicke, *The Marrying*, p. 151.
16. Scarisbrick, *Henry VIII*, pp. 372–3.
17. Schofield, *Thomas Cromwell*, p. 238. On the circumstances under which William had inherited Gelderland, see Warnicke, *The Marrying*, p. 238.

18. Elton, 'Thomas Cromwell's decline and fall' in *Studies in Tudor and Stuart Politics and Government*, I (1974), p. 203. *L & P*, XIV, i, no. 672.

19. TNA SP1/140, f. 197. *L & P*, XIV, i, nos 634, 645. Chistopher More to Cromwell, March 1539.

20. Alasdair Hawkyard, 'The Court, the Household and Parliament in the Mid-Tudor Period', *The Court Historian*, 16, 2011, pp. 159–75.

21. Cromwell was not taken by surprise by the royal agenda for this parliament. Among his remembrances for early March is a note for 'a device in the parliament for the unity in religion'. *L & P*, XIV, i, no. 655. Elton, 'Decline and fall...', pp. 205–7.

22. Statute 31 Henry VIII, c. 14. *Statutes of the Realm*, III, pp. 739–43.

23. Foxe, *Acts and Monuments* (1583), p. 1192.

24. *Lords Journals*, I, pp. 128–9, where it is rendered in Latin, although delivered in English. The translation is from Elton, 'Decline and Fall...', p. 216.

25. *Ibid.*, pp. 217–8.

26. *Lords Journals*, I, p. 133.

27. R. S. Schofield, 'Taxation and the political limits of the Tudor State' in *Law and Government under the Tudors*, pp. 257–66. Schofield, 'Parliamentary Lay Taxation, 1485–1547' (Cambridge Univerisity PhD, 1963).

28. Elton, 'Decline and Fall...', pp. 219–20.

29. Loades, *Cardinal Wolsey* (2008), pp. 28–32. P. J. Gwyn, *The King's Cardinal*, pp. 630–2.

30. Merriman, *Life and Letters*, I, p. 285. P. Van Dyke, *Renascence Portraits* (1905), pp. 237 *et seq.*

31. Sadler did, however, bare Cromwell's last letters to Henry. F. S. Stoney, *Life and Times of the Right Honourable Sir Ralph Sadler* (1877), p. 68.

32. More strictly, he was under house arrest. *State Papers*, 1, pp. 627–8.

33. Elton, 'Decline and Fall...', p. 192

34. *L & P*, XII, no. 27, XIII, no. 143. Elton, 'Decline and Fall...', pp. 220–1.

35. Schofield, *Thomas Cromwell*, pp. 296–9.

36. *Ibid.*, p. 297. For Norfolk's attitude to Irish affairs, see Ellis, *Tudor Ireland*, p. 123.

37. *L & P*, XII, ii, no. 249.

38. TNA SP1/105, f. 245. *L & P*, XI, no. 233. It is alleged that one of the factors turning Norfolk against Cromwell in 1540 was the dissolution of Thetford Abbey in February, while the duke was in France.

39. TNA SP1/106, f.157. *L & P*, XI, no. 434.

40. TNA SP1/106, f.183. *L & P*, XI, no. 470.

41. *L & P.*, XI, no. 576.

42. Elton, 'Decline and Fall...', p. 195.

43. The letter was actually drafted by Wriothesley, which makes Cromwell's role in its contents all the more obvious. *L & P*, XI, nos 777, 809, 810, 863.

44. *L & P*, XII, ii, no. 291. Elton, 'Decline and Fall...' p. 196 and n. 4

45. *L & P*, XIV, i, no. 541.

46. Elton, 'Decline and Fall...' pp. 196–7.

47. G. Redworth, *In Defence of the Church Catholic*, pp. 59–61. J. A. Muller, *Stephen Gardiner and the Tudor Reaction* (1926), pp. 55 *et seq.*

48. The nature of Cromwell's relationship with Gardiner is fairly reflected in the former's letter of 5 July 1536. BL Add. MS 25114, f. 175. Merriman, *Life and Letters*, pp. 19–21.
49. *L & P*, IX, no. 1039. Merriman, *Life and Letters*, I, pp. 439–40. *Ibid.*, II, p. 20.
50. 12 June 1537. *L & P*, XII, ii, no. 78.
51. Cromwell to Gardiner, 15 February 1538. BL Add. MS 25,114, f. 286. Merrimen, *Life and Letters*, II, pp. 115–6.
52. Burnet, *History of the Reformation*, 1, p. 425.
53. A view held by Chapuys, *L & P*, X, nos 351, 688, XI, no. 40; and Castillon, *Ibid.*, XIII, i, nos 995,1101–2. 1135. Merriman, *Life and Letters*, I, pp. 233–4.
54. Elton, 'Decline and Fall...', p. 219.
55. Merriman, I, p. 287.
56. *L & P*, XV, nos 334, 425.
57. *Ibid.*, no. 486.
58. *Ibid.*, no. 429.
59. *L & P*, XV, no. 437. Elton, 'Decline and Fall...', pp. 215–6. Schofield, *Thomas Cromwell*, pp. 374–5.
60. *L & P*, XV, nos 540–1. Edward Hall, *Chronicle*, p. 838. For the idea that this was a deliberate snub to Norfolk, see D. Head, *Ebbs and Flows of Fortune; the Life of Thomas Howard, third Duke of Norfolk* (1995), p. 170.
61. Marillac to Francis I, 1 June 1540. *L & P*, XV, no. 736. Sampson was arrested some time between 25 and 28 May.
62. *L & P*, XV, no. 373
63. *L & P*, XIV, i, nos 1108, 1152, 1156. M. St Clare Byrne, *The Lisle Letters* (1983), pp. 476–99.
64. *L & P*, XV, nos 766–7.
65. The Emperor and the King of France were also members of the Order Schofield, *Thomas Cromwell*, pp. 392–3. Hutchinson, *Thomas Cromwell*, pp. 238–9. Although he did not speak for him, Ralph Sadler did at least bear Cromwell's final plea for mercy to the king. This may have contributed to a loss of favour, because he spent a period in the Tower in 1541. A. J. Slavin, *Politics and Profit* (1966).
66. Scarisbrick, *Henry VIII*, pp. 372–3. Wamicke, *Marrying of Anne of Cleves*, pp. 202–3. Wriothesley's deposition, made after Cromwell's fall. *L & P*, XV, no. 850 (II), printed by Strype, *Ecclesiastical Memorials*, I, Records, cxiv, no. 9.
67. Hutchinson, *Thomas Cromwell*, pp. 222–3. Loades, *Catherine Howard* (2012), pp. 96–7.
68. *L & P*, XV, n. 766. Henry VIII to Marillac. Schofield, *Thomas Cromwell*, pp. 391–2.
69. Elton, 'Decline and Fall...', pp. 225–6.
70. Schofield, *Thomas Cromwell*, p. 392.
71. Hall, *Chronicle*, p. 838.
72. *State Papers*, VIII, pp. 364–5.
73. *L & P*, XV, no. 364. T. B. and T. J. Howell, *Complete Collection of State Trials* (1828), I, p. 455.

74. *L & P*, XV, no. 785. *State Papers*, VIII, p. 264.
75. BL Cotton MS Titus B 1, f. 273. Merriman, *Life and Letters*, II, pp. 264–7.
76. Schofield, *Thomas Cromwell*, p. 403.
77. *L & P*, XV, no. 823. Merriman, *Life and Letters*, pp. 268–73.
78. Elton, 'Decline and Fall...', p. 221.
79. The Act is printed in full by Burnet, *History of the Reformation*, IV, p. 415
80. *Ibid.*, clause 3.
81. *Ibid.*, clause 10.
82. Elton, 'Decline and Fall...', p. 225.
83. *L & P*, XV, no. 804.
84. Richard Hilles to Bullinger, *L & P*, XVI, p. 270
85. Burnet, *History of the Reformation*, I, i, bk iii, p. 206.
86. R. A. Rebholtz, *The Complete Poems of Thomas Wyatt* (1978), p. 86.
87. *L & P*, XV, no. 498. S. E. Lehmberg, *The Later Parliaments of Henry VIII, 1536–1547* (1977), p. 111.
88. Schofield, *Thomas Cromwell*, p. 408.
89. *Ibid.*, p. 415.

8 Cromwell and the State

1. Reginald Pole, 'Apologia ad Carolum Quint Caesarem', *Epistolarum... Pars Prima*, ed. Qurini (1744), p. 133. G. R. Elton, 'The Political Creed of Thomas Cromwell', *Studies in Tudor and Stuart Politics and Government* (1974), II, pp. 216–8.
2. Pole, 'Apologia', p. 133.
3. *England in the Reign of King Henry the Eighth*, ed. S. J. Herrtage and J. M. Cooper (EETS, 1878), p. xv.
4. In the Reformation statutes he was always careful to emphasise that the law so created was consistent with the law of God – although not, of course, with the canon law, which was merely of human invention.
5. Elton, 'The Political Creed...', pp. 228–9.
6. *Ibid.*, p. 230. Henry, Lord Morley, wrote to Cromwell in February 1539, sending him a copy of the *History of Florence* (in Italian), and commending *The Prince* to his attention, in case he was unfamiliar with it. *L & P*, XIV, i, no. 285.
7. Schofield, *Thomas Cromwell*, pp. 110–24.
8. Cromwell to the Council of Calais, 27 May 1539. Merriman, *Life and Letters*, II, pp. 222–4. See also, *ibid.*, p. 112. *Lords Journals*, I, p. 128.
9. Alexander Alesius, *Of the authoritie of the word of god against* the *bishop of London* (?1540), RSTC 292. *Letters and Papers*, XII, i, no. 790.
10. *Lords Journals*, I, p. 128. For a full consideration of the punishments which he inspired, see G. R. Elton, *Policy and Police*, pp. 327–83.
11. Cromwell to Fisher, February 1534. Merriman, *Life and Letters*, I, p. 376.
12. Cromwell's use of attainder was attacked by no less a Common Lawyer than Sir Edward Coke, who certainly did not regard it as a gesture of respect! G. R. Elton, *The Tudor Constitution*, p. 172.
13. While it is true that the common law did not recognise slander as an offence,

there was nevertheless a form of action devised called 'trespass on the case', whereby the offender was deemed to have trespassed upon the plaintiff's reputation. Marjorie Blatcher, *The Court of King's Bench 1450–1550* (1978), p. 25.

14. Elton, *Tudor Constitution*, p. 340.

15. *Letters and Papers*, XIII, i, no. 120. F. Schultz, 'Bracton on Kingship', *English Historical Review*, 60, 1945.

16. All that is known of this story comes from the depositions collected by the commissioners. TNA SP1/131, ff. 23–31. *L & P*, XIII, i, no. 686.

17. *Ibid.*

18. Elton, *Policy and Police*, p. 93.

19. The discontented monk informed Lord Stourton, who passed the matter on to Cromwell. TNA SP1/76, f. 84. *L & P*, VI, no. 510.

20. Henry Ellis, *Original Letters relating to the English Reformation* (1846), 11, ii, p. 130. A letter from his brother Alan.

21. *L & P, Addenda*, nos 1056–7, 1063, 1075.

22. Elton, *Policy and Police*, p. 109.

23. *L & P*, VI, no. 433. TNA SP6/1, no. 19.

24. *L & P*, VI, no. 412. TNA SP1/75, f.229.

25. Elton, *Policy and Police*, p. 116,

26. *Ibid.*, pp. 116–7. *L & P*, VI, no. 799 (2).

27. *L & P*, VI, no 932.The old book of prophecies appears to have been the 'Book of Merlin', attributed to Geoffrey of Monmouth. Rupert Taylor, *Political Prophecy in England* (1911), pp. 48 *et seq.*

28. Dobson's collection of prophecies included bits of Merlin and Thomas of Erceldoune, but this reference to 'the Crumme' he would appear to have made up himself. Taylor, *Political Prophecy*, pp. 48–58, 62–71.

29. *L & P*, XII, ii, no. 1212; XIII, i, nos 107, 705. TNA SP1/127, ff. 63–7, 128, ff. 124, 131, f. 56.

30. See the careful examinations of Henry's foreign policy contained in Scarisbrick, *Henry VIII*, pp. 355–83 and Loades, *Henry VIII*, pp. 261–98.

31. Loades, *Mary Tudor*, pp. 99–103.

32. Chapuys was withdrawn in the spring of 1539 and Cromwell does not seem to have established a similar relationship with his successor, Mendoza.

33. Scarisbrick, *Henry* VIII, p. 367.

34. Thomas Cromwell to Christopher Mont and Thomas Paynell, 10 March 1539. Merriman, *Life and Letters*, II, pp. 186–90.

35. For example, Sir George Lawson to Cromwell, 24 January 1537, *L & P*, XII, ii, no. 219. Lawson was not the only one to appeal to Cromwell for funds. In January 1538 Sir Brian Tuke, the Treasurer of the Chamber, begged to be allowed £20,000 of the subsidy money, because he was out of funds. *L & P*, XIII, i, no. 47.

36. Merriman, I, p. 27.

37. G. Cavendish, *The Life and Death of Cardinal Wolsey*, ed. R. S. Sylvester and D. P. Harding (1962), p. 116.

38. Elton, 'The Political Creed...', p. 225.

39. G. W. Bernard, *The Late Medieval English Church* (2012), p. 34.

40. *Statutes of the Realm*, III and IV.

41. Merriman, *Life and Letters*, I, p. 409.

42. G. R. Elton, 'Henry VIII's Act of Proclamations', *Studies*, I, pp. 339–54.

43. I. D. Thornley, 'The Treason Legislation of Henry VIII', *Transactions of the Royal Historical Society* (1917), pp. 87–111.

44. Statute 26 Henry VIII, c. 13. *Statutes of the Realm*, III, pp. 508–9.

45. Herrtage and Cooper, *England in the reign of Henry VIII*, p. lxxi.

46. F. L. Baumer, 'Thomas Starkey and Marsiglio of Padua', *Politica*, 2, 1936, p. 188. *L & P*, VII, nos 422–3.

47. Ewart Lewis, *Medieval Political Ideas* (1954), p. 543. S. Lockwood, 'Marsilius of Padua and the case for the royal ecclesiastical supremacy', *Transactions of the Royal Historical Society*, 6th series, 1, 1991. Elton, 'The Political Creed...', p. 229.

48. *Ibid.*, p. 230.

49. *The Defence of Peace* (1535), RSTC 17817, ff. 27, 28, 45.

50. 'Free though he was with deferential remarks about the Imperial Crown, it was not in a despotic king that he saw the law-giver...', Elton, 'The Political Creed...', p. 233.

51. Statute 24 Henry VIII, c. 12. *Statutes of the Realm*, III, p. 427.

52. Lewis, *Medieval Political Ideas*, pp. 430 *et seq.*

53. Statute 25 Henry VIII, c. 21. *Statutes of the Realm*, III, p. 464.

54. For example, *L & P*, XIII, i, nos 677–9.

55. Goronwy Edwards, 'The Principality of Wales, 1267–1967', *Transactions of the Caernarfonshire Historical Society*, 1969. R. R. Davies, *The Age of Conquest: Wales 1063–1415* (1992).

56. Loades, *Tudor Government* (1997), p. 131. R. Somerville, *A History of the Duchy of Lancaster* (1953).

57. Statute 27 Henry VIII, c. 24. *Statutes of the Realm*, III, pp. 555–8.

58. *Ibid.*, para xix.

59. W. S. K. Thomas, *Tudor Wales* (1983), pp. 49–54. P. R. Roberts, 'The "Act of Union" in Welsh History', *Transactions of the Honourable Society of Cymmrodorion* (1972–3), p. 49.

60. Loades, *Tudor Government*, p. 51.

61. J. R. Tanner, *Tudor Constitutional Documents* (1951), pp. 473–4. Statute 11 Henry VII, c. 2. *Statutes of the Realm*, II, p. 569.

62. Tanner, pp. 475–9. Statute 22 Henry VIII, c. 12. *Statutes of the Realm*, III, p. 328.

63. *Ibid.*, p. 558. Statute 27 Henry VIII, c. 25. Tanner, pp. 479–81.

64. *Ibid.*, para xiii.

65. E. Hatcher, *Plague, Population and the English Economy: 1348–1530* (1977). E. A. Wrigley and R. S. Schofield, *The Population History of England, 1541–1871: A Reconstruction* (1981). Susan Brigden, *New Worlds, Lost Worlds* (2000).

66. By abolishing the office of Lord Chamberlain, and placing the Chamber and the Household together under the control of a Lord Great Master. This was a reform which lasted only three years, from 1540 to 1543. Loades, *The Tudor Court* (1986), pp. 203–4.

67. G. R. Elton, 'King or Minister? The Man behind the Henrician Reformation', *Studies*, I, pp. 173–88.

68. For example, Mary, Duchess of Richmond, wrote to Cromwell in April 1538, expressing her gratitude for all his kindness to her, and sending him a 'small token'. *L & P*, XIII, i, no. 876.

9 Historiography

1. Richard Morison, *A remedy for sedition* (1536), *RSTC* 18113.5. Thomas Starkey, An *exhortation to the people instructynge them to Unitie and Obedience* (1536), *RSTC* 23236. Sir Thomas Elyot, *Pasquil the playne* (1533), *RSTC* 7672.
2. *Letters and Papers*, IX, no. 862. Printed by Merriman in *Life and Letters,* I, pp. 17–18.
3. For Chapuys's attitude to Cromwell see Elton, *Tudor Revolution in Government*, pp. 71–4.
4. *Epistolarum Reginaldi Poll*, ed. A. M. Quirini (1744–57). For a full discussion of the Exeter Conspiracy, see Hazel Pierce, *Margaret Pole, Countess of Salisbury* (2003).
5. For Henry's reputation in Europe, see Scarisbrick, *Henry VIII,* pp. 355–83.
6. Hall, *Chronicle*, p. 838.
7. *L & P*, XVI, no. 590.
8. Bound volumes of printed broadsides, Volume I, Henry VIII to Elizabeth, folio 4. Society of Antiquaries of London. Hutchinson. *Thomas Cromwell*, p. 264.
9. Broadsides, folio 5.
10. One of the reasons why the nobility hated Cromwell was because he imitated the lifestyle of a peer long before he was created one. Beckingsale, *Thomas Cromwell*, pp. 61–5. His largesse far outdid that of the Bishop of Winchester's house in Southwark. John Stow, *Survey of London* (ed. 1908), pp. 89, 91. Schofield, *Thomas Cromwell*, p. 286.
11. If these grants had been made on Cromwell's personal initiative, there would have been some chance that they would have been invalidated by his fall. This did not happen because he was always careful to ensure that grants were made by royal warrant. However the anxiety remained. Schofield, *Thomas Cromwell*, pp. 61–5.
12. John Foxe, *Acts and Monuments* (1583), p. 1188. D. Loades, 'Henry VIII and John Foxe', *The John Foxe Bulletin*, I (2002), pp. 5–12
13. Foxe, *Acts and Monuments*, p. 1177.
14. Foxe was born into the middle-class establishment of Boston in the year 1517 and moved to Coningsby while he was still very young, but he stayed in touch with his Boston roots. It cannot be proved that he knew Geoffrey Chamber's family, but it is a reasonable supposition, and would explain the interest which he showed in this event.
15. Foxe, *Acts and Monuments*, p. 1181.
16. *Ibid.*, p. 1184
17. *Ibid.*, p. 1187
18. *Ibid.*, p. 1190. It seems that this prayer was taken from Hall, with whom it is almost identical.
19. Raphael Holinshed, *Chronicles of England, Scotland and Ireland* (ed. 1807–8), p. 818.

20. *RSTC* 7204.5

21. 'Charles Dodds' was the pseudonym of Hugh Tootel, and his work was probably published in London.

22. William Stubbs, *Lectures on Medieval and Modern History* (1887), p. 281.

23. J. A. Froude, *History of England* (1864), II, pp. 531–2. J. R. Green, *A Short History of the English People* (1874), pp. 331–2. The editions of Foxe were by S. R. Cattley and George Townsend (1837–41) and by Josiah Pratt (1870).

24. R. B. Merriman, *Life and Letters of Thomas Cromwell* (1902), I, passim.

25. *Ibid.*, pp. 85–6.

26. *Ibid.*, p. 86.

27. *Ibid.* The two letters are printed as nos 163 and 180. G. R. Elton argued that they were both forgeries, but without citing his evidence. Elton, *Thomas Cromwell* (ed. 2008), p. 19.

28. John, Abbot of Fountains, to Cromwell, 16 March 1536, L & P, X, no. 484. He was also, for instance, Warden of the forests north of the Trent, Dean of Wells and Recorder of Bristol. Beckingsale, *Thomas Cromwell*, p. 119

29. Merriman, *Life and Letters*, I, pp. 112–46.

30. G. R. Elton, *Reform and Renewal*, pp. 81–2.

31. G. R. Elton, *The Tudor Revolution in Government*, passim.

32. *Ibid.*, pp. 423–4.

33. G. R. Elton, 'Tudor Politics: the points of contact: 1. The Parliament', *Transactions of the Royal Historical Society*, 5th series, 24, 1974, pp. 183–200.

34. For example the first Chancellor was Richard Rich. Elton, *The Tudor Revolution*, pp. 215–9.

35. Scarisbrick, *Henry VIII*, p. 471.

36. Gerald Harriss and Penry Williams, 'A Revolution in Tudor History?', *Past and Present*, 25, 1963. Penry Williams, *The Tudor Regime* (1979), pp. 41–2.

37. Elton, *Reform and Renewal*, pp. 9–37.

38. *Ibid.*, pp. 122–6.

39. D. Starkey, *Revolution Reassessed* (1986), particularly Chapter 2, and the introduction to his *The English Court from the Wars of the Roses to the Civil War* (1987). D. Starkey, 'Intimacy and innovation; the rise of the Privy Chamber 1485–1547', in *The English Court*, pp. 71–118.

40. J. A. Guy, 'The Privy Council; revolution or evolution?' in *Revolution Reassessed*.

41. G. R. Elton, *Policy and Police*, pp. 327–82.

42. For a discussion of Cromwell's doctrinal position, see A. G. Dickens, *Thomas Cromwell and the English Reformation* (1959), pp. 141–53.

43. Elton, *Reform and Reformation* (1977), pp. 5–6.

44. Published originally in the *Transactions of the Royal Historical Society*, 5th series, Volume 6, 1956, pp. 69–92, and reprinted in *Studies*, II, pp. 215–35.

45. Dickens, *Thomas Cromwell and the English Reformation*, p. 142.

46. Glyn Redworth, *In Defence of the Church Catholic; a life of Stephen Gardiner* (1990), pp. 105–27.

47. G. R. Elton, *Thomas Cromwell* (ed. 2008), p. 13.
48. *Ibid.*
49. Schofield. *Thomas Cromwell*, pp. 100–106.
50. Robert Hutchinson, *Thomas Cromwell*, pp. 264–70. Schofield, *Thomas Cromwell*, pp. 414–20. J. P. Coby, *Thomas Cromwell* (2012), pp. 232–5.

BIBLIOGRAPHY

Manuscripts

The National Archives

E36
E344
E361
SP1/76, 96, 101, 105, 106, 109, 110, 112, 119, 124, 131,138, 139, 140
DL 5/6, 12/7

British Library

Cotton Cleopatra E iv
Cotton Otho C x
Cotton Titus B i
Additional 8715
Arundel 152
Lansdowne 156

Contemporary Printed Works

Alesius, Alexander, *Of the Authority of the Word of God against the Bishop of London*, RSTC 292.
Bandello, M., Novella XXIV in *Tutte le Opere* (ed. 1966).
Elyot, Sir Thomas, *Pasquil the Playne* (1533), RSTC 7672.
Foxe, John, *The Acts and Monuments of the English Martyrs* (1583), RSTC 11225.

Hall, Edward, *Chronicle* (ed. 1809).

Harpesfield, Nicholas, *The Life and Death of Sir Thomas More*, ed. E. Hitchcock and R. W. Chambers (Early English Text Society, 186, 1932).

Marsilius of Padua, *The Defence of Peace*, trans. W. Marshall (1535), *RSTC* 17817.

Morison, R., *A Remedy for Sedition* (1536), RSTC 18113.5.

The Necessary Doctrine and Erudition for any Christian Man (1543), *RSTC* 5168.

Pole, Reginald, *Apologia ad Carolum Quintum Caesarem*, Epistolarum, pars 1 (ed. 1744).

Robholtz, R. A., *The Complete Poems of Sir Thomas Wyatt* (ed. 1978).

Roper, W., *The Life of Sir Thomas More*, ed. E. Hitchcock (Early English Text Society, 1935).

Schofield, R. S. and D. P. Harding, *Cavendish's Life and Death of Cardinal Wolsey* (ed. 1962).

Singer, S. W., *The Life and Death of Cardinal Wolsey by George Cavendish* (ed. 1827).

Starkey, Thomas, *An Exhortation to the People, urging them to Unity and Obedience* (1536), RSTC 23236.

Taverner, Richard, *The Confession of the Faith of the Germans* (1536), RSTC 909.

Tyndale, W., *The Practice of Prelates* in *The Whole Works of W. Tyndall, John Frith and Doctor Barnes* (1573), RSTC 24436.

Wriothesley, Charles, *A Chronicle of England 1485–1559*, ed. W. D. Hamilton (Camden Society, 1875).

Calendars and Works of Reference

Bray, Gerald, *Tudor Church Reform: The Henrician Canons* (2000).

Byrne, M. St Clare, *The Lisle Letters* (1983).

Calendar of State Papers, Spanish, ed. R. Tyler *et al.* (1862–1954).

Calendar of State Papers, Venetian, ed. R. Brown *et al.* (1864–98).

Ellis, Sir Henry, *Original Letters Illustrative of English History* (1846).

Frere, W. H. and W. M. Kennedy, *Visitation Articles and Injunctions of the Period of the Reformation* (Alcuin Club, 1910).

Hart, C. A., *The English Works of John Fisher, Bishop of Rochester* (2002).

Howell, T. B. and J. J., *A Complete Collection of State Trials* (1828).

Hughes, P. L. and J. F. Larkin, *Tudor Royal Proclamations* (1964).

Letters and Papers ... of the Reign of Henry VIII, ed. J. S. Brewer *et al.* (1867–1910).

Lloyd, C., *Formularies of the Faith put forth by Authority during the Reign of Henry VIII* (1825).

Lords Journals (1846).

Mayer, T. F., *The Correspondence of Reginald Pole*, Vol. I, A Calendar 1518–1548 (2002).

Oxford Dictionary of National Biography.

Pollard, A. F., *Tudor Tracts* (1903).

Bibliography

Rogers, E. F., *The Correspondence of Thomas More* (1947).
Royal Historical Society Handbook of Dates (1978).
Rymer, T., *Foedera, Conventiones etc.* (1704–35).
State Papers of the Reign of Henry VIII (1830–52).
Statutes of the Realm, ed. A. Luders *et al.* (1810–28).
Tanner, J. R., *Tudor Constitutional Documents* (1951).
Valor Ecclesiasticus, ed. John Coley and Josiah Hunter, 6 volumes (1810–34).
Wilkins, D., *Concilia Magnae Brittaniae et Hiberniae* (1737).
Wright, Thomas, *Three Chapters Relating to the Dissolution of the Monasteries* (Camden Society, 1843).

Secondary Works

Alsop, J. D., 'Innovation in Tudor Taxation', *English Historical Review*, 99, 1984.
Anglo, S., *Spectacle, Pageantry and Early Tudor Policy* (1969).
Anglo, S., *Images of Tudor Kingship* (1992).
Baumer, F. L., 'Thomas Starkey and Marsilius of Padua', *Politica*, I, 1936.
Baumer, F. L., *The Early Tudor Theory of Kingship* (1940).
Beckinsale, B. W., *Thomas Cromwell: Tudor Minister* (1978).
Bedouelle, G. and P. Le Gal, *Le 'Divorce' du roi Henry VIII* (1987).
Bellamy, J. G., *The Law of Treason in the Later Middle Ages* (1970).
Bernard, G. W., *War and Taxation in Early Tudor England* (1986).
Bernard, G. W., *The King's Reformation* (2005).
Bernard, G. W., *Anne Boleyn: Fatal Attractions* (2010).
Bernard, G. W., *The Late Medieval English Church* (2012).
Bindoff, S. T., *The House of Commons, 1509–1558* (1982).
Binns, J., 'Scarborough and the Pilgrimage of Grace', *Scarborough Archaeological and History Society*, 53, 1997, pp. 23–39.
Blatcher, M., *The Court of King's Bench, 1450–1550* (1978).
Bradshaw, B., 'George Browne, the First Reformation Archbishop of Dublin', *Journal of Ecclesiastical History*, 21, 1970, pp. 310–30.
Bradshaw, B., 'Cromwell's Reforms and the Origins of the Kildare Rebellion', *Transactions of the Royal Historical Society*, 1977, pp. 69–94.
Bradshaw, B., *The Irish Constitutional Revolution of the Sixteenth Century* (1979).
Brigden, Susan, *New Worlds, Lost Worlds* (2000).
Burnet, Gilbert, *The History of the Reformation of the Church of England* (ed. 1841).
Cavill, Paul R., *The English Parliaments of Henry VII, 1485–1504* (2009).
Cavill, Paul R., '"The Enemy of God and His Church": James Hobart, Praemunire, and the Clergy of Norwich Diocese', *Journal of Legal History*, 32, 2011, pp. 127–50.
Cavill, Paul R., 'A Lollard of Coventry: A source on Robert Silkby', *Midland History*, 38, 2012, pp. 226–31.
Cavill, Paul R., 'A Perspective on the Church–State Confrontation of 1515: The Passage of 4 Henry VIII c.2', *Journal of Ecclesiastical History*, 63, 2012, pp.

655–70.

Coby, J. P., *Thomas Cromwell* (2012).

Colvin, H. M., *A History of the King's Works, Vol. IV: 1485–1660* (1982).

Daniell, David, *William Tyndale, a Biography* (1994).

Daniell, David, *The Bible in English; Its History and Influence* (2003).

Davies, R. R., *The Age of Conquest: Wales 1063–1415* (1992).

Davis, T. F., 'Lollards, Reformers and St Thomas of Canterbury', *University of Birmingham Historical Journal*, 9, 1963, pp. 1–25.

Deansley, M., *The Lollard Bible* (1920).

Dickens, A. G., *Thomas Cromwell and the English Reformation* (1959).

Dickens, A. G., *The English Reformation* (1964).

Dietz, F. C., *English Government Finance, 1485–1558* (1964).

Edwards, Goronwy, 'The Principality of Wales, 1267–1967', *Transactions of the Caernarfonshire Historical Society*, 1969.

Ellis, S. G., 'The Kildare Rebellion and the early Henrician Reformation', *Historical Journal*, 19, 1976, pp. 807–30.

Ellis, S. G., 'Tudor Policy and the Kildare Ascendancy in the Lordship of Ireland', *Irish Historical Studies*, 20.

Ellis, S. G., *Tudor Ireland* (1985).

Elton, G. R., *The Tudor Revolution in Government* (1953).

Elton, G. R., *Policy and Police* (1972).

Elton, G. R., 'King or Minister? The man behind the Henrician Reformation', *Studies in Tudor and Stuart Government and Politics*, I, 1974, pp. 173–88.

Elton, G. R., 'The Commons Supplication against the Ordinaries; Parliamentary manoeuvres in the reign of Henry VIII', *Studies*, III, 1974, pp. 107–37.

Elton, G. R., 'Thomas Cromwell's Decline and Fall', *Studies*, I, pp. 189–230.

Elton, G. R., 'The Political Creed of Thomas Cromwell', *Studies*, II, pp. 215–35.

Elton, G. R., 'Henry VIII's Act of Proclamations', *Studies*, I, pp. 339–54.

Elton, G. R., *The Tudor Constitution* (1982).

Elton, G. R., *Thomas Cromwell* (2008).

Fissell, M. C., *English Warfare, 1511–1642* (2001).

Guy, J. A., 'The Privy Council; revolution or evolution?' in *Revolution Reassessed* ed. D. Starkey and C. Coleman (1986).

Gwyn, Peter, *The King's Cardinal* (1990).

Hatcher, E., *Plague, Population and the English Economy, 1348–1530* (1977).

Head, D., *Ebbs and Flows of Fortune; the Life of Thomas Howard, third Duke of Norfolk* (1995).

Herrtage, S. J. and J. M. Cooper, *England in the Reign of Henry VIII* (Early English Text Society, 1878).

Hicks, Michael, *False, fleeting, perjur'd Clarence': George, Duke of Clarence, 1449–1478* (2014).

Hollger, Christopher, 'Reginald Pole and the Legations of 1537 and 1539; Diplomatic and Polemical responses to the break with Rome' (Oxford University, D.Phil., 1989).

Hoyle, R. W., *The Pilgrimage of Grace and the Politics of the 1530s* (2001).

Hutchinson, Robert, *Thomas Cromwell* (2007).

Ives, E. W., *The Life and Death of Anne Boleyn* (2004).

Knecht, R. J., *Francis I* (1982).

Knowles, D., *The Religious Orders in England*, Vol. 3, The Tudor Age (1959).

Lehmberg, S. E., *The Reformation Parliament 1529–1536* (1970).

Lehmberg, S. E., *The Later Parliaments of Henry VIII 1536–1547* (1977).

Lewis, Evert, *Medieval Political Ideas* (1954).

Loades, D., *Politics and the Nation, 1450–1660* (1974, 1999).

Loades, D., *The Reign of Mary Tudor* (1979, 1991).

Loades, D., *The Tudor Court* (1986).

Loades, D., *Mary Tudor; a Life* (1989).

Loades, D., *Tudor Government* (1997).

Loades, D., 'Henry VIII and John Foxe', *The John Foxe Bulletin*, I, 2002, pp. 5–12.

Loades, D., *Cardinal Wolsey* (2008).

Loades, D., *The Tudor Queens of England* (2009).

Loades, D., *The Boleyns* (2011).

Loades, D., *Henry VIII* (2011).

Loades, D., *Jane Seymour* (2013).

Lockwood, S., 'Marsilius of Padua and the Royal Ecclesiastical Supremacy', *Transactions of the Royal Historical Society*, 1991.

Logan, F., 'Thomas Cromwell and the Viceregency in Spirituals; a revisitation', *English Historical Review*, 103, 1988, pp. 568–87.

Maas, K. D., *The Reformation and Robert Barnes* (2010).

MacCulloch, D., *Thomas Cranmer* (1996).

McEntellgert, Rory, *Henry VIII, the League of Schmalkalden and the English Reformation* (2002).

Mantel, Hilary, *Wolf Hall* (2009).

Mantel, Hilary, *Bring up the Bodies* (2012).

Mattingly, Garrett, *Catherine of Aragon* (ed. 1965).

Mayer, T. F., *Reginald Pole, Prince and Prophet* (2000).

Merriman, R. B., *The Life and Letters of Thomas Cromwell* (1902, 1968).

Muller, J. A., *Stephen Gardiner and the Tudor Reaction* (1926).

Murphy, B., *Bastard Prince; Henry VIII's Lost Son* (2001).

Neame, A., *The Holy Maid of Kent; the Life of Elizabeth Barton 1506–1534* (1979).

Nicholson, Graham, 'The Act of Appeals and the English Reformation' in *Law and Government under the Tudors*, ed. C. Cross, D. Loades and J. Scarisbrick (1988).

Pardue, Brad C., *Printing, Power and Piety. Appeals to the Public during the early years of the English Reformation* (2012).

Paul, J. E., *Catherine of Aragon and her Friends* (1966).

Pierce, Hazel, *Margaret Pole, Countess of Salisbury, 1473–1541* (2003).

Redworth, Glyn, *In Defence of the Church Catholic; a life of Stephen Gardiner* (1990).

Rees, D., *The Son of Prophecy. Henry Tudor's road to Bosworth* (1985).

Roberts, P. R., 'The "Act of Union" in Welsh History', *Transactions of the Honourable Society of Cymrodorion*, 1972–3.

Rowley-Williams, Jenny, *Ladies of the Tudor Court* (2014).

Samman, N., *Henry VIII and Wolsey: The Tudor Court and Royal Progresses, 1509–1547* (2014).

Scarisbrick, J. J., *Henry VIII* (1968).

Scarisbrick, J. J., 'Fisher, Henry VIII and the Reformation Crisis', *Humanism, Reform and Reformation; the career of Bishop John Fisher*, ed. B. Bradshaw and E. Duffy (1989).

Schenk, W., *Reginald Pole, Cardinal of England* (1950).

Schofield, John, *Thomas Cromwell; Henry VIII's Most Faithful Servant* (2008).

Schofield, R. S., 'Parliamentary Lay Taxation, 1485–1547' (University of Cambridge, PhD, 1963).

Schofield, R. S., 'Taxation and the Political limits of the Tudor State', and *Law Government under the Tudors* (1988).

Schultz, F., 'Bracton on Kingship', *English Historical Review*, 60, 1945.

Somerville, R., *A History of the Duchy of Lancaster* (1953).

Sowerby, Tracey, *Renaissance and Reform in Tudor England: The career of Sir Richard Morison, 1536–1556* (2010).

Starkey, D. and C. Coleman, *Revolution Reassessed* (1986).

Starkey, D., *The English Court from the Wars of the Roses to the Civil War* (1987).

Storey, F. S., *The Life and Times of the Right Honourable Sir Ralph Sadler* (1877).

Strype, J., *Ecclesiastical Memorials* (ed. 1822).

Taylor, Robert, *Political Prophecy in England* (1911).

Thomas, W. S. K., *Tudor Wales* (1983).

Van Dyke, P., *Renasence Portraits* (1906).

Warnicke, Retha M., *The Marrying of Anne of Cleves* (2000).

Whatmore, L. E., 'The sermon against the Holy Maid of Kent and her adherents', *English Historical Review*, 58, 1943, pp. 463–75.

Williams, Penry, *The Council in the Marches of Wales under Elizabeth* (1958).

Williams, Penry, *The Tudor Regime* (1979).

Wrigley, E. A. and R. S. Schofield, *The Population History of England 1541–1871; a Reconstruction* (1981).

Youings. J., *The Dissolution of the Monasteries* (1975).

LIST OF ILLUSTRATIONS

1. Henry VIII by Holbein. Courtesy of Jonathan Reeve JR951b53p505 15001550.
2. Anne Boleyn. Courtesy of Ripon Cathedral.
3. Arthur, Henry VII's first son and Henry VIII's elder brother. Courtesy of David Baldwin.
4. Anne of Cleves. Courtesy of Amberley Archive.
5. Anne Boleyn's father, Thomas Boleyn, the Earl of Wiltshire. Courtesy of Elizabeth Norton.
6. Henry VII. Courtesy of Elizabeth Norton.
7. Jane Seymour, Henry's third wife. Courtesy of Stephen Porter.
8. Edward, Henry VIII's son by Jane Seymour. Courtesy of Stephen Porter.
9. Erasmus in an iconic woodcut by Dürer. Courtesy of Jonathan Reeve JR 1160B4P600 15001550.
10. *An Allegory of the Tudor Succession* depicting the family of Henry VIII. Courtesy of Yale Center for British Art, Paul Mellon Collection.
11. Statue of Catherine of Aragon. Courtesy of Patrick Williams.
12. Thomas Wolsey, from a drawing by Jacques le Boucq. Courtesy of Jonathan Reeve JR1169b2p7 15001550.
13. Tomb of Thomas Howard, 3rd Duke of Norfolk. Courtesy of Elizabeth Norton.
14. Thomas Cranmer from a painting by Gerhard Flicke. Courtesy of Elizabeth Norton.
15. Thomas Wyatt, poet and friend of Cromwell. Courtesy of Elizabeth Norton
16. A view of the Tudor palace at Greenwich. Courtesy of Jonathan Reeve JR944b46fp180 14501500.
17. The Tower of London. Courtesy of Stephen Porter.
18. The Traitor's Gate at the Tower of London. Courtesy of Elizabeth Norton.
19. London Bridge. Courtesy of Stephen Porter.

20. A plan of Westminster Palace. Courtesy of Jonathan Reeve JRCD2b20p769 15501600.

21. A view of Westminster, *c.* 1550, by Anthony van Wyngaerde. Courtesy of Jonathan Reeve JR1872b46fp16 13001350.

22. Whitehall Palace, *c.* 1550, also by van Wyngaerde. Courtesy of Jonathan Reeve JR1884b46fp192 15001550.

23. A drawing for the painting of Sir Thomas More and his family by Hans Holbein, *c.* 1527. Courtesy of Elizabeth Norton.

24. Windsor Castle. Courtesy of Elizabeth Norton.

25. A copy of Pope Clement VII's 'definitive sentence' in favour of Catherine of Aragon and against Henry VIII. Courtesy of Jonathan Reeve JR1171b2p45 15001550.

26. Henry VIII in council. Courtesy of Jonathan Reeve JRCD3b20p910 15001550.

27. Title page from the Great Bible, printed by Richard Grafton and Edward Whitchurch, 1539. Courtesy of Jonathan Reeve JRCD2b20p929 15001550.

Tudor History from Amberley Publishing

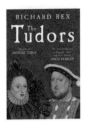
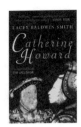

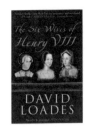

THE TUDORS
Richard Rex

'The best introduction to England's most important dynasty'
DAVID STARKEY
'Gripping and told with enviable narrative skill... a delight'
THES
'Vivid, entertaining and carrying its learning lightly'
EAMON DUFFY
'A lively overview' **THE GUARDIAN**
£9.99   978-1-4456-0700-9   256 pages PB 143 illus., 66 col

MARGARET OF YORK
Christine Weightman

'A pioneering biography of the Tudor dynasty's most
dangerous enemy'
PROFESSOR MICHAEL HICKS
'Christine Weightman brings Margaret alive once more'
THE YORKSHIRE POST
'A fascinating account of a remarkable woman'
THE BIRMINGHAM POST
£10.99   978-1-4456-0819-8   256 pages PB 51 illus

CATHERINE HOWARD
Lacey Baldwin Smith

'A brilliant, compelling account' **ALISON WEIR**
'A faultless book' **THE SPECTATOR**
'Lacey Baldwin Smith has so excellently caught the
atmosphere of the Tudor age' **THE OBSERVER**
£9.99   978-1-84868-521-5   256 pages PB 25 col illus

THE SIX WIVES OF HENRY VIII
David Loades

'Neither Starkey nor Weir has the assurance and command
of Loades' **SIMON HEFFER, LITERARY REVIEW**
'Incisive and profound. I warmly recommend this book'
ALISON WEIR
£9.99   978-1-4456-0049-9   256 pages PB 55 illus, 31 col

MARY ROSE
David Loades

£20.00 978-1-4456-0622-4
272 pages HB 17 col illus

MARY BOLEYN
Josephine Wilkinson

£9.99 978-1-84868-525-3
208 pages PB 22 illus, 10 col

JANE SEYMOUR
Elizabeth Norton

£9.99 978-1-84868-527-7
224 pages PB 53 illus, 26 col

HENRY VIII
Richard Rex

£9.99 978-1-84868-098-2
192 pages PB 81 illus, 48 col

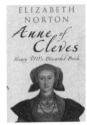

ANNE BOLEYN THE YOUNG QUEEN TO BE
Josephine Wilkinson
£9.99 978-1-4456-0395-7
208 pages PB 34 illus (19 col)

ELIZABETH I
Richard Rex

£9.99 978-1-84868-423-2
192 pages PB 75 illus

ANNE OF CLEVES
Elizabeth Norton

£9.99 978-1-4456-0183-0
224 pages HB 54 illus, 27 col

Available from all good bookshops or to order direct
Please call **01453-847-800 www.amberleybooks.com**

More Tudor History from Amberley Publishing

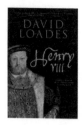

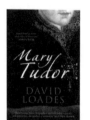

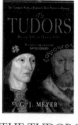

HENRY VIII
David Loades

'David Loades Tudor biographies are both highly enjoyable and instructive, the perfect combination' *ANTONIA FRASER*

£12.99 978-1-4456-0704-7 512 pages HB 113 illus, 49 col

THE TUDORS VOL 1
G. J. Meyer

'His style is crisp and popular'
PROFESSOR DAVID LOADES

£12.99 978-1-4456-0143-4 384 pages PB 72 illus, 54 col

ANNE BOLEYN
Elizabeth Norton

'Meticulously researched and a great read'
THEANNEBOLEYNFILES.COM

£9.99 978-1-84868-514-7 264 pages PB 47 illus, 26 col

THE TUDORS VOL 2
G. J. Meyer

'A sweeping history of the gloriously infamous Tudor era'
KIRKUS REVIEW

£12.99 978-1-4456-0144-1 352 pages PB 53 illus, 15 col

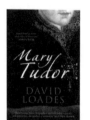

ANNE BOLEYN
P. Friedmann

'A compelling and lively biography... meticulously researched and supremely readable classic of Tudor biography' *DR RICHARD REX*
'The first scholarly biography' *THE FINANCIAL TIMES*

£20.00 978-1-84868-827-8 352 pages HB 47 illus, 20 col

CATHERINE PARR
Elizabeth Norton

'Norton cuts an admirably clear path through tangled Tudor intrigues'
JENNY UGLOW
'Wonderful... a joy to read'
HERSTORIA

£9.99 978-1-4456-0383-4 312 pages HB 49 illus, 30 col

MARY TUDOR
David Loades

£12.99 978-1-4456-0818-1 328 pages HB 59 illus, 10 col

MARGARET BEAUFORT
Elizabeth Norton

£9.99 978-1-4456-0578-4 256 pages HB 70 illus, 40 col

IN BED WITH THE TUDORS
Amy Licence

£20.00 978-1-4456-0693-4
272 pages HB 30 illus, 20 col

THE BOLEYNS
David Loades

£10.99 978-1-4456-0958-4
312 pages HB 34 illus, 33 col

BESSIE BLOUNT
Elizabeth Norton

£25.00 978-1-84868-870-4
384 pages HB 77 illus, 75 col

ANNE BOLEYN
Norah Lofts

£18.99 978-1-4456-0619-4
208 pages HB 75 illus, 46 col

Available from all good bookshops or to order direct
Please call **01453-847-800 www.amberleybooks.com**

More Tudor History from Amberley Publishing

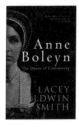
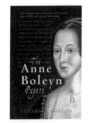
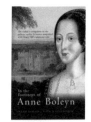

ANNE BOLEYN
Lacey Baldwin Smith

'The perfect introduction'
SUZANNAH LIPSCOMBE

£20.00   978-1-4456-1023-8   240 pages HB 60 illus, 40 col

INSIDE THE TUDOR COURT
Lauren MacKay

'Superb... highly recommended'
ALISON WEIR

Feb 2014 £20.00   978-1-4456-0957-7   240 pages HB

THE ANNE BOLEYN PAPERS
Elizabeth Norton

'A very useful compilation of source material on Anne'
ALISON WEIR

£12.99   978-1-4456-1288-1   384 pages PB

IN THE FOOTSTEPS OF ANNE BOLEYN
Sarah Morris & Natalie Grueninger

£20.00   978-1-4456-0782-5   288 pages HB 100 illus, 70 col

KATHARINE OF ARAGON
Patrick Williams

£25.00   978-1-84868-325-9   512 pages HB 70 col illus

THOMAS CROMWELL
J. Patrick Coby

£20.00   978-1-4456-0775-7   292 pages HB 30 illus, 10 col

ELIZABETH OF YORK
Amy Licence

£20.00   978-1-4456-0961-4   272 pages HB 40 illus, 10 col

CATHERINE HOWARD
David Loades

£20.00   978-1-4456-0768-9   240 pages HB 27 illus, 19 col

JANE SEYMOUR
David Loades

£20.00   978-1-4456-1157-0
192 pages HB   40 illus, 20 col

THE BOLEYN WOMEN
Elizabeth Norton

£20.00   978-1-84868-988-6
304 pages HB   40 illus, 20 col

Available from all good bookshops or to order direct
Please call **01453-847-800 www.amberleybooks.com**

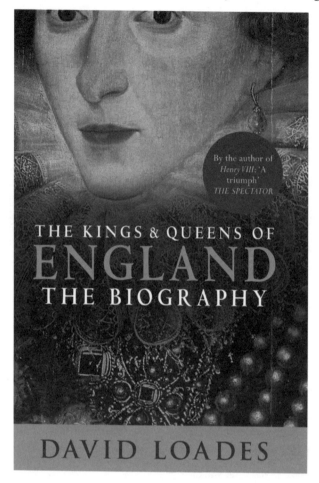

INDEX